W9-ANK-699

The Perversion of Virtue

The Perversion of Virtue

Understanding Murder-Suicide

THOMAS JOINER, PhD

OXFORD
UNIVERSITY PRESS

OXFORD
UNIVERSITY PRESS

Oxford University Press is a department of the University of Oxford.
It furthers the University's objective of excellence in research, scholarship,
and education by publishing worldwide.

Oxford   New York
Auckland   Cape Town   Dar es Salaam   Hong Kong   Karachi
Kuala Lumpur   Madrid   Melbourne   Mexico City   Nairobi
New Delhi   Shanghai   Taipei   Toronto

With offices in
Argentina   Austria   Brazil   Chile   Czech Republic   France   Greece
Guatemala   Hungary   Italy   Japan   Poland   Portugal   Singapore
South Korea   Switzerland   Thailand   Turkey   Ukraine   Vietnam

Oxford is a registered trademark of Oxford University Press
in the UK and certain other countries.

Published in the United States of America by
Oxford University Press
198 Madison Avenue, New York, NY 10016

© Oxford University Press 2014

Library of Congress Cataloging-in-Publication Data
Joiner, Thomas E.
The perversion of virtue : understanding murder-suicide / Thomas Joiner.
    pages cm
Includes bibliographical references and index.
ISBN 978-0-19-933455-1 (hardback)
1. Suicide—United States.   2. Homicide—United States.   I. Title.
HV6545.J649 2014
362.28—dc23
2013028785

9 8 7 6 5 4 3 2 1
Printed in the United States of America
on acid-free paper

Contents

Preface *vii*

Section 1   **Introductory Material**

ONE   Murder-Suicide: Prevalence, Characteristics, and Initial Conceptualization   3

TWO   Understanding Murder   53

THREE   Understanding Suicide   75

FOUR   Understanding Virtue   106

Section 2   **Understanding Murder-Suicide as a Perversion of Virtue**

FIVE   A Perversion of Mercy   121

SIX   A Perversion of Justice   141

SEVEN   A Perversion of Duty   163

EIGHT   A Perversion of Heroic Glory   171

NINE The Neighboring but Distinct Categories of
Perverting Self-Control and Fate 177

Section 3 Implications and Conclusions

TEN Prevention, Clinical, and Other Real-World
Applications 193

ELEVEN Conclusion: Human Nature and the
Perversion of Virtue 202

Notes 213

References 235

Index 245

Preface

This book is ambitious and single-minded about a grave subject. The goal of the book is to develop and defend a specific perspective on murder-suicide, one that borrows on established knowledge and concepts, but one that reorganizes and extends them into a coherent and incrementally novel understanding of the horror that is murder-suicide. By the book's end, I hope to have persuaded readers that the perspective developed in the book is viable, incremental beyond past work, and crucially, now ready to face off empirically with other perspectives.

The bootstrapping nature of this process deserves emphasis. The argument begins with facts, moves to conjecture, and builds from there to establish a theory of what defines murder-suicide and the thought processes that underlie it. The approach is inherently conjectural, as theory-building by definition is. My goal is to introduce a contender into the race to explain murder-suicide, not to call the race as finished.

In a field such as this, the race clearly is not finished, a main reason for which is the extent and quality of extant data on the phenomenon. Unsurprisingly, illuminating data on the mindset of the murder-suicide perpetrator are rare, and when available, incomplete. To this point, Liem and Nieuwbeerta state, "Most existing studies on homicide-suicide do not focus on determinants and explanatory mechanisms...The few studies that do examine explanations of homicide-suicide are (qualitatively) descriptive in nature and include only a small number of homicide-suicide cases."[1]

This state of affairs affects the current project as it would any project on murder-suicide, but it should be acknowledged that this book is acutely affected by this issue because the book's goal is to characterize the true mindset of the murder-suicide perpetrator. My approach is to work with what data are available, which often involve things like notes left behind by perpetrators, as well as behavioral observations made by those who knew the perpetrator. These can be quite revealing but have drawbacks as sole sources of data, as do purely anecdotal sources of information more generally. The gaps in the record are sometimes extensive enough that I speculate on the state of mind of the individuals involved. I attempt to make the tentative nature of these speculations clear and have confidence that readers can decide on their own whether they are plausible or not.

Inevitably, and I think naturally enough, the book, to a degree, favors its own argument. This would be natural enough even if there were many existing theories of the phenomenon of murder-suicide, but as the book shows, there are not. The book advocates for a particular perspective—an initial theoretical conjecture in the midst of a relative conceptual vacuum—and trusts readers' discernment regarding the merits or lack thereof of the explanation developed in what follows.

Section 1
Introductory Material

Murder-Suicide: Prevalence, Characteristics, and Initial Conceptualization

IN CONNECTICUT IN 1782, LYDIA BEADLE WAS MURDERED, as were her four children, who ranged in age from 6 to 11. Her headstone reads, "Fell by the hands of William Beadle/an infatuated Man who closed the/horrid sacrifice of his Wife/& Children with his own destruction."[1] If William Beadle were intent on suicide, one might ask, why would he first kill his wife and children? Or, alternatively, did he kill his family rashly and then, in despair and as a consequence, kill himself? The headstone describes William Beadle as "infatuated"—what does this mean precisely? Why, fundamentally, did William Beadle perpetrate this appalling incident?

Crime perpetrated by one of us on a fellow human being opens up a unique window on our very souls. The ancient Roman playwright Terence wrote "Homo sum: humani nil a me alienum puto" ("I am human and nothing human is alien to me").[2] Around two thousand years later, the psychiatrist Harry Stack Sullivan said, "we are all much more simply human than otherwise."[3] Violent crime forces a mirror on us: Why did he do that? What could have driven someone to such lengths? Given certain circumstances, do I have that in me?

In what follows, I propose some answers to these questions—answers that may surprise, maybe even shock. Truth regularly has this character. In fact, in his poignant *A Mathematician's Apology*,[4] the eminent English mathematician G. H. Hardy described true—even beautiful—mathematical concepts as being initially surprising, but then, upon reflection and in retrospect, familiar, even obvious. The power of truth and beauty, in part, is that in rapid succession they startle us and then they ground us.

Mathematicians have perhaps more opportunities to understand and experience this power, but they have not cornered the market. Darwin's "bulldog," Thomas Henry Huxley, upon perceiving the core idea of Darwin's masterpiece and experiencing the attendant surprise, pleasure, and then familiarity, stated, "How extremely stupid not to have thought of that!"[5]

I have posed concepts in previous books that, although not Darwinian in profundity, I nevertheless contend have this character of initial surprise followed by knowing understanding. In *Why People Die By Suicide*,[6] I argued that a kind of fearlessness is required to voluntarily face the daunting prospect of one's death, and that doing so necessarily involves a fight against ancient, ingrained, and powerful self-preservation instincts. Many are initially startled by this perspective on suicidal behavior—the concepts of fearlessness and suicide tend not to co-occur in the public mind—but upon reflection, it is conceptually obvious that confronting an extremely fearsome thing requires a certain fearlessness, just as it is empirically obvious that many highly suicidal people shrink from enacting their own deaths, despite genuine desire and intent to die, the obstacle being an uncontrollable fear of death. This perspective surprises people at almost the same time it induces them to say things like, "oh, yes, of course."

In *Myths About Suicide*,[7] I argued that death by suicide is neither cowardly, vengeful, controlling, nor selfish. Here too, these claims contradict certainties in the public mind, and thus are received with surprise. And yet, regarding for example the question of selfishness, when it is documented that most if not all suicide decedents believe (wrongly and tragically) that they are doing everyone a favor, and that many take planful steps to lessen the massive blow of their deaths on others, selfishness seems, at first surprisingly and then in retrospect clearly, to have no role.

In the current book on murder-suicide, I believe I have similar claims in store—conjectures that may surprise somewhat, but that I hope will have the ring of truth upon reflection. In response to the assertion "I see that suicide is not cowardly, vengeful, or selfish, but murder-suicide obviously is," I respond: "it depends on the motive, and most, perhaps all, motives for murder-suicide—at least as understood by the person enacting it—are neither cowardly, vengeful, nor selfish."

On the contrary, the motives for murder-suicide involve virtue.

To mention virtue's involvement in atrocity is surprising, and indeed, many cringe reading that last sentence, understandably, because something as seemingly senseless and (often) as brutal as murder-suicide seems far from virtuous. But, as I will show in what follows, murder-suicide is not senseless, if what is meant by "senseless" is "impossible to make sense of." From the perspective of the person engaging in murder-suicide, the act is subject to a tractable and internally coherent logic.[8] This logic is underlain by appeals to virtue—a perverted and horribly distorted version of it to be sure— but, perhaps uncomfortably, a version of it that retains its essence as virtue even despite the distortions and perversions. This view will take us on a journey that involves understanding murder *per se*, suicide *per se*, their convergence in often horrible incidents of murder-suicide, the essence and types of virtue, and crucially, how the perversion of virtue is the *sine qua non* of genuine murder-suicide.

To get an initial sense of this approach, imagine, for instance, that you are completely certain that someone you care for is suffering intolerably, that her agony will only increase, and that her death, though assured, is still days or perhaps even weeks away. Imagine further that you are quite certain that she has signaled her wish for you to help her in dying (even if at the moment she is uncommunicative due to her condition). Would you find it virtuous to do so?

On behalf of some of their physicians, the people of Oregon (and now also those of Washington state and Vermont, and functionally though not affirmatively legally, Montana) have answered "yes."[9] Under Oregon's Death with Dignity Act, passed in 1997 and enacted in 1998, terminally ill patients may make a written request to die, and then another, and the requests must be separated by at least 15 days.

Certification by a physician that the patient is mentally competent to make the decision to die, and that the patient does not have a mental disorder like depression, is also required. In such cases, physicians may write prescriptions for lethal doses of medication; it is up to the individual to actually ingest the medication (and not all who are written prescriptions follow through, sometimes because natural death intervenes, but also because people waver in their resolve...[10] as is only natural: resolve to die is inherently difficult to sustain, and this is true for everyone, even the terminally ill and the suicidal).

In writing prescriptions for lethal doses of medication, what are physicians' motives? One motive is written into the very name of the law—that is, concern for people's dignity. Two other motives are clearly involved as well, namely mercy and respect for self-determination. The causing of the death is justified with an appeal to virtues like mercy.

Now, imagine a very different scenario, but with many of the same parameters—that you are sure that people you care for will suffer badly, and that death will bring a quick end to their ongoing ordeal. Imagine further that you are quite certain that death is best for them. This is the situation not only of some physicians in Oregon working under the Death with Dignity Act, but also of two California parents who decided to kill their five young children before killing themselves.[11]

It is jarring to read of physicians and these parents as comparable because, in so many ways, they are not. But that should not obscure a crucial similarity: in both scenarios, the causing of the death is justified by appeals to virtues such as mercy. This is a fundamental motive for Oregon physicians, just as it was, *in their minds*, of Ervin Antonio Lupoe and his wife, who, according to a letter left by Lupoe, decided together that they and their children should die following numerous family stresses and strains, including the fact that both parents had recently lost their jobs. In the letter, Lupoe termed the family's life a "horrendous ordeal" and explained that he and his wife "felt it better to end our lives" and would not think of leaving their children behind to suffer the ongoing, cruel ordeal that fate had bestowed on them. The five children ranged in age from 2 to 8.

The Lupoes killed their children not out of anger, cruelty, or sadism. Neither did they kill them out of insanity, if that term is meant to convey the kind of psychosis that can occur, for example, in postpartum psychoses during which mothers occasionally kill their infants because they believe that they were instructed to do so by God or that the baby is possessed by the devil. Rather, the Lupoes believed that killing their children was the merciful thing to do. The Lupoes probably did not misunderstand mercy itself, for, as occurs in Oregon, causing death can indeed be viewed as legitimately merciful; instead, they profoundly and tragically misunderstood their current situation and their children's future.

Though it can be hard to see it through the haze of horror, the logic of mercy is intact in the Lupoes' actions. Given first principles or assumptions of irremediable agony and needless suffering, some view death as merciful, including some Oregon physicians and parents like the Lupoes. The considerable difference between the two groups inheres not in their understanding of mercy but in their understanding of first principles. The Lupoes were mistaken in their assumption of the irremediable agony and needless suffering of their children; once they had made that assumption, however, there was an internally consistent logic to their actions, and the virtue of mercy was central to that logic. That this is uncomfortable to ponder does not make it untrue.

Of course, not all murder-suicides can be laid at the doorstep of misapplied mercy; other virtues are involved too. Indeed, the identification of the specific virtues involved in various murder-suicide incidents produces a comprehensive yet parsimonious typology of murder-suicide and may shed light on the nature of virtue itself.

A typology with these characteristics is sorely needed, for three reasons. First, accurate description is a necessary precondition to deep understanding, and previous descriptive frameworks have been bedeviled, at least to a degree, by inaccuracy, unwieldiness, or both. As will be expanded upon at the beginning of Section 2, past typology efforts[12] focus on the identity of the victim (e.g., spouse vs. extrafamilial) and on an array of motives and other factors (e.g., euthanasia, altruism, substance abuse, psychosis, seizure disorder). In my opinion, past frameworks are descriptive (perhaps overly so)[13] but not explanatory. The taxonomy presented in this book represents an attempt at a novel and useful scholarly contribution, geared toward valid and parsimonious description as well as toward explanation.

Second and relatedly, an accurate descriptive framework can establish the foundation on which to understand the specific thought processes in the murder-suicide perpetrator's mind—essential to a full understanding of the phenomenon and, to a degree at least, isomorphic with developing a new theory of murder-suicide. Third, as one of the book's concluding chapters will show, this taxonomy has potential utility in clinical and law enforcement contexts in that it may aid in the identification and thus potential prevention of unfolding murder-suicide incidents. Useful applied and clinical implications tend to flow from valid descriptive frameworks (e.g., Kraepelinian approaches to mental disorders as seen in the modern DSM, controversies regarding DSM-5 notwithstanding).

Four Virtues Are Perverted in Murder-Suicides

The typology proposed in this book includes six categories, four of which, I contend, represent true species of murder-suicide, and two of which contain neighboring phenomena, which, though they share some features with true murder-suicides, are nevertheless distinct. The four categories of true murder-suicides correspond to the misapplied virtues of mercy, justice, duty, and glory. True murder-suicides, this book will argue, always involve the perversion of one of these four virtues. The perversion does not distort the four virtues beyond recognition; instead, it involves the gross misperception of when and how virtue should be applied.

Notice something, incidentally, about these four virtues. Unlike virtues such as freedom or autonomy, mercy, justice, duty, and glory are *interpersonal* virtues. In my judgment, this is not coincidental, a point that is expanded upon later in the book.

A fifth category lies just outside the boundaries of true murder-suicide. Consider an incident in which a person plans another's murder and also plans to then escape to another country and assume a new identity. The murder occurs but the plan for escape falls apart. With the police closing in on him, the murderer kills himself. A murder has occurred, as has a suicide, and thus it is not hard to imagine why some would classify this as a murder-suicide.

But, according to the perspective developed here, it is not. In forensics, in courtrooms, in clinics, and elsewhere, an essential issue regarding violence, either other- or self-directed, involves *motive*.

A companion concept is *intent*. Incidents such as a planned murder followed by a botched escape, and then and only then, suicide, are primarily about murder. Indeed, they would be *only* about murder were it not for the happenstance of the failed escape. The motive— the intent—is murder, and it is inaccurate to characterize suicide in these incidents as primary. To do so would give suicide a weight in these incidents that it does not deserve; as grave as it is, suicide is nevertheless peripheral in these instances.

By contrast, in true murder-suicides, at least according to this book's perspective, suicide is not only primary, but it is also the source of all that follows, especially including the appalling murders; in murder-suicide, murder occurs because of suicide, as a consequence of suicide having been settled on, and as a result of perpetrators perverting virtue along the lines of "If I am to die it is virtuous that they do too."

A sixth category will be discussed as well, a type in which the intent is suicide, there is no thought that it would be virtuous to kill others, but others are killed nevertheless. This latter category can be viewed as a perversion of fate and involves suicides that unintentionally cause other people's deaths. Of the million or so deaths by suicide that occur worldwide each year, a few accidentally also cause someone else's death. For example, those who jump from the upper floors of a building risk landing on someone who has walked out the building's ground-floor door, killing both people. Alas, this very thing occurs, though it is mercifully rare. Of course, this category does not fit the definition of murder-suicide *per se*, which involves both intentional homicide and suicide—the technical term for this phenomenon, I suppose, is manslaughter-suicide, an even more chilling phrasing than murder-suicide. It is consistent with this book's thesis that a phenomenon in which virtue is not involved—fate is not a virtue—is also one that clearly does not qualify as murder-suicide *per se*.

Of the four misapplied virtues involved in true murder-suicides, justice and mercy represent the two most common types. For the individual contemplating a murder-suicide that he[14] thinks is about justice, the line of thinking is along the lines of "Soon I'll be dead. But is it fair that I suffer that end, while those who have deeply wronged me go unpunished and happily live on? Certainly not. But that is what will happen unless I deliver justice myself." Here, as with the virtue of mercy and the horrible end of the Lupoe family, it is not the virtue that is misunderstood, because justice should be swiftly applied to those who have deeply wronged. Rather, it is the surrounding circumstances that are misunderstood, and that exert a distorting effect on the virtue in question.

Murder-suicides involving perversions of mercy and justice are horrible; they leave numerous people dead—the incident involving the Lupoe family took seven lives—not to mention the effects on family, friends, witnesses, and investigators, and not to mention the costs of lost years of productivity, funerals, insurance settlements, police and other investigations, and so on. Much the same can be said of incidents in which the virtue of duty is perverted.[15] On all these parameters, as bad as murder-suicides distorting mercy, justice, and duty are, they are often outpaced by those involving a perverted sense of glory.

As well known as the incident at Columbine High School in Colorado is, relatively few seem to grasp the shooters' fundamental motives. Fifteen people lost their lives at Columbine (including shooters Eric Harris and Dylan Klebold, who killed 13 people before killing themselves), and many more were injured. Many, including most in the media, viewed the incident, to use the terminology and framework developed in this book, as murder-suicide based on the perversion of the virtue of justice. That is, many media outlets reported that the two shooters had been bullied and otherwise victimized by particular subgroups of other students, especially athletes. In the incident, so the reporting said, athletes were singled out for revenge—a perversion of justice.

However, this is not what happened. None of those killed were singled out because they were athletes;[16] and, as the journals and videotapes the boys left behind demonstrate in disturbing detail, their motive was a perverted version of glory. Their explicit goal was to outdo Timothy McVeigh (who was responsible for 168 deaths in the Oklahoma City bombing); the boys easily would have done this had their bombs not malfunctioned. Their goal was to be remembered forever—perverted glory.

As will be drawn out in the chapter on perverted glory, the Columbine tragedy illustrates a fundamental property of murder-suicide, at least as viewed here. The evidence clearly suggests that the boys' suicidality formed first, well before plans for the shooting. Suicide was primary for both boys; homicide—and in their distorted view of it, glory—came later. This represents a general principle applicable, I will argue throughout the book, to all true murder-suicides. Suicide is always primary; it is decided on first and thus becomes part of the "first principles" assumptions that perpetrators of murder-suicide make.[17] In the case of the Lupoes, their logic about their children's future flowed from the primary decision that the Lupoes themselves would not be around to fend for the children, because the Lupoes had decided on suicide—the note they left makes this clear. Demographic research on murder-suicide affirms this view, in that those who enact murder-suicide have demographic profiles that resemble those of suicide decedents more so than they do those of murderers.[18] As will be drawn out in a later chapter on the applied implications of the model developed here, if it can be shown that suicide is fundamental in murder-suicide, then suicide prevention is also murder-suicide prevention.

As alluded to already, there is a category of incidents in which people purposefully kill others and then kill themselves, but which, according to the view articulated in this book, do not qualify as genuine murder-suicide. The "Santa Claus" killer fit this type.[19] In December 2008, Bruce Pardo donned a Santa Claus suit and went on a shooting rampage at a party, killing his ex-wife, her parents, and several others. As he was shooting, he sprayed racing fuel throughout the house and set it ablaze. His body was later discovered approximately 25 miles from the scene; he had died from a self-inflicted gunshot wound.

The description of this incident thus far makes it sound like a "justice"-type murder-suicide; perhaps Pardo was intent on his own death but believed that if he were to die, it would only be fair for others who had wronged him, such as his ex-wife and her family, to die too. But there is a key difference between "justice"-type murder-suicides and the incident perpetrated by Pardo. In genuine "justice"-type incidents, the perpetrator plans his suicide and, as a consequence thereof, plans others' deaths. But Pardo didn't plan his suicide; he planned his escape (to Canada) following the killings.

His plans went awry; in the course of spraying the house with racing fuel, he accidentally soaked his Santa Claus suit with the fuel. The fuel in the suit ignited, searing it into Pardo's skin and causing third-degree burns. He was injured severely enough that escape to

Canada became impossible. He had a backup plan, and that involved death by a self-inflicted gunshot wound.

Suicide emerged in the mix of Pardo's planning, but it was secondary to escape. If things had gone according to his preferred (and horrible) plan, suicide would not have entered into it at all. He appeared to use an "if-then" kind of reasoning, along the lines of "if I perpetrate these murders and if escape fails, then I will take things into my own hands and kill myself." It is the "take things into my own hands" impulse—and its corollary "avoid dealing with public scorn, the authorities, and prison"—that I suggest puts this category adjacent to but outside the realm of true murder-suicide. It is adjacent because a virtue and its perversion can be discerned; namely, self-control or autonomy in the "take things into my own hands and die" line of thought (a line of thought, as we will see, that can be involved in genuine murder-suicides involving the perversion of justice). It is outside the realm, though, because unlike true murder-suicides, these incidents prioritize murder, and also because, to the degree that a distorted virtue is involved, it is a self-focused, non-interpersonal virtue.

Genuine murder-suicides, the present perspective asserts, start with the decision to die by suicide, which leads to the perversion of an interpersonal virtue, which leads, in turn, to murder. The interpersonal nature of the implicated virtues is expanded upon throughout the book; to briefly foreshadow this aspect of the argument, the distortion of specifically *interpersonal* virtues is involved in part because murder is involved, and murder, of course, is interpersonal, intimately and horribly so.

The "Santa Claus" incident illustrates another theme that will recur throughout the chapters that follow. Although my claim is that all murder-suicides can be classified within a taxonomy based on distorted virtue and most fit cleanly within one category, some events span categories. The Pardo incident would not have included suicide at all if not for his failed escape plan and his invoking self-control in his decision to kill himself, and so it belongs outside the category of true murder-suicide. But there are clear elements as well having to do with Pardo's distorted sense of justice. He meted out revenge—his version of justice—on his ex-wife and her family. Indeed, had Pardo's awful plan worked, the incident would have been like most murders—killings perpetrated in anger for the sake of revenge...[20]

another reason to ultimately classify this incident as outside the realm of murder-suicide *per se*.

Nature can be like that—even true categories have fuzzy edges, and occasionally the edges of adjoining categories overlap.[21] This speaks to a potential advantage of the taxonomy that this book will propose and defend: despite nature's fuzzy edges, virtually all murder-suicides fit neatly within the proposed categories. Of course, it is also possible that the fuzziness has to do not with nature, but with a weakness of the framework developed here, a possibility explored further in this book's final chapter.

The Virginia Tech killer fits well within one of the four core areas of true murder-suicide, but with some undertones of a second core area. His primary motive, he genuinely believed, was justice, but there were undertones of glory in his way of thinking as well. As with Columbine, the true motives in the Virginia Tech incident have been obscured somewhat by the media's coverage and interpretation of the event, and, also as with Columbine, reference to the virtue-based typology proposed here would bring the killer's motive into clearer focus.

In the videos he recorded and in his suicide note, Cho voiced his contempt for wealthy people, complaining about his peers as "rich kids" and "deceitful charlatans" and as regularly engaging in "debauchery." In those same materials, Cho compared himself to Jesus Christ, in that, by killing the "rich kids," he would become "the savior of the oppressed, the downtrodden, the poor, and the rejected."[22]

In his comparison of himself to Christ, and in some of the other materials Cho sent to NBC, references to the virtue of glory can occasionally be detected. But, in Cho's mind, the reason he would receive glory is because he would deliver justice; the virtue of justice was primary for him (and grossly perverted by him).

The panel that investigated the incident foreshadowed the prevailing theme of this book. They wrote of Cho, "his thought processes were so distorted that he began arguing to himself that his *evil* plan was actually doing good."[23] President Obama said much the same thing about the Ft. Hood psychiatrist who, in 2009, killed 13 people (apparently expecting that he too would be killed in the process; he nearly was, but survived). The President characterized the incident as involving "twisted logic"—stated differently, the perversion of virtue.[24]

The Definition of Genuine Murder-Suicide

What is a murder-suicide; what is its technical definition? This may seem an achingly obvious question—it is simply an occasion when someone perpetrates one or more murders followed by his/her own suicide, right? The opening quotation to Hervey Cleckley's[25] *The Mask of Sanity*—a work to which we will return—is "Non teneas aururn totum quod splendet ut aururn," attributed to Alanus de Insulis, and translated "Do not hold as gold all that shines as gold."

In some ways, "a murder followed by a suicide" is a quite true and serviceable definition, but it nevertheless glosses over some important details and thus can be viewed as fool's gold. For example, what of the legal distinction between murder and, for instance, unpremeditated homicide (or for that matter manslaughter)? What of circumstances in which an individual kills others, and then dies by suicide a year later...or ten years later?

I have already alluded to one characteristic of promising intellectual ideas—they surprise and quickly thereafter produce the thought "of course, how could it be otherwise?" My claim is that viewing murder-suicide as a perversion of virtue has this characteristic, a claim I will attempt to deliver on in the pages and chapters that follow.

Another feature of promising intellectual ideas is that they are born into a sea of problems that they themselves help to solve— they serve as a lever in the Archimedean sense of "Give me a lever long enough and a fulcrum on which to place it, and I shall move the world."[26] A very satisfying example from the history of science involves the unusual orbit of Mercury. In the last half of the 19th century, this anomaly was recognized as a serious problem for Newtonian physics, which expected an elliptical orbit for Mercury (and for the other planets too)—and there were additional problems for Newtonian physics beyond Mercury's puzzling orbit. Einstein's theory of general relativity was born into this sea of problems and in quick order solved many of them. Why is Mercury's orbit unusual? What, from a Newtonian perspective, is befuddling is, from Einstein's theory, not only explicable but predicted: the Sun's strong gravity has many effects, including the curvature of space. These effects are especially strong "locally," and Mercury, the closest planet to the Sun, is local. One consequence for Mercury of being local is a noticeable alteration in its orbit. The effects of the Sun's gravity, of course, do not stop at Mercury; the orbits of the other planets are altered, too, but they are far away enough from the Sun that the effects are difficult to detect. Einstein's theory, developed in the early 1900s, can precisely predict alterations in celestial objects' orbits, such as those of the dwarf planets Pluto and Eris, which were not discovered until decades later. Powerful theories thus not only solve problems that have puzzled people for years or decades, but they also lay in wait to solve problems of which people are not yet even aware. Einstein's work is a towering example of a theoretical model's explanatory power (and of imperfection even in towering work, as subsequent work in physics has shown regarding some of Einstein's views).

I am not aiming to explain the mysteries of the universe, but nevertheless, can the model I am proposing here solve some of the problems it was born into, like the definitional ones involving the legal distinction between murder and unpremeditated homicide, and the "time lag" problem?

I believe it can, although it is also bound to have its own imperfections. If, as this book contends, suicide is always decided on first in murder-suicide incidents, and thus is a point of departure from which perpetrators of murder-suicide plan others' deaths, then the question of premeditation is solved. Murder-suicides are inherently premeditated. "Murder-suicide" is thus a defensible term; expanding the term—as some have suggested—to something like "homicide-suicide" is not only unwieldy but could also be viewed as inaccurate.

It is interesting to consider the premeditated nature of murder-suicide in light of Meloy's[27] distinction between predatory and affective violence.[28] Affective violence, according to this perspective, is emotional and reactive, involving high autonomic arousal, and with threat reduction as a main motive. Predatory violence, by contrast, is relatively unemotional and is planned and purposeful (this account is compatible with those that emphasize instrumental/proactive vs. reactive forms of violence).[29] The present perspective on murder-suicide includes both affective and predatory elements. The emphasis is on premeditation, a key aspect of the predatory type; however, because of the involvement of virtue and its perversion, emotion runs very hot, a key aspect of the affective type.

This perspective also illuminates, and perhaps solves, the "time lag" problem. Any murder that is planned as an antecedent to suicide, and that in the process perverts virtue, qualifies as a murder-suicide incident according to this book's perspective, and this is true irrespective of the time interval between the murder and the suicide. Given the contingent nature of suicide and murder in these incidents, and given that both are tied together in perpetrators' minds by a perversion of virtue, it is no surprise that the time interval between murder(s) and suicide is almost always on the order of minutes or hours.

But it need not be. This framework allows for the rare possibility of an interval of days or even longer. For example, the following scenario would qualify as a murder-suicide, despite a week-long interval. A man living in California decides on suicide and plans his death for a specific California location. But, in a perversion of the virtue of justice, he believes his ex-wife, now living in New York, should die too. The man travels to New York, perpetrates the murder, and takes several days traveling back to California. Once there, he spends two days attending to final affairs and then dies by suicide as planned, a full week after his wife's death. The time lag in this example, though considerable, does not alter the essential nature of this incident as a murder-suicide: premeditated murder occurred and was preceded by plans for death by suicide, all in the name of virtue as understood by the perpetrator.

Death by Suicide, Far from Being Impulsive, Is Premeditated, as Is Murder-Suicide

Time elapsed between murder and suicide is thus not a fundamental aspect of the definition of murder-suicide. This is a refrain of a related truth regarding suicide *per se*, a truth that is very widely misunderstood, and one that I will dwell on here because it informs an understanding of murder-suicide as well. Understanding suicide *per se* is essential to the argument of this book for many reasons, including that the framework developed here views murder-suicide as a subset of suicide in general.

Many people assume, quite wrongly, that suicide occurs literally impulsively, on a whim, in true "spur-of-the-moment" fashion. Consider, to take just one of many possible examples, the following passage from a book that is otherwise well done; the passage is discussing the nature of suicide: "For some, it is a daring recreational maneuver that goes a little too far, often in the setting of drunkenness or a drug high. Momentary desperation impels others to jump off a cliff, a building, or a bridge or in front of an oncoming train or bus. If one is faced with a lethal opportunity in the here and now, death can be achieved impulsively, courtesy of an instantaneous decision."[30] This is just not so; if it were, one would expect the majority of suicide decedents to have alcohol or drugs of abuse in their systems at the time of death as revealed by toxicology reports. But the clear minority do—another surprising and underappreciated fact and one that will be expanded upon later in the book.

Compare the foregoing passage on "impulsive suicide" to the following account from *An Unquiet Mind* by Kay Redfield Jamison,[31] about her own experience with suicidal behavior: "for many months I went to the eighth floor of the stairwell of the UCLA hospital and, repeatedly, only just resisted throwing myself off the ledge."[32] Eric Wilson's[33] memoir *The Mercy of Eternity* contains several passages on suicidal thinking that also ring true and, not coincidentally, also contradict the notion of "suicide on a whim." For instance, describing the many times he had imagined his death by hanging, he wrote, "I witnessed myself hanging from one of the rafters in our basement. I was swaying dead from side to side, the wood squeaking slowly. A naked lightbulb glared on my shocked blind eyes."[34]

These are the true signatures of serious suicidal behavior: a long (months-long in Jamison's and Wilson's experience) process of thought and behavior, in complete contradistinction to the notion of death by suicide on a mere whim.[35]

A similarly informative example, and one that is particularly haunting and tragic as well, occurred in the Boston area. A man in his 30s approached Harvard Yard, scaled the steps of Memorial Church, and fired one gunshot into his temple. One might conjecture that the man impulsively decided to enact his death on this particular day, but such supposition could not be more contradicted by the facts. For the previous five years, the man had worked on his suicide note, which, when finished, totaled 1,905 pages and contained 1,433 footnotes and a 20-page bibliography.[36] An essential point is that, as extreme as the preparation of a books-length note is, it is far *more* representative of death by suicide than is the notion that suicide occurs on a whim (a true example of which I have been challenging audiences to point me to for years, and to date I have been persuaded of no such cases, while all the while cases involving deliberation and planning happen daily). Imagine, incidentally and hypothetically, that the man's very long suicide note had never been discovered, and that he had disclosed his years-long suicidal process to no one. His death, under that scenario, could appear to have been impulsive, when it was no such thing.

In actual fact, death by suicide—like the phenomenon of murder-suicide—is an extremely fearsome and daunting thing and thus requires considerable thought, planning, and resolve. And even when these have occurred, even when people are, by all accounts, expressly and deeply suicidal, even then, many people back away from death at the last moment. Or, people wish they could back out at the last moment but cannot because they have already initiated a sequence that should lead to their deaths, as the accounts of the very few people who survive a jump from the Golden Gate Bridge show. These lucky few report a profound regret at their decision, in mid-air, during the four seconds the fall takes (and this fact illustrates one of the many deep tragedies of suicide, because it indicates that a large proportion of those who die likely regretted their decision too).[37] This is only as it should be in creatures evolved to be self-preserving.

The myth that suicide occurs impulsively in "spur-of-the-moment" fashion is deeply entrenched in the public mind. I anticipate, therefore, that a similar misunderstanding exists regarding murder-suicide, and thus it is worthwhile to explore this issue in some depth at this juncture, first as regards suicide *per se* and then using that discussion as a lens through which to understand the same issue as applied to murder-suicide.

People view death by suicide as occurring rashly for a few reasons. First, suicide can genuinely surprise decedents' loved ones, seeming to come completely from "out of the blue." "Spur of the moment" and "out of the blue" have an understandable conceptual compatibility in people's minds: things that come from "out of the blue" impinge on our awareness suddenly, and suddenness is a feature of true "spur-of-the-moment" phenomena. An essential distinction, however, is between the suddenness of the phenomenon in question and the suddenness with which it enters our awareness. Small meteors come literally "out of the blue" and quite suddenly enter the awareness of happenstance observers, but it is inaccurate to describe them as "spur-of-the-moment" things (especially considering the eons-long journeys of many of them). Similarly, death by suicide can shock a decedent's loved ones *and* be planned for weeks, months, or even years. This is because of the human capacity, quite stunning in some cases, for privacy and secrecy.

Thus, a first reason that the "impulsive suicide" myth persists is that people cannot believe that a loved one planned something so momentous as death and kept the process private. A second and closely related reason is that it can be extremely disconcerting for family members to consider that they did not know *everything* about their loved one, now lost to suicide. I have spoken to bereaved people who are absolutely certain that suicide is an inherently impulsive act, because to think otherwise is to allow that their loved one harbored life-and-death thoughts and kept them private. This understandable reaction occurs in many but especially in the parents of female teens or young women who have died by suicide; like many (but certainly not all) parents of girls, they came to expect an openness about even very sensitive things. They assume—alas, wrongly, I am afraid—that this openness would attach to every last thing, to include plans for suicide. This assumption of complete openness is, of course, theirs to include as they wish as part of the narrative of their loved one's death; some seem to find considerable comfort in the view, and those bereaved by suicide need comfort (and are often denied it).

A similar assumption is held by some clinicians who have lost a patient to death by suicide. They believed that the therapeutic work was going well, and they noticed their patient making future plans for things big and small, including scheduling next week's therapy appointment. The fact that the patient was dead by suicide before next week's appointment indicates to them that the death was impulsive and, further, inherently unpreventable.

But clinicians should know of people's capacity for secrecy, and also for simultaneously planning contradictory things, like suicide and attending next week's therapy appointment. Moreover, to insist on unpreventability as a general principle is a breach of practice standards, not to mention a public health menace. Even further still, there is at least one health plan in the United States that has adopted a "zero suicide" policy—a policy in which the stated goal is to prevent all suicides within the system. This program claims zero suicides over the course of 30 months or so, and this among a large, at-risk population.[38] The details of this claim are, to my knowledge, not publicly available and therefore are hard to evaluate, it should be acknowledged. But apart from the essential question of effectiveness, notice the difference in attitude between clinicians who insist on unpreventability, on the one hand, and a sizable health plan in the United States, on the other hand, that views suicide as preventable enough that they are striving for complete elimination of deaths by suicide among their patients.

The proper attitude, then, is to promote prevention, which saves lives every day, to rigorously adhere to clinical standards, and also to acknowledge that the mental disorders that spur suicide are forces of nature, strong enough that in our battle with them, we may lose on occasion (as happens in cardiology, oncology, and many other areas of health care). But we will win many, too, and the crucial thing is we do not know in advance which are winnable and which are not, and so we have to fight all of them as if they are winnable. There are few things more tragic than a fight against misery that is both winnable and unfought.

One understands why assumptions like transparency of intention crop up—they provide a kind of comfort and solace—but these kinds of assumptions are untenable. As already alluded to, such assumptions construe humans as transparent creatures, with every thought or feeling readily apparent to others. A moment's reflection on one's own mental experiences, and how many of them are kept private even from very close intimates, will rapidly undo this assumption.

"Flash-in-the-Pan" Suicidal Thoughts, Including When on a High Place

I have delved into this issue of suicide being misunderstood as "spur of the moment" because the issue informs murder-suicide too; I am suggesting in this book that, like suicide, murder-suicide, far from being impulsive, is planned well in advance of the act. I will return to murder-suicide shortly, but there is yet another informative aspect of suicide that deserves attention. Still another source for the myth that death by suicide is an inherently impulsive act comes from the phenomenon, relatively widely experienced in the general population, of "flash-in-the-pan" suicidal thoughts, often when on a high place. A surprisingly high proportion of people report the impulse to jump as they cross a bridge, or are on the balcony of a high building.

It is important to emphasize that a majority of people who have this experience are neither depressed nor suicidal at the time.

This experience has been used to defend a view that I think is not only in error but also confused (bringing to mind the Baconian dictum that truth emerges more readily from the former than from the latter;[39] I believe Sir Karl Popper would agree)—namely, that we all have a little death wish in us. This folly, although it started with or at least was greatly popularized by psychoanalysts, has crept far beyond psychoanalytic or even academic-clinical circles to influence the wider culture. A representative example appeared in the May 2010 issue of *GQ*, in an article on a man in China who patrols bridges in an effort to prevent suicides therefrom. The article's author, in a meditation on suicide in general, wrote, "One's reasons for being on the bridge belonged to the mysterious underworld in all of us...what would it feel like to fly, to prove you could? The mere glimmer seemed almost too dangerous to consider. If you let it in, is that when you started to feel the pull of this other force? Could it be stopped?"

A "death force" *can* be stopped, easily, as can most things that do not exist in the first place (I resist saying "everything that does not exist can be stopped," because, alas, many falsehoods have virus-like staying power). The notion of a death force is implausible, and in this, Hervey Cleckley agreed. In his book *The Mask of Sanity*, he wrote, "The concept of an active death instinct postulated by Freud has been utilized by some to account for socially self-destructive reactions. I have never been able to discover in the writings of Freud or any of his followers real evidence to confirm this assumption."[40] Moreover, to imagine a generalized death wish is to misunderstand, among other things, one of the most important ideas in history, evolution by natural selection.[41] What is really happening, then, when a person in a more-or-less normal state of mind walks across a high bridge and finds herself inexplicably concerned with jumping?

An example from a different context may be illuminating. Those who work in the wild in settings with lots of snakes regularly report the following experience. They are strolling along, when their body all of a sudden reacts, for example, by leaping backward; only then, after a half-second or so, does the snake enter into their conscious awareness. An excerpt from Percy Fawcett's journals, published posthumously in 1953, and cited in Lynne Isbell's 2010 book *The Fruit, the Tree, and the Serpent: Why We See So Well*, gives an account of this intriguing experience: "What amazed me more than anything was the warning of my subconscious mind, and the instant muscular response. [These snakes] are reputed to be lightning strikers, and they aim hip-high. I had not seen it till it flashed between my legs, but the `inner man'—if I can call it that—not only saw it in time, but judged its striking height and distance exactly, and issued commands to the body accordingly."[42]

We have evolved some systems of perception and thought that are extremely fast and automatic but are "dumb" in the sense that they cannot be modulated, that they are not subject to conscious control. And we have other systems too, which, while relatively slow, are "smart" because they can be subjected to reflection and thus can be modulated.[43] Like a lot of evolved systems, the interplay of these two sets of systems is quite workable (fit enough to have survived, thus their current existence) but not 100% harmonized.

Concern about jumping from bridges represents an instance when these systems are not optimally harmonized. To put it somewhat crudely, I believe this experience stems from one's amygdala, the brain's fear-processing center, sending a message in its usual rapid and terse way along the lines of "high place, back up, you might fall." And the person does back away, even before the thought enters awareness—this is how our brains are wired to work under conditions of danger. The person is perplexed; from her experience, her body backed away and then there was a thought in her head about "you might fall," just as the field researcher leaps first and then is aware of the snake.

People doing research in the wild and who confront snakes there tend to be educated about evolution, nature, brain systems, and the like, and they tend not to buy into ideas like death wishes and psychoanalysis. And so to my knowledge, they never experience a line of thought like "my body reacted to a snake even before I had the image in my head, and then the image was there and I viewed it with fear…that must mean that I have a death wish involving snakes." They would endorse the motto of one of George Orwell's favorite childhood teachers: "No one can understand difficult things like their own lives unless they understand simpler things like animals and birds first."[44]

People walking across bridges are a more varied lot, not on average trained in evolution and brain systems and the like, and are quite

subject to general notions floating around in the culture like unconscious death wishes as a part of human nature. They therefore are
prone to lines of thought like "I flinched and was suddenly aware of
the possibility of falling; but of course I can't fall, there's a railing and
I'm feet from it…this must mean that I have a death wish involving
heights." Because the thought seems to arise suddenly, it tends to
encourage the unfortunate idea that suicidal phenomena are inherently impulsive.

The bridge-walker's mistake is to imagine that the ancient
fast-path fear reaction should be subject to reason, should care that
there's a railing. But it doesn't care; it is, in a sense, "dumb" and cannot handle rational information like "no need to worry, the railing
will protect me." Railings did not exist hundreds of millions of years
ago, when this module evolved in mammals and became very sensitive and attuned to vision in certain primates, including our ancient
ancestors. The bridge-walker is hearing her amygdala but misattrib-
uting it to a death wish.

This phenomenon of "high place suicidal impulses" has been
speculated about often, but with scant data to rein in or inform speculation. A study by Hames and colleagues[45] aimed to redress the lack
of data on the "high place phenomenon." Over 400 college students
were asked questions like "When standing on the edge of a tall building or walking past a bridge, have you ever had the urge to jump?
How often has this happened in your lifetime?" and "When you are
inside a tall building have you ever imagined jumping out a window? How often has this happened in your lifetime?" The students
responded using the following rating scale: 1 = never; 2 = very rarely;
3 = rarely; 4 = occasionally; 5 = frequently; 6 = very frequently.

Across all such questions, the *lowest* percentage of people who
endorsed experiencing the "high place" phenomenon of the urge to
jump was 25%. For some questions, the corresponding percentage
was 50%. More than 10%, on average, endorsed undergoing this
experience "occasionally," "frequently," or "very frequently." It is
plainly not a rare phenomenon. What is more, these high percentages rule out the possibility that suicidal people are the ones endorsing the items; the percentages are too high for this to be plausible.
To make this especially clear, analyses were conducted on people
who, on a distinct measure of general suicidal ideation, indicated
that they experienced absolutely no suicidal ideation. Among these

non-suicidal undergraduates, the "high place" phenomenon was common, occurring in, at minimum, 23% of them.

Implicit in my approach to the "high place" phenomenon and in the questions Hames and colleagues posed to participants is the idea that all of us humans are wired to be afraid of a fall from a high place. If this were so, one might expect that everyone would overestimate the distance of a fall, viewing it as more dangerous than it actually is. And this is, in fact, the case. Writing of research on this topic in his book *On Second Thought*, Wray Herbert[46] states, "on the most fundamental level, we're all afraid of falling; it's a basic heuristic-driven survival mechanism, engrained over eons of evolution. It's a cognitive strategy for safety and self-preservation."[47] The cognitive strategy Herbert refers to is very rapid, virtually automatic. Its message is "danger!" It is a misinterpretation—one characteristic of aspects of our culture obsessed with death and sex—to view this safety signal as a death wish.

A similar—and similarly reasonably common—phenomenon occurs in religious settings, when someone about to kill himself hears the voice of God telling him not to (a thing, as we shall see in the chapter on murder, that also occasionally occurs when a person is about to kill someone else). The book *Salvation on Sand Mountain*,[48] which, interestingly enough in the context of the current discussion, is about snakes—more specifically, snake-handling in religious settings—includes an example. One of the people described in the book reoriented his entire life toward religion and snake-handling after an incident in which he was desperately suicidal and resolved to shoot himself. As he began to lift the gun to his head, he heard the voice of God telling him not to, to turn instead to religion and snake-handling. I believe he heard a voice, but I do not believe it was the voice of God; it was the voice of his amygdala, misattributed to God. It is interesting in this context, incidentally, how frequently snakes and religion are intertwined, from the Garden of Eden to snake-handling. These phenomena make one wonder if the amygdala's "voice" is the very source of religion itself.[49]

Should you care to test out this ancient fear module in yourself, and furthermore, should you wish to prove to yourself that it is operative beyond just high places, take a trip to the zoo. Place your face near the glass of a snake enclosure, and try to control your reaction should one of the snakes strike at you. You will likely fail, as did

Darwin himself. He reported in his 1872 book *The Expression of the Emotions in Man and Animals,* "our reason telling us that there is no danger does not suffice. I may mention a trifling fact, illustrating this point, and which at the time amused me. I put my face close to the thick glass-plate in front of a puff-adder in the Zoological Gardens, with the firm determination of not starting back if the snake struck at me; but, as soon as the blow was struck, my resolution went for nothing, and I jumped a yard or two backwards with astonishing rapidity. My will and reason were powerless against the imagination of a danger which had never been experienced."[50]

Darwin was interested in snakes and if asked would probably say that he even "liked" them; his amygdala, however, saw things differently, as indeed it was designed to do. By direct contrast, a woman described in the December 2010 issue of *Current Biology* stated that she "hated" snakes and spiders.[51] Yet, when researchers accompanied her to a local pet store, she made her way directly toward the snake terrariums, and when asked by an employee if she would like to hold one of the snakes, she readily agreed. She touched the snake's flicking tongue and looked on in delight as the snake slithered through her hands. Employees had to frequently warn her from touching other snakes that were venomous, as well as a high-risk arachnid. The researchers also accompanied the woman to a haunted house during Halloween. Not only was she unafraid of the hidden monsters who popped out to scare her, she even scared one of the monsters by poking it in the head out of curiosity.

Charles Darwin would say he "likes" snakes, yet cannot control his automatic fear response to them; the woman says she "hates" snakes and yet shows no fear in their presence (and no fear of anything else). What is the difference between them? In a phrase, an intact amygdala. Presumably, Darwin's amygdala functioned normally; by contrast, the woman had experienced bilateral damage to hers (due to Urbach-Wiethe disease, a rare congenital genetic disorder). The woman experienced other emotions normally, but her fear reactions were very blunted if not altogether absent. There can be a natural and normal disharmony in people such that fast and automatic systems override more deliberate ones; in this woman, there is an unnatural disharmony—she "hates" snakes but behaviorally is attracted to them—due to impaired amygdala functioning. Virtually all the people I know who have reported the inexplicable urge to jump from a high place are people with alarmist amygdalae. They are temperamentally fearful and have a lot of fears, including of course of heights.

In this book, and in my previous ones, my suspicion of psychoanalysis is readily apparent. This does not mean, however, that I think that every utterance issued forth from the mouth or pen of a psychoanalyst is incoherent or absurd. In my opinion, the individual psychoanalyst who most regularly said revealing and helpful things was Harry Stack Sullivan (not exactly an orthodox psychoanalyst for his time, a fact that I believe is not coincidental; D. W. Winnicott is in Sullivan's league on this dimension of insightful coherence, and he, too, was not particularly orthodox). I have already quoted Sullivan's statement that "we are all much more simply human than otherwise,"[52] a phrasing that I think combines parsimony with beauty. He said something else as well: "The [suicidal] revery studies danger, personal probabilities, with, as an unwitting goal, a goal that is not noticed by the person who is entertaining the suicidal fantasy, the prevention of this very act of self-destruction. The prevention of the hostile-destructive act is the unwitting goal, the unnoticed goal, of the revery process."[53] Sullivan argued that what is *experienced* as an urge toward death *begins* as an impulse toward safety.

Which, then, is the more believable account of the "high place" phenomenon? Do you think it is that we all, each and every one of us, have something inside that harbors a secret wish to die? Or do you think it is a perspective that in one form or another was written about and personally experienced by Charles Darwin, is expectable based on modern neuroscience, explains phenomena in settings as diverse as urban bridges and the snake-infested wild, is compatible with the theory of evolution, and was independently arrived at by Harry Stack Sullivan?

I think it is the latter, and this is one front in the assault I am making on the idea that suicide—and murder-suicide—are impulsive, spur-of-the-moment things, subject to whimsy much as is the casting off of peanut shells at the ballpark. The idea is ludicrous[54] and obscures genuine understanding of phenomena like murder-suicide.

In May 2011, a murder-suicide occurred in Florida; a man and his wife, both in their 20s, were visiting the home of relatives. Police concluded, after interviews with the relatives and with neighbors, that an argument between the man and his wife occurred during which the man shot his wife multiple times and then died by a self-inflicted gunshot wound. A neighbor interviewed by local media expressed surprise that the incident occurred while the couple were visiting relatives, rather than, for example, at the couple's own home. A police spokesperson remarked, "This is a crime of passion."[55]

These two details—the neighbor's surprise at the death's location and the spokesperson's comment on "crime of passion"—intimate that this event occurred rashly, without forethought, in the heat of an argument. A point of my work is to show how exceedingly unlikely this is. After all, the man had his weapon on him, and media reports revealed that he had threatened to shoot his wife before. The couple's relationship was marked by many disputes, including those involving escalating violence.[56] Further still, the man had very likely pondered his and his wife's death many times before. Had he not, he would be, I assert, simply unprepared to enact something as fearsome and daunting as killing someone else and then facing his own death.

Proper Terminology, the Primacy of Suicide in Murder-Suicide, and the Time Lag Problem

To return to murder-suicide's precise definition, the preceding discussion has set us up to reiterate a key point: Suicides in general, as well as a subset of them—murder-suicides in particular—are *premeditated*. We are not discussing manslaughter here, nor are we discussing homicide generally. According to the framework developed in this book, it is murder, plain and simple, premeditated and planned out to satisfy a virtue—either mercy, justice, glory, or duty (virtues about which, it should be remembered, people can be passionate indeed). The virtue is perverted, true, but in the mind of the murderer (and soon the suicide decedent), it is a virtue nonetheless.

I therefore suggest that the term "murder-suicide" is the most apt description.[57] A rival contender is "suicide-murder;" the advantage of this latter term is that it gets the mental sequencing right.[58] A disadvantage of this term, of course, is that it does not reflect the behavioral sequencing. That is, needless to say, the murder occurs first, then the suicide; thus the term "murder-suicide."[59] I am satisfied with either term, as long as the primacy of suicide in mental sequencing is acknowledged. Since it is an established term of art, I use "murder-suicide" throughout this book, from the title onward.

The primacy of suicide in murder-suicide suggests that if the murder rate changed and the suicide rate remained steady, the murder-suicide rate might also remain level. In fact, this very pattern has emerged in the United States. Evidence suggests a considerable decrease in murders over the last 20 years,[60] whereas the suicide and the murder-suicide rates have not decreased. The primacy of suicide in murder-suicide can also be glimpsed in day-of-week patterns: murder occurs more frequently on Saturdays and Sundays;[61] by contrast, suicide[62] and murder-suicide[63] are more likely to occur on Mondays and Tuesdays.

The primacy of suicide in the contemplation of murder-suicide can also be seen in the ruminations of a young man in England, described in the biography *Stuart: A Life Backwards:*[64] "there are times regular when I sit in this flat and I look around, and I look what's here in my life—do I really want to be here? If I've got my drink inside me I sit here having mad conversations with meself, talking about mutilating myself, killing myself, killing those who I think have done me wrong."[65] The mention of suicide precedes the mention of murder, not coincidentally I assert. This young man changed his mind about murder, but not about suicide—in an act that was anything but impulsive, he died in his 30s by stepping in front of an oncoming train.

In the usage of the term "murder-suicide," I both agree with and dissent from a 1992 statement from Marzuk and colleagues that appeared in the illustrious *Journal of the American Medical Association.* They said, "we continue to use the term murder-suicide in accordance with the predominant nomenclature in the literature…" With this portion of their statement I agree. But they continue, "…although we recognize that generically homicide-suicide is more applicable. Murder is a degree of homicide defined by statute in each of the United States."[66] "Homicide-suicide" would indeed be more applicable *if* some involved unpremeditated killing followed by suicide. But, it is argued here, the essence of genuine murder-suicide involves a premeditated appeal to perverted virtue. If so, the term "homicide-suicide" is inaccurate.

To get a further sense of the importance of this distinction, consider an incident that occurred in Wyoming in November 2011. A young man had decided, according to all of the available evidence, to die by driving his car into oncoming traffic. He did exactly this and killed himself and four other people in the process. The young man was traveling nearly 100 miles per hour at the time of impact; he did not brake the vehicle at all; there were no skid marks left by the vehicle; and the young man had sent numerous text messages about personal problems in the hour or so before his death (he was not texting as he was driving, however). On this basis, the coroner quite reasonably decided that the manner of the young man's death was suicide. A law enforcement officer remarked, again quite reasonably, "He picked the next vehicle that was coming down the road, is what it looked like to us."

If it is true that the young man "picked the next vehicle that was coming down the road," did he commit murder? Clearly he killed people, but did he do so with "malice aforethought" (a common definition of murder)? The Wyoming coroner ruled that he did, and this is a clearly defensible decision, in part because wanton recklessness can qualify under the law as malice aforethought, and the young man's actions were certainly reckless. But I would like to suggest a different possibility: that the young man's attention was so focused on his own death that he did not attend to anything else, including harming others. *Should* he have thought of others? Obviously. But did he? I doubt it. On this view, this incident would represent a different phenomenon than do clear murder-suicides in which the perpetrator plans out a specific individual's death because he believes it is the virtuous thing to do. That this latter possibility is not only viable but likely to be true is a point that I will develop throughout the book.[67]

The Role of Alcohol and Mental Disorders in Homicide, Suicide, and Murder-Suicide

A common aspect of unpremeditated killing is the involvement of alcohol. In his *Reflections on the Guillotine*, Albert Camus[68] wrote that it has been "estimated that [alcohol] is a factor in 60 percent of all crimes of blood."[69] More recent figures are compatible with this estimate. If, as I am arguing here, premeditation is a particular signature of murder-suicide, then one might predict that alcohol is more of a factor in homicide than it is in murder-suicide. And such is definitely the case. In a 2009 article in the *Journal of the American Academy of Psychiatry & Law*, Scott Eliason wrote, "Most of the information from murder-suicide studies showed that substance involvement in murder-suicide was about half that found in homicide alone."[70] Additionally, using this same logic that murder-suicide is a subset of suicide rather than of murder, one might expect that the involvement of alcohol in murder-suicide is roughly equivalent to that in suicide *per se*. Again, this is the case: a 2005 study in the *American Journal of Geriatric Psychiatry* reported a rate of alcohol detected in the bodies of murder-suicide perpetrators to be 15%, equal to the percentage detected in suicide decedents.[71] Taken together, research in this area indicates that the involvement of alcohol (and drugs of abuse) is higher in murder and homicide in general than it is in suicide and murder-suicide.

The result of 15% with above-zero blood alcohol content (BAC), incidentally, debunks the myth that most suicide decedents are intoxicated at the time of death—not at all true. In the study just mentioned, 15% had above-zero alcohol levels; the figure would be even lower still regarding those with levels above legal limits of intoxication. My colleagues and I are in the process of meta-analyzing this literature; to date, we have compiled studies including more than 100,000 suicide decedents for whom BAC was recorded at autopsy, and the percent with any alcohol detectable was 26%. Here again, this figure would be far lower regarding those whose levels were above a threshold like 0.08%. When other drugs of abuse are considered, it remains the case that the modal suicide decedent has a clean toxicology report (although, unsurprisingly, many have antidepressant and anti-anxiety medications in their systems).[72] Just as it is a misconception that people die by suicide on an impulsive whim, it is a falsehood that it is common for people to die by suicide while intoxicated. These two myths, each treated at length in my book *Myths About Suicide*,[73] encourage one another, leading to explanations along the lines of "he must have been drunk and because of that impulsively decided to die." When intoxicated, people sometimes impulsively decide to do *easy* things (e.g., urinate on the street; get fast food); they tend not to decide, impulsively or otherwise, to do daunting things (e.g., write serious literature; suicide). Intoxicated people may *say* they will do these things (and may do them when not intoxicated) but tend not to actually do them when intoxicated, in part because it is too hard to do so.

The BAC data of murder-suicide perpetrators resemble those of suicide decedents more so than those of murder perpetrators. This is yet another strand of evidence in the case built here that murder-suicide represents a sequence beginning with suicide.

Just as murder absent suicide often involves alcohol whereas suicide relatively rarely does, murder absent suicide rarely involves mood disorder whereas suicide, including murder-suicide, often does. Data from a Dutch forensic hospital corroborate this claim.[74] Researchers compared 297 individuals who killed an intimate partner, but did not attempt or die by suicide themselves, to 44 people who killed an intimate partner followed by a suicide attempt or death by suicide. One of the strongest differences between the two groups was that the latter had substantially higher rates of depressive illness. They were also much more likely to have threatened suicide in the past. Here again, the findings combine with those already touched on to show that murder-suicide, characterized as it often is by depression and suicide history, is more accurately viewed as a subcategory of suicide than of murder.

In this context, the role of mental disorders in murder-suicide deserves comment. The view articulated in this book is that what applies to suicide as a general category also applies to murder-suicide because the latter is a subcategory of the former. It is uncontroversial that easily 90% of suicide decedents experienced a mental disorder at the time of death. The careful and comprehensive psychological autopsy study carried out by Eli Robins and summarized in the 1981 book *The Final Months* returned a rate of 94%. My own view is that the more accurate figure, when all mental disorders and their subclinical variants are considered, is 100%.[75] This would suggest, then, that 100% of the perpetrators of murder-suicides experienced a mental disorder at the time of the incident.

Why not then develop a framework explaining murder-suicide by pointing to the role of mental disorders? In fact, some have tried[76], just as some have attempted to attribute suicide to mental disorders. These approaches emphasize an important truth—mental disorders play an essential role—but they founder on a key fact: Mental disorders are extremely common, suicide and murder-suicide much less so. Much the same can be said about attempts to attribute suicide and murder-suicide to things like relationship or financial problems. The latter can play a role but cannot constitute full explanations because they are so common and the outcome they are supposed to explain is so rare.

The virtue-based framework touched on above and developed throughout this book has, I would suggest, already delivered on a promise of incremental intellectual ideas—it has solved or at least suggested a plausible solution for a very basic definitional issue: What counts and what does not count as a genuine murder-suicide? The framework has the same promise with regard to another vexing definitional issue: the time lag between the murder and the suicide.

There are very clear instances in which an individual has committed a murder and has later died by suicide but that no one would identify as a true murder-suicide. For example, consider a person who killed someone when he was 17 years old, served 45 years in prison for the crime, was released, and then died by suicide 10 years after release, at age 72. The person killed someone and himself, and yet this is not a murder-suicide incident. This example seems easy to exclude from the categorization of murder-suicide because the time lag between the murder and the suicide was so long—55 years in this example. Of course, it is not just the time lag that suggests the independence of the two acts; it is also a discontinuity in the process. Whatever occasioned the murder seems discontinuous from whatever led to suicide. Continuity of process is essential to the definition of murder-suicide.

Fifty-five years is clearly too long a lag; so is 40; so is 30 and so on…but "so on" to what amount of time? A year seems a long lag but not impossibly so. Eighteen months? Two years? This, in my view, is an obviously futile exercise due to its necessarily arbitrary nature and to the related problem of "$N + 1$." That is, pick an amount of time N as the maximum lag time between a murder and a suicide in supposedly true murder-suicide incidents. Doing so would force the designation of a murder followed by a suicide N amount of time later as a true murder-suicide, but would force the exclusion from the murder-suicide category of the exact same kind of incident with a time lag of $N + 1$ day. This approach is doomed to failure and thus suggests that time lag *per se* is not an essential aspect of the definition of murder-suicide.[77]

Imagine, as another example, a scenario in which a man decides on murder-suicide involving his wife, kills her, but blanches at the prospect of his own death. He stores his wife's body in a freezer and approximately 2 years later sends a letter to police describing his original plan for murder-suicide. He then dies by self-inflicted gunshot wound.

You need not overtax your imagination in trying to conceive of such a horror, because it actually occurred in the Las Vegas area in September 2009.[78] The man's letter to police illustrated some rather important truths. First, it confirms that the incident was a murder-suicide. Therefore, and second, this was a murder-suicide with a two-year lag between murder and suicide, showing that time lag is not a very useful aspect of the definition of murder-suicide. Third, the man did not hesitate in killing his wife but did hesitate in killing himself, one possible interpretation of which is that killing oneself is even harder than killing someone else (though both things are difficult, to put it mildly)—a point that will be emphasized throughout the book.

The goal of this book is to argue that what *is* an essential aspect of the definition of murder-suicide is the reasoning that one's impending suicide necessitates, through an appeal to virtue, the death of at least one other person. The nature of these appeals often lends itself to fast timeframes, for at least two reasons.

First, the virtue-based mental process in genuine murder-suicide is along the lines of "I'm ready to die now but I have one last thing on this earth to see to." Once that last thing—the murder—is seen to, the final barrier to suicide is removed in the perpetrator's mind, and thus suicide usually follows very quickly upon the murder(s) in true acts of murder-suicide. Second, an enormously important and somewhat overlooked law of nature is that "killing of one's own species is hard to do."[79] Should you doubt this law, consider the many instances in war in which sworn enemies are shooting at each other from a distance of several yards, with no fatalities, or that physicians who participate in euthanasia are often troubled by it for years.[80] Furthermore, consider why several species very capable of inflicting lethal wounds on their own kind in the course of inevitable disputes about food, mates, or territory engage instead in methods of conflict resolution that are charmingly non-lethal (e.g., rattlesnakes wrestle; piranhas have "sword fights" with their tails). We will return to this law and its corollaries in future chapters, where we will see that it affects even people who are resolutely intent on killing someone else or on killing themselves.

Someone who has just perpetrated a murder is therefore in a unique state of mind. He has broken the barrier against killing. Moreover, he is in the state of physiological arousal that accompanies killing, a time-limited state, and a state that I believe is necessary for death by suicide (which is why, in the moments before their deaths, suicide decedents are almost never described as "sluggish" and very regularly are described as "agitated"). This arousal opens a window for suicide; because this state is time-limited, suicide following murder usually occurs within minutes or hours.

In pondering the question of time lag in murder-suicide, an analogy to chess may be helpful. Some chess games are lightning quick, finished in a minute or so; some chess games go on and on, sometimes even for days. This temporal aspect is not an especially useful feature in defining a "proper" chess game. Time elapsed is really beside the point. Analogously, time elapsed between a murder and a suicide is not essential to the definition of murder-suicide. By contrast, *continuity of process* is a core element in both chess and murder-suicide. In chess, one move follows upon another, according to a fixed set of rules, making for a continuous process. Analogously, murder-suicide involves a continuous process initiated by the decision to die by suicide, followed by the thought that one's decision to die necessarily dictates the death of at least one other person (a decision that involves an appeal to virtue), and followed finally by the murder and then the suicide. It is a premeditated, uninterrupted process, and whether it takes minutes or days or even longer is not very relevant.

In genuine murder-suicides, both suicide and murder occur as a function of a single continuous process. By contrast, some individuals have perpetrated a murder in their past, and then some time later, die by suicide, and these events are independent, having nothing to do with one another, *not* reflective of a single underlying process.

The chances of independent phenomena happening to the same person are calculated by multiplying the probability of the one by the probability of the other. Two successive coin flips are independent of one another, and the chance of tossing heads on successive tries is 25% or the probability of heads on the first toss (50%) times the probability of heads on the second toss (50%). If, unlike in coin tosses, the probability of the individual outcomes are both rare, the probability of their joint occurrence is geometrically so. Being struck by lightning twice is thus incredibly rare (mercifully). Also very rare is the phenomenon of perpetrating a murder, and then, in an independent process, later dying by suicide.

Importantly, this logic holds for *independent* phenomena. In genuine murder-suicide, the processes are not independent, and thus their co-occurrence is not as rare. This produces two insights: (1) the vast majority of instances in which an individual has perpetrated a murder and a suicide are genuine murder-suicides; (2) in rare instances, however, murders and suicides occur independently in the same individual. In past theorizing, these latter instances have been lumped together with true murder-suicides, which I believe is a mistake.

Most such mistakes are accounted for by murders followed by suicides that mimic true murder-suicides in some ways but do not meet the definition in other, essential ways. We have already encountered one such incident, that involving the "Santa Claus" killer. This horrible crime displayed some features of true murder-suicides, in that murders were perpetrated and shortly thereafter death by suicide was enacted.

Discontinuity of Process Rules out Murder-Suicide

Crucially, in the Santa Claus killer's case, there was a discontinuity in process. The original process in the killer's mind involved murder and then escape to another country. That process was interrupted by injuries sustained by the perpetrator in the fire he set. A second, distinct process then kicked in, involving death by suicide.

There are other examples like this as well. Professional basketball player Brian Williams (who changed his name to Bison Dele) was killed by his brother, who had joined Dele on his yacht for a trip around the South Pacific. Also killed were Dele's girlfriend and the yacht's captain. The brother's motive is a little hard to discern, but his jealousy of Dele's ability, wealth, and fame was well known. In the months after the murder, the brother used Dele's identification and forged Dele's signature to buy over $150,000 in gold, which led authorities to his trail. Police later learned that the brother had lived for a time following the murders in Mexico. This sad saga ended with the brother's death by suicide several months after the murders. The last person who had heard from the brother reported he said he felt he could not survive prison. In this incident, the time Dele's brother spent in Mexico, using Dele's identification and so on, represented a discontinuity between the murders and the suicide, ruling the case out as a genuine murder-suicide.[81]

The fact that Dele's brother escaped to Mexico and lived there for a time is reminiscent of the facts in the "Santa Claus" killer case, except that in the latter incident, the perpetrator was unable to make his escape to a foreign country due to his injuries. The cases resemble one another in another way too: both men killed themselves not as the primary act in their appalling plans and behavior, but because their primary plans unraveled and became untenable.

Here, too, notice that time lag is not a particularly helpful concept. The "Santa Claus" case as well as that involving Dele's brother were *not* murder-suicides, at least according to the view developed in this book. The lag in the Dele case—several months—fits with this view comfortably. But focusing on time lag in the "Santa Claus" killer incident would be deceiving: the time lag resembles that of most genuine murder-suicides, and yet, if the killer had had his way, there would be no time lag, because there would be no suicide.

Physician Richard Sharpe perpetrated a murder and later died by suicide, but like the incidents involving Dele's brother and the "Santa Claus" killer, this was no murder-suicide. Sharpe was a dermatologist on the faculty of Harvard Medical School and had invested his earnings well, earning him millions in the stock market. In July 2000, he shot his estranged wife to death, which earned him life in prison. The case became even more notorious because of Sharpe's unusual demeanor and appearance during the trial, and especially because reports and photographs emerged regarding his propensity for cross-dressing. In a suit to gain control of his fortune filed by his children (who ranged in age from four to 27 at the time), it was revealed that Sharpe injected himself with female hormones and stole underwear for his cross-dressing from his wife and eldest daughter. Almost nine years after the shooting, Sharpe hanged himself in prison.[82] Here, as in the incidents involving Dele's brother and the "Santa Claus" killer, it is wrong to view Sharpe's actions as murder-suicide. He perpetrated murder, no doubt; he died by suicide, no doubt. But these were independent processes, separated in time by many years.

The case of Amy Bishop also illustrates these principles. Bishop was a biology professor at the University of Alabama at Huntsville, where she attended a faculty meeting, sat calmly for several minutes, and then pulled out a gun and opened fire on her colleagues, killing three and wounding others. This occurred in the context of a contentious process determining whether or not Bishop would receive tenure at the university, a process that was unlikely to go her way. In the aftermath of the shootings, those looking into her background discovered that the gun-related deaths in Huntsville were not the first in which Bishop was involved. Approximately 20 years before the Huntsville shootings, she shot her brother to death. At the time, the shooting was ruled accidental, but that case is being reopened, as there is evidence that the incident was purposeful.

While imprisoned for the Alabama killings, Bishop survived a suicide attempt[83] and thus was trending toward someone who might be considered the perpetrator of a murder-suicide. Even had she killed herself, however, the facts of the case suggest that the murders and her death should have been considered as separate. This is clearly the case regarding the death of her brother. It is also the case regarding the Alabama shootings, because the process involved in the murders and that involved in her suicide attempt were distinct and discontinuous.

People like Bishop, Sharpe, Dele's brother, and the "Santa Claus" killer are primarily murderers and in a real sense are only incidentally suicide decedents (or in Bishop's case, a suicide attempter). Therefore, I would predict that they have past histories of behavior much more similar to those of murderers than to those of suicide decedents. Suicide decedents, unsurprisingly, often have significant histories of suicidal ideation and behavior, even well before their lethal attempt,[84] whereas murderers, again unsurprisingly, often have significant life histories of violence toward others, previous to the murder(s).[85] If, as this book argues, suicide is primary in true murder-suicides, then those who perpetrate murder-suicide should resemble suicide decedents more so than they resemble murderers, regarding past history of suicidality versus violence toward others. This prediction has "risky" properties—"risky" in the philosophy-of-science sense of putting ideas through very rigorous tests—because there is overlap between having a history of suicidal behavior and of violent behavior. That is, the one is a risk factor for the other. Despite the risk inherent in this prediction, it is borne out. As noted before, those who enact murder-suicides have past histories more similar to suicide decedents than to murderers.[86]

In the preceding section, I have considered incidents that, though they have included both a suicide and murder, are not properly viewed as genuine murder-suicides. The examples summarized above involve clear discontinuities between the murder and the suicide, each of which was conceived as an independent process in the mind of the perpetrator/decedent-attempter. Are there other kinds of incidents that have the superficial appearance of a true murder-suicide but, when examined in depth, are revealed to be otherwise?

Is Suicide Terrorism Murder-Suicide?

Besides events like those summarized above (and which are by far the main category of such phenomena that may appear to be but are really not genuine murder-suicides), a distinct phenomenon in which a person causes both his own death and those of others is suicide terrorism. Is suicide terrorism murder-suicide?

In suicide terrorism, the main intent is probably political, not personal (though, in the chapter on perverted glory, this issue will be revisited, including recent scholarship on suicide terrorism that views it as a form of suicide *qua* suicide; on this view, suicide terrorism is personal and only incidentally political). In a 2003 paper entitled "The strategic logic of suicide terrorism," Robert Pape analyzed every act of suicide terrorism that occurred between 1980 and 2001 (there were 187 such acts). He argued that explanations emphasizing religion and personal circumstances did not square with the evidence.[87] For instance, regarding religion, it happens that the group that has perpetrated the most suicide terrorism is decidedly not religious at all (Sri Lanka's Tamil Tigers, who adhere to a Marxist/Leninist view). Explanations based on the impoverished backgrounds of future terrorists are contradicted by evidence that such people come from all kinds of backgrounds; if anything, there is a recent trend for them to hail from relatively higher, not lower, socioeconomic levels. Pape concludes, "In contrast to the existing explanations...suicide terrorism follows a strategic logic, one specifically designed to coerce modern liberal democracies to make significant territorial concessions."[88] Moreover, he asserts, suicide terrorists perpetrate their crimes because they "have learned that it pays...The pattern of making concessions to suicide terrorist organizations over the past two decades has probably encouraged terrorist groups to pursue even more ambitious suicide campaigns."[89]

Both suicide terrorism and murder-suicide involve an appeal to virtue, usually some form of glory and justice in the case of suicide terrorism. But the differences may outweigh this similarity. Just as suicide terrorism is probably political and not personal, true murder-suicide is deeply (and horribly) personal and usually has little to do with the political. Far from being primary in suicide terrorism, suicide is merely incidental to the act of suicide terrorism, a means to a political end (though again, as we will see, some have contested this view by arguing that suicide terrorism is primarily a form of suicide; see Monahan, 2012, for a recent treatment of risk assessment of potential for terroristic violence). By contrast, in genuine murder-suicide, suicide is the alpha and the omega—it is the starting point, the foundation, as well as the culmination. It is an awful thought, and only partially true, but if anything, murder is incidental in murder-suicide—in a true sense, it is an afterthought to the decision to die by suicide. What is awful about that thought is to consider someone's death as an incidental afterthought; the thought is only partially true, because it is not really proportionate to view murder as this trivial in the process of murder-suicide. True, suicide is primary; but it is also true that once suicide is decided on in cases of murder-suicide, the perpetrator's every thought and effort turns to murder, because he, like this book, views it as part and parcel of a unitary and ongoing process.

Therefore, I believe it is mostly inaccurate to view suicide terrorism as a true instance of murder-suicide. At best, it is a fringe phenomenon, on the periphery of the core concept of murder-suicide. Importantly, a property of penetrating conceptual frameworks is that they illuminate even fringe phenomena. Should it be insisted that suicide terrorism counts as murder-suicide, the perspective presented here has two responses: (1) No, it is not, because of the numerous differences between the two phenomena, such as political versus personal motive and method choice (so often guns in murder-suicide and so often bombs in suicide terrorism) and many others; and (2) even so, suicide terrorism can be understood within this book's approach as a perversion of the virtue of glory with undertones of justice—the suicide terrorist may be reasoning, as do some of those who perpetrate murder-suicide, along the lines of "I have decided on suicide, but as long as I am to die, it is virtuous that I use my death for the glory of my society and for revenge and justice too."

To summarize the preceding discussion, very basic definitional questions have lingered in past work on the topic of murder-suicide. What counts as a true murder-suicide incident? Does time elapsed between murder and suicide enter into the definition? Is "murder-suicide" even the proper name for the phenomenon? The framework developed in this book strives to resolve these questions, defining genuine murder-suicide as a murder that is both derivative of a decision to die by suicide and based on an appeal to perverted virtue, excluding time lag as an essential aspect of the core definition and instead placing the emphasis on continuity of process, and affirming "murder-suicide" as the phenomenon's most apt name.

Figure 1.1 provides a visual summary of this book's perspective on the relations between murder-suicide and its components.

Some features of the figure deserve comment. First and foremost, the subcategory of murder-suicide, depicted in the black oval, is fully contained within the larger "parent" category of suicide (depicted by the white circle). Second, the area of "eclipse" between the "suicide" category and the "murder" category is intended to denote the fact that those who perpetrate murder at one point in time may later die by suicide, with the two behaviors being causally independent. That is, incidents like those involving the "Santa Claus" killer would be placed in the small area of overlap between the white and gray circles. Finally, the relative sizes of the figure's features are intentional, in

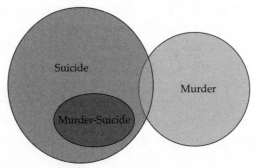

FIGURE 1.1 Relationships between murder-suicide and its components.

that they correspond (though not precisely) to the relative frequency of each category of occurrence. Death by suicide is the most common occurrence, followed by murder, followed by murder-suicide, followed lastly by the rare phenomenon of the causally independent co-occurrence of murder and suicide, like in the case of the "Santa Claus" killer.

The Demographics of Murder-Suicide

How common is murder-suicide? I am aware of very few books that are directly on the topic. An important early work was provided by West,[90] a work referred to throughout the book. Another is a novel; fiction, for all its merits, is just as likely to obscure as to illuminate a topic like murder-suicide. Still another, *Death by Domestic Violence*,[91] is on actual murder-suicides, but only those occurring between romantic partners. Attention to the topic of domestic violence is laudable, but murder-suicides occurring within intimate relationships do not, I think, represent a useful categorization of murder-suicides: some such incidents are motivated by perverted justice, some by perverted mercy, and moreover, these same motives can be discerned in murder-suicides occurring outside of intimate relationships.

Given that there are so few books on the topic, one may assume that murder-suicide is very rare. Alas, no. Most studies that have examined this question on U.S. samples have produced a figure of between 0.2 and 0.4 murder-suicide incidents per year per 100,000 people.[92] In 24 U.S. samples studied by Large and colleagues, the range was from 0.17 to 0.55 per 100,000, with a mean value of 0.32 (SD = 0.09).[93] Therefore, a reasonable lower-bound estimate of the annual U.S. murder-suicide rate is 0.25 per 100,000 people. As I write this in late 2012, the U.S. Census Bureau's population clock shows that there are 314,900,628 people in the United States. An annual murder-suicide rate of 0.25 incidents per 100,000 people thus translates into 787 murder-suicide incidents. Of the approximately 38,500 deaths by suicide in the U.S. annually,[94] approximately 787 are murder-suicides; that is, 2% of all U.S. suicides are murder-suicides.

Importantly, even if somewhat obviously, each incident results in the death of at least two people, and so a reasonable lower-bound estimate for the number of people in the U.S. who die in murder-suicide incidents each year is 1,574. Put differently, we lose at least four of our fellow Americans in murder-suicide incidents each and every day. This estimate is consistent with a *Time* magazine survey focusing on all deaths by firearms, which appeared in July 1989. The survey covered a one-week time frame and identified 11 murder-suicides using firearms. Extrapolation of this finding into annual rates reveals between 1,000 and 1,500 U.S. deaths in murder-suicide incidents each year, somewhat lower than the total of 1,574 noted above—as it should be, as the survey was conducted at a time when the U.S. population was smaller, and as the *Time* survey only covered murder-suicides involving firearms. This method, as we shall see, is very common in the United States, but it is not the only method.

The Violence Policy Center in the United States produced similar rates in a study using a national newspaper clipping service, in which reports of murder-suicides were culled from news reports.[95] The study focused on the first six months of 2011 and defined a murder-suicide as one or more murder(s) followed by a death by suicide within 72 hours—a definition I have already noted is somewhat problematic. The study uncovered 691 murder-suicide deaths, which included 313 suicides and 378 homicides; by definition, then, the 691 total deaths resulted from a total of 313 murder-suicide incidents. In each of these incidents, an average of just over two people were killed, indicating that in the majority of incidents, one person was murdered by the perpetrator, who later died by suicide, but that in a minority of incidents (approximately 65 of the 313, or around a fifth), more than one person was murdered by the perpetrator. Recall that these figures are for a six-month interval, and therefore the annual rates produced by the study would be 1,382 murder-suicide deaths occurring in 626 murder-suicide incidents—put differently, well over one every single day of the year, and over a dozen each and every week.

Another informative angle on the murder-suicide rate is to compare it to the suicide rate. If we take the figure of 626 murder-suicide incidents per year as numerator, and use 38,500 suicide deaths per year (which is the approximate annual U.S. count) as denominator, we find that 1.6% of all suicides are murder-suicides. In his in-depth study of a series of 134 cases of death by suicide in his book *The Final Months*, Eli Robins[96] noted 4 murder-suicide incidents; 4 of 134 produces a rate of 2.99%—a similar if slightly higher rate.

The Violence Policy Center study revealed interesting patterns involving gender and whether children were victimized. Of the 313 perpetrators in that study, only 30 were female; over 90% of those who enact murder-suicides are men. This gender ratio is higher than that for both suicide and murder *per se* (for which both rates are between 80% and 90% in the United States); murder-suicide, then, is even more male-linked than obviously male-linked behaviors like suicide and murder. A reasonable conclusion is that among those who decide to die by suicide in the United States (a total of around 38,500 per year), several hundred also decide to kill someone else; of these several hundred who so decide, virtually all, more than 9 of 10, are men.

Of the 378 homicides in this study (and recall this is for a 6-month time frame), the majority of victims were female; specifically, 288 of the 378 victims, or 76%, were female. This is a remarkable fact, because it is so different from victimhood rates in murder *per se*. In murder *per se*, the chance that the victim is *male* is at least 75%; in murder-suicide, the chance that the victim is *female* is approximately 75%.

What to make of this striking discrepancy? One clear conclusion is that murder-suicide is not best viewed as a subset of murder; the victim profiles in the two sets of phenomena are simply too different. A second implication is that perverted virtue in murder-suicide involves mostly men perpetrating the deaths of mostly women. Some suicidal males, in a distorted appeal to either justice, mercy, duty, or glory, believe that their suicide morally entails the murder of someone else, usually female.

Murder *qua* murder is very male-linked; as already pointed out, nearly 90% of murderers are men. But an additional perspective on just how male-linked murder is derives from the fact that far more than 99% of people executed for murder are men. The disproportionate number of men among the executed is explained by the facts that male murderers, as compared to female murderers, are more likely to commit aggravated acts of violence and to have past histories of criminality. These facts understandably influence juries. But they also show just how male-linked murder is. That murder-suicide is even more male-linked than murder is thus all the more remarkable.

In context of the virtue-based taxonomy to be developed in this book, it is of interest that murder-suicide is almost always perpetrated by men, and that several of the implicated virtues can be viewed as linked more to typical male than to typical female psychology (e.g., glory through violence). The fact that women are so commonly victims may relate to men's sense of justice in situations of perceived betrayal, and to men feeling (distorted) mercy for women. Still another advantage of the framework developed in this book is its potential to shed new light on the demographic pattern of murder-suicide.

As just noted, of these four virtues, justice—or rather its perversion—predominates in scenarios in which men decide on suicide and based thereon decide on the murder of a woman. Most of these instances involve men who have been jilted by the woman; the man decides to kill himself but then thinks how unfair it seems that he will be dead when his ex as well as her new romantic interest can live happily ever after. That is not just, or so he thinks. And so, in an appeal to distorted justice, he takes matters into his own hands and kills her (and sometimes the new boyfriend) before killing himself. Of the victims in murder-suicide, many of the 25% who are male are caught up in perverted justice incidents; they are the new romantic interest.

It is rare, fortunately, for youth to be victims in murder-suicide incidents, but it does occur. In the Violence Policy Center study summarized above, 55 of the 378 victims, or approximately 14%, were younger than 18 years old. Many of these were involved in "mercy"-related events, I surmise based on the conceptualization advanced in this book. That is, the parents have decided to die by suicide and based thereon think to themselves that it would be most unmerciful to leave their children behind to suffer the slings and arrows of the future's cruel fate. The thing to do—the merciful thing to do, or so they think—is to prevent the children's future ordeal by killing them now.

Overall, the Violence Policy Center study uncovered an annual rate of well over 1,300 deaths in murder-suicide incidents over a year-long timeframe. The study's authors state, "Due to the necessary limitations of our incident-collection method, this is most likely an underestimate. Anecdotal evidence suggests that our study may have missed a small percentage of murder-suicides. Whether this would be the result of an incident not being reported, not being reported as a murder-suicide, not falling within our self-imposed time frame, or not being published in a local newspaper is not known. In the absence of a national surveillance system, there is no means available for a complete and accurate count."

The authors are right to point to these sources of error, including the self-imposed timeframe of 72 hours—that is, they counted an incident as a murder-suicide only if the suicide followed within 72 hours upon the murder. On the one hand, this is a workable approach, in that the vast majority of true murder-suicide incidents conform to this timeframe; they do so because of the principle of *continuity of process*. On the other hand, as alluded to already, the "N + 1" problem affects this approach, in that an incident with a time interval of 72 hours would be counted as a genuine murder-suicide, whereas the same incident with a time interval of an hour or even a minute more would not. The arbitrary quality of this definition does not render it useless for the purposes of the study summarized above, but it does render it unworkable as a general definition.

Murder-Suicide Around the World

It is not just Americans who are affected by this troubling phenomenon. Though the data are somewhat sparse, there is an indication of some international similarity in murder-suicide rates, at least in the 10 countries studied by Coid in a 1983 report. A review by Large and colleagues, however, returned a rate of 0.15 per 100,000 in 40 non-U.S. regions, as compared to a rate of about twice that in U.S. studies (0.32 per 100,000).[97] Using the same population clock mentioned above, there are 7,058,306,501 people in the world; an annual, international lower-bound murder-suicide rate of 0.15 per 100,000 therefore translates into 10,578 murder-suicide incidents each year worldwide, or about 29 incidents per day. Here again, each incident results in the death of at least two people, and so a reasonable lower-bound estimate for the number of people in the world who die in murder-suicide incidents each year is 21,175. Put differently, we lose at least 58 of our fellow citizens of the world in murder-suicide incidents each and every day.

In one sense, then, murder-suicide is shockingly common—a daily occurrence that kills well over 21,000 people around the world annually. From a broader perspective, however, it is important to keep in mind that this cause of death is, in relative terms, quite rare. It can seem odd to speak of the cause of over 21,000 deaths per year as rare, but it is, at least as compared to causes of death such as heart disease, cancer, and stroke, which contribute to a yearly death rate of over

56 million. Indeed, far more people die worldwide every *day* (more than 150,000) than die in murder-suicide incidents in an entire year.

In *American Homicide*, Randolph Roth[98] documents the staggering difference between the United States and other affluent democracies in murder rates, with the United States having rates many times those of comparison countries. In the review by Large and colleagues, the U.S. murder rate was six times that of non-U.S. regions.[99] This is an interesting fact in general, but it assumes particular importance in the context of the earlier discussion of the primacy of suicide versus murder in murder-suicide incidents. If murder were primary in murder-suicide, then it would be expected that countries' murder-suicide rates would track their murder rates. By contrast, if suicide is primary in murder-suicide, countries' murder-suicide rates would track their suicide rates.

There is some supportive evidence for the view that murder-suicide rates track the suicide rates more than they do the murder rates. For example, as alluded to earlier, over the last 20 years, the murder-suicide rate has tracked the suicide rate (both have remained stable), whereas the murder rate has declined considerably.[100] In addition, the murder rates in Australia, Denmark, and Germany are about a quarter of the U.S. murder rate, but the suicide and murder-suicide rates in the four countries are more concordant.[101] Taken together, this suggests that the murder-suicide rate across societies may mirror the suicide rate more so than the murder rate, consistent with the primacy of suicide in murder-suicide advanced by the conceptualization developed here.[102] Barber and colleagues'[103] finding that suicide decedents and murder-suicide perpetrators were similar with regard to antidepressant use can be interpreted as further corroboration of a link between suicide and murder-suicide.[104]

However, there is also evidence that contradicts this view. Large and colleagues[105] found that homicide-suicide (their term) rates tracked homicide rates more than they tracked suicide rates.[106] Future research is needed to fully resolve this question.

The statistics on rates also affirm a different aspect of the framework presented in this book. As alluded to earlier, a key element of the definition of a murder-suicide has to do with its continuity of process. Put differently, the murder and suicide are not independent events; rather, they are contingent, in that the murder is predicated, via an appeal to perverted virtue, upon the decision to die by suicide.

If these were independent events, much as is a coin toss independent from a subsequent toss, then the rate for murder-suicides could be calculated by multiplying the chances of dying by suicide by the chances of perpetrating a murder. Rough and round estimates for the United States regarding the suicide rate and the murder rate are 10 per 100,000 per year, and 5 per 100,000 per year, respectively. Under the (mistaken) assumption that these are truly independent, the chances of perpetrating a murder and dying by suicide would be low indeed, 5 per 1,000,000,000. If this were the rate, there would be around 2 murder-suicides per year in the United States; in reality, there are well over 700 per year. Taken together, this analysis refutes the independence of these events and supports the view that genuine murder-suicide is characterized by a contingent continuity of process between the murder and the suicide.

Method Choice in Murder-Suicide

What are the usual methods used to enact suicide, and how do they compare to those used to perpetrate murder and murder-suicide? In the United States, firearms tend to be involved across the three categories of deaths. Both murder *per se* and suicide *per se* involve firearms between 55% and 70% of the time. The rate in murder-suicide is considerably higher, with some studies returning rates approaching 100%. For example, a study from Oklahoma determined that 97.3% of murder-suicides involved guns, and a study from Florida on older adults actually did return a rate of 100% involvement of guns. Other studies have reported slightly lower rates, but it is rare that a percentage less than 80% is detected.

One such instance involved the 4 murder-suicides in the series of 134 suicides described by Eli Robins in his 1981 book *The Final Months*. I quote Robins' descriptions at length because, characteristic of his writing and thought, they are succinct but illuminating:

"Subject with affective disorder killed wife with ax just prior to suicide;"

"Subject with alcoholism shot wife in presence of their four-year-old child just prior to suicide;"

"Subject with undiagnosed psychiatric illness (alcoholic symptoms) shot estranged wife from a hiding place outside the window of her house just prior to suicide;"

"Subject with undiagnosed psychiatric illness (affective disorder symptoms) shot divorced wife, with whom he was residing in their daughter's home, just prior to suicide."[107]

The rate of firearm use in this series is 75%, somewhat lower than usual for U.S. samples, but likely attributable to the small numbers involved. Incidentally, this series is revealing for other reasons: (1) as is so often the case, these incidents involve male perpetrators and female victims; (2) these examples are all likely perversion-of-justice kinds of cases, consistent with the fact that, of the four kinds of murder-suicide described in this book—perversions of justice, mercy, duty, and glory—the justice-related type is the most common;[108] (3) in each of these cases, the murder and the suicide occurred on the same day, with an interval between murder and suicide being seconds or at most a few minutes, consistent with the usual time-related signature of murder-suicide; and (4) each of the four perpetrators had a mental disorder of some sort, consistent with my view that suicide decedents suffer from some form of mental disorder in the hours and days (if not much longer) preceding their suicide, and since I view murder-suicide as a subset of suicide, this applies to perpetrators of murder-suicide as well.

Method choice represents an instance in which there is a commonality between murder *per se* and suicide *per se* (with gunshot rates of 55% to 70%),[109] with murder-suicide being the "odd phenomenon out" (with even higher rates of gun involvement).[110] This pattern is an exception to the rule: as we have seen, as a rule, suicide and murder-suicide show compatibilities. Here, however, it is murder and suicide *per se* that show similar patterns, and murder-suicide stands out. How to understand this particular pattern, this exception to the prevailing rule of murder standing out from suicide and from murder-suicide?

Regarding guns, there is perhaps a pragmatic reason for their very high rate of involvement in murder-suicide. Someone planning murder-suicide has at least two killings to consider: the murder of at least one other person followed by his own death by suicide.[111] Although it is chilling to do so, think of it as a problem in probabilities. As we have already seen and will see again, killing is very hard to do. Therefore, the probability of enacting a killing is less than 100%, and this is so regarding both murder and suicide, as those who survive close calls from these can attest (e.g., the death rate in self-inflicted gunshot incidents is clearly less than 100%). The probability of enacting two killings is (as long as the probability of enacting either one is less than 100%), by definition, considerably less than enacting one. For instance, if the probability of enacting one killing is 90%, the probability of enacting two is 90% × 90% = 81%. As the probability of enacting one decreases, the joint probability of enacting two decreases disproportionately; for instance, if the probability of one is 60%, the joint probability is 60% × 60% = 36%.

A probability of 36% is highly incompatible with the mindset of the person contemplating murder-suicide. Certainty is inherent to the process; an individual in this state of mind is so sure of his desire to die that it has become a foundation on which he has planned murder—a murder that, in his mind, is necessary as a matter of virtue. Even as compared to suicide *per se* and murder *per se*, the perpetrator of murder-suicide is intent on completion. The awful logic of very high intent leads to the choice of a maximally lethal method: gunshot. Poisoning someone and then poisoning oneself could lead to deaths in both instances, but with only moderate certainty; the same could be said about use of a knife, perhaps with lethality being a little higher but still far from certain. Firearms, though not absolutely lethal, represent the most certain option, and certainty is central to the mindset of the murder-suicide perpetrator. As already noted, surveys on the topic of method choice in murder-suicide routinely return rates of gun use of over 90%. The rate is not 100%, indicating that other methods, though rare, are occasionally involved. For example, in March 2011 in the Bronx, a man stabbed his estranged wife with a syringe filled with cyanide, and then he drank from a bottle of cyanide. Both died within minutes.[112]

The foregoing discussion assumes that one will use the same method for both murder and suicide, when of course it is possible to use different methods. But murder-suicides in which the perpetrator kills using one method and dies by suicide using another are quite rare. Why would this be so? I believe the answer derives from the basic and illuminating principle that killing is very hard to do. Doing a hard thing in one domain does not ensure that one can do a hard thing in another, even in another domain that is closely connected to the first. In a very different context, Michael Jordan learned this lesson when, after doing a hard thing in one sport (i.e., basketball, in which his team won many championships and he many MVP awards), he was unable to do so in another (i.e., baseball). This same principle would either thwart altogether or make exceedingly difficult the plan of a murder-suicide perpetrator to kill someone using one method and then kill himself using another...as evidenced by the fact that this occurs only very rarely. Having killed someone with, for example, a gun chips away at the natural barrier against killing with guns, making a subsequent gun killing (here, the suicide) not easy by any means, but easier. Changing methods would mean having to overcome a new and difficult barrier. In the example alluded to above of the man who perpetrated a murder-suicide using cyanide, not only did his killing of his wife likely facilitate his own killing, but before the incident, the man was very familiar with cyanide. He was a jeweler, and jewelers frequently use cyanide as a cleaner for their wares.

Another harrowing example from June 2011 illustrates this same principle. A man killed his wife and his young son by bludgeoning them with a baseball bat. Death by suicide with a baseball bat would be exceedingly difficult to enact; indeed, though I am aware of many unusual suicide methods, I have never come across a death involving self-bludgeoning with an object like a baseball bat. The man in this case did nevertheless arrange that he be bludgeoned to death: he placed himself in front of an oncoming passenger train.[113]

The media reporting of this event was unusually incisive. The chief executive of the county emergency services was described as saying that "parents who kill their own children often...are acting out of total despair. When suicidal people take the life of their loved ones it is because they believe that their son or daughter or wife are better off dead than living without them...In the case of children, a parent often thinks the child would suffer without a parent, and that in the parent's mind the murder is an act of mercy." The chairman of the county suicide prevention team sounded a very similar note; he stated, "in the mind of that father, when some people, particularly men, get suicidal and decide the world would be better off without them, they believe those close to them would be better off not to be here too."[114] These statements are highly consistent with this book's framework, and moreover contain many facts, including the primacy of suicide in murder-suicide, the involvement of "others-better-off"

calculations in suicidal thinking, the preponderance of male perpetrators, and the role of perverted virtue (here, mercy).

The claim that the individual planning murder-suicide is even
more committed to the acts than someone pondering murder or
suicide alone is supported by the extreme rarity of a person who
plans murder-suicide, commits murder, and then backs away from
suicide. This is a rare enough phenomenon that I am aware of very
few cases actually having occurred—though we have already seen
a case in which the perpetrator hesitated in his suicide, following
the murder of his wife, for two years, and there are occasional cases
in which perpetrators back away from suicide entirely. By contrast,
backing away from death occurs quite regularly regarding suicide;
many very suicidal people plan their deaths and even take steps to
enact their deaths but back off at the last minute, sometimes at the
last instant.

I began this chapter—and this book—with the inscription on the
headstone of a woman named Lydia Beadle, who was killed by her
husband in 1782. Her husband also killed their four children before
killing himself. This specific incident epitomizes some aspects of
murder-suicide—for example, it was perpetrated by a man and
against a woman (and, in this case, against their children). The headstone inscription describes the perpetrator as an "infatuated man."
Infatuation and fanaticism can be viewed as similar; regarding the
latter, George Santayana's[115] useful maxim was that fanatics have
lost sight of their goal but redoubled their efforts.

But I do not believe this maxim applies to the perpetrators of
murder-suicide. They have not forgotten their awful goal; on the
contrary, they are uniquely focused on it. The conceptualization
offered here narrows the interpretation of "infatuation" to mean the
perversion of the virtues of justice, mercy, glory, and/or duty. The
following chapters further present and defend this perspective.

Roadmap for the Rest of the Book

To fully understand murder-suicide in general, as well as the view
of it presented here in particular, a firm grasp of the constituents
of the framework is needed. The next chapter, therefore, delves into
the topic of murder *per se*. The following chapter does the same

regarding suicide *per se*, and subsequent chapters examine the essence and types of virtue. These reflections on murder, suicide, and virtue are intended to position us to understand their convergence in murder-suicide and how the perversion of virtue, at least according to this book, is the *sine qua non* of genuine murder-suicide.

Understanding Murder

"No matter how much you feed him, he keeps looking at the forest."—Russian proverb, usually said with reference to wolves

"…ask now the beasts, and they shall teach thee."—*Job*, 12:7

AS WAS DOCUMENTED IN THE PRECEDING CHAPTER, there is a considerable collection of facts and concepts indicating that murder-suicide is best viewed as a subset of suicide, not of murder. Nevertheless, and needless to say, murder is involved. Therefore, it stands to reason that some consideration of murder *per se* may provide important context for a comprehensive understanding of murder-suicide.

If you perchance are so inclined, try this macabre little experiment with your friends. Ask them to name as many serial killers as they can. Usually you will get five or so names: Jack the Ripper, the Boston Strangler, Ted Bundy, Jeffrey Dahmer, and the Zodiac killer represent common answers. Now, ask your friends to name a serial killer who has also died by suicide. Virtually all of them will draw a blank, and this fact, I believe, is telling—those who perpetrate serial killings are, in general, a different breed than those who enact suicide and its subset, murder-suicide.

There are, of course, exceptions (as there essentially always are in matters of human nature). Though not an example of genuine murder-suicide, a serial killer who died by suicide is England's Frederick West, who killed at least 12 people, many of whom were found buried in his yard. One of West's victims was his own daughter, whom he buried in a spot in the yard where the family barbeque grill was later located.[1] West hanged himself in prison in 1995.

This case, however, harkens back to those discussed in the last chapter, in which the process connecting the murders and the suicide is discontinuous. Serial killers like West kill for excitement, thrill, and pleasure. Though excitement, thrill, and pleasure are positive experiences, they are not virtues as the term is used in this book. The behavior of serial killers can be understood as a perversion, to be sure, but not as a perversion of virtue. The perversion of virtue is a signature not of killing in general, but of murder-suicide in particular, at least according to the perspective articulated in this book.

The Natural Barrier Against Within-Species Killing

At one particular Civil War skirmish at Vicksburg, as at numerous battle scenes, sworn enemies were squared off and shooting at each other at relatively close range, but could not bring themselves to kill each other and shot into the ground or into the air instead.[2] Like Civil War soldiers, piranha and rattlesnakes do not violently kill each other even in the midst of serious conflicts; instead, even though they have ready access to lethal means in the form of venomous fangs or razor-sharp teeth, rattlesnakes wrestle and piranha have "swordfights" with their tails to resolve disputes.[3] "In general, animals avoid conflicts whenever possible because fighting hurts, and the margins in the wild are simply too tight."[4]

We need to study various forms of killing so as to prevent them, much as we need to study various forms of cancer so as to prevent them. As written in our very cells and souls, killing one's own— including one's own self—is extremely hard to do, as evidenced not just by soldiers, piranha, and rattlesnakes, but throughout nature. To take another example from nature, bull elk are massive creatures, with lethal hooves and antlers. An all-out fight between two such animals would end in a very grisly scene of, in the best-case scenario, one elk dead and the other wounded to the point of near-death.[5]

Like rattlesnakes, they choose to wrestle instead, locking horns with one another and pushing each other to and fro. This pushing contest, somewhat like arm wrestling in humans, decides a winner with no need for death or injury, and no need even for the expenditure of much energy. Hervey Cleckely, in his 1941 book *The Mask of Sanity*, provides an entertaining example of these kinds of displays, in discussing a psychopathic patient he had encountered: "He was found in the custody of the police, against whom he had made some resistance but much more vocal uproar. The resistance actually was only a show of resistance consisting for the most part of dramatically aggressive gestures made while he was too securely held to fight and extravagant boasts of his physical prowess and savage temper. His general demeanor in this episode suggested the familiar picture of small boys, held fast by peacemakers, who wax ever more eloquently militant as the possibilities of actual conflict diminish."[6]

Nature has evolved efficient ways of resolving conflicts over food, territory, and mates, and thus has made killing one's own hard to do. Of course, nature includes a lot of killing, "red in tooth and claw," but virtually all of this killing is across-species, not within-species. Consider the remarks of a combat veteran who was describing how hard it was to kill even a deeply hated enemy in World War II: "I had to pretend I was killing a cobra—coiled to strike. If I didn't, it was almost impossible to take that first shot."[7] This veteran pretended to kill across-species to facilitate killing within-species, which otherwise would be too hard to do.[8]

It was too hard for George Orwell (the pen name for Eric Blair). He wrote in his 1943 essay "Looking Back on the Spanish Civil War," "a man presumably carrying a message to an officer, jumped out of the trench and ran along the top of the parapet in full view. He was half-dressed and was holding up his trousers with both hands as he ran. I refrained from shooting at him...I did not shoot partly because of that detail about the trousers. I had come here to shoot at 'Fascists'; but a man who is holding up his trousers isn't a 'Fascist,' he is visibly a fellow-creature, similar to yourself, and you don't feel like shooting at him." As John Wayne said in his last movie, *The Shootist*,[9] "It's not always being fast or even accurate that counts. It's being *willing*."

Of course, as these words imply, killing one's own is not impossible to do. This includes killing one's own self. And, virtually needless to say, it is not impossible for people to occasionally be able to kill one another. This happens in war, though the reality of how few actually kill in war is important to appreciate; it happens too, alas, in murder, but here again, the perpetrators of the act have unique characteristics that set them apart from others. This is, in a way, a quite obvious statement, but what is less obvious is precisely how such others are unique and different from everyone else.

In his 2004 book *War and Redemption*, Larry Dewey wrote of his work in Veterans Administration hospitals: "Before I started working with combat vets, I imagined that the fear of being killed was the hardest thing to face in war. Fear of death is difficult to face and conquer, but for most men the loathing of killing is even harder to overcome."[10] In *Exodus*, midwives were ordered by no less than the Pharaoh himself to kill baby boys born to Jewish women. The first chapter of *Exodus* continues, "The midwives, however, feared God and did not do what the king of Egypt had told them to do; they let the boys live. Then the king of Egypt summoned the midwives and asked them, `Why have you done this? Why have you let the boys live?' The midwives answered Pharaoh, `Hebrew women are not like Egyptian women; they are vigorous and give birth before the midwives arrive.'"

I have no doubt that the midwives feared God, and no doubt that they feared the Pharaoh (thus their excuse to him about vigor and fast birth). But an even more basic element—one that existed even before *Exodus* was written—and a main explanation for the midwives' behavior was that they were afraid of killing.

Killing is loathsome. This applies to killing oneself and to killing others (in fact, killing oneself combines the loathsomeness of killing with the fear of one's own death, an important and unique aspect of suicide to which we will return in the next chapter). Killing is hard enough to do that most soldiers in combat, as we have seen, simply will not do it. Dave Grossman, in his 1995 book *On Killing*, states that "only 1% of U.S. fighter pilots accounted for nearly 40% of all enemy pilots shot down in World War II: the majority apparently did not shoot anyone down or even try to,"[11] illustrating that even those killing at a distance struggle with the ingrained dictate not to kill. Similarly, and perhaps even more astonishing, Dewey[12] reviews evidence from World War II indicating that a *maximum* of 20% of those in infantry combat shot to kill. This fact is worth dwelling on. In war, in which a main point is to kill the enemy—an enemy that is usually vilified—*at most* one in five trained combatants will kill. There are only two conceivable explanations for this stunning fact: either humans are deeply cowardly, or killing is simply beyond most people's capacity. Reams of evidence support the latter view.

Military combatants are often drafted into service; many of them do not voluntarily seek out the role of soldier, with all that it involves, including potentially killing another person (in addition to potentially being killed). One might imagine, therefore, that a reluctance to kill would not surface in those who voluntarily seek out roles in which killing might be involved. It appears, however, that the reluctance to kill still emerges in the U.S. military, a volunteer force, as evidenced by anecdotal reports from Operations Desert Storm, Enduring Freedom, and Iraqi Freedom.

Additionally, consider law enforcement officers in this context. The FBI publishes an annual report on incidents in which police are either assaulted or killed. In recent years, the annual number of instances per year in which officers are assaulted is approximately 60,000 (or around 7 per hour every hour of every day, a rate that inspires sympathy and respect for police officers, if any more inspiration were needed), with approximately 10,000 of these events involving assaults with weapons. Of these 10,000 events involving assaults with weapons on police officers, approximately 3,000 involved the use of firearms.[13]

In these situations in which their lives are clearly in danger, as sometimes are the lives of bystanders, how often do people who sought out police work and who have been trained in the use of deadly force actually discharge their own weapons? To quote a 2008 summary of the findings,[14] "Most people outside the law enforcement community generally do not realize that many officers, given circumstances where they could employ deadly force, refrain and hesitate until the last possible moment or do not use it at all." In fact, the average annual number of people who police shoot and kill is approximately 350, or about 10% of incidents in which police personnel are directly threatened with a firearm.[15] This figure squares well with that mentioned above from World War II, in which a maximum of 20% of those in combat shot to kill.

There are, it should be acknowledged, many reasons that an officer refrains from shooting, but a very likely candidate for a main reason is that it is simply very hard to kill, even when one has volunteered for it, has trained for it, and is being actively threatened with death itself. And death itself definitely occurs for police officers who refrain from shooting: The annual FBI report documents multiple incidents per year in which an officer and an assailant are pointing weapons at each other, the officer issues several commands to put down the gun, after which the assailant shoots and kills the officer.

As this fact about police dying in the line of duty shows, killing is beyond most people, but not beyond everyone, mostly a tragic fact but occasionally not. In an example of the latter, Dewey[16] quotes a veteran who stated, "I killed everyone my squad killed. If I hadn't been there, my squad would all be dead. A few would never fire more than into the air. The rest would point in the general direction of the enemy and close their eyes and pull the trigger."[17] This soldier served his country admirably and saved many of those in his squadron. Did he do so because he callously enjoyed killing? His PTSD symptoms decades later suggest not. Rather, he did it because it had to be done.

Still, why him, and why not one of the others in the unit? Another example, this one far more sinister, raises a similar question. In his 2003 book *Under the Banner of Heaven*, Jon Krakauer describes two brothers, intent on killing their sister-in-law. These two brothers were under the impression that God had instructed them to kill their brother's sister, and as they were brutally assaulting her, one of the two men tied something around the woman's neck. As one of the brothers later recounted, "another fascinating thing took place: as he attempted to put the cord around her neck, some unseen force pushed him away from her. He turned and looked at me and says, 'Did you see that?!' I said, 'Yes, I did. Apparently this is not for you to do. Give me the cord.' I wrapped it around her neck twice and tied it very tightly."[18] He then killed his sister-in-law and her baby.

The depravities in this tale are legion, making even a starting point for its analysis challenging. Leaving aside such issues as why also kill the baby, and why God would choose two such as these with whom to communicate, and, having made that very dubious choice, why God would then communicate such a heinous set of instructions, let's focus our energies instead on two issues: the choice of the phrase "another fascinating thing" and the nature of the "unseen force" that intervened (which intervention, of course, did not prevent two appalling murders). These two things are sides of the same coin.

The "unseen force," which the brothers (characteristically) misunderstood as God, is indeed a force and is indeed unseen, but it is not God. Rather, it is the same force that bull elk, rattlesnakes, piranhas, and soldiers feel: the ancient and ingrained reluctance to kill one's own. One brother felt it and it stopped him. The other brother, however, was unmoved by this same force and took over for his brother and proceeded to perpetrate the murders of a woman and a baby.

This same man who perpetrated the killings later referred to the incident of his brother being stopped short as "another fascinating thing." Provided that the listener possesses skill, it is remarkable how just a few words can illuminate an entire personality. I am not the only one who holds this opinion; in his 2008 *Not With a Bang But a Whimper*, Theodore Dalrymple writes how a recent medical case reminded him "of how sharply a few words can bring into relief an entire attitude toward life and shed light on an entire mental hinterland."[19] Given due attention, each of the three words "another fascinating thing" drips with evil. To describe an aspect of these murders as a "thing" is to reveal the deeply callous character of the speaker. To use the word "another" is to imply that there were many things about this scene of horror, not just the supposed intervention of God, that the speaker found intriguing. And to describe anything about this act as "fascinating" is an obscenity. The person who uttered this obscenity—who murdered a woman and her infant—is, in addition to revealing the deranged nature of his mind, also telling an important if unsettling truth. I believe him that he found the series of events leading up to and including the killings "fascinating." That he found it so sets him apart, even from his own brother, who attempted but was revolted by the acts.

The two brothers are on either side of a threshold—an essential threshold to understand when it comes to killing in all of its varieties. On the one side of the threshold is the brother who paused, the one who, despite thinking it was a fine idea to kill a woman and her baby, and who participated very enthusiastically up to a point, nevertheless blanched at the crucial moment. In this respect, he is like the rest of us: afraid of killing deep down in his bones. In numerous other respects, he is not like the rest of us, in that, for example, he believes that God speaks specifically to him and commands execrable acts in God's name. The fact that we and this brother are in so many ways deeply different and yet in a few ways fundamentally the same speaks to the universality of some features of human nature. There are very basic things that we all share—we all have bones and blood. Almost as universal as bones and blood is the reluctance—perhaps more accurately, the incapacity—to kill our own.

Alas, the incapacity is not universal, as the murderous brother amply demonstrated. This brother is on the other side of the threshold from his reluctant sibling (and from the rest of us), and this is obvious not only in his actions but in his words—specifically, words like "fascinating." What one brother finds abhorrent another finds fascinating. One explanation for this situation would be that these two brothers are just inherently different from each other, perhaps genetically or temperamentally. Although that might be quite true, it is not a particularly satisfying explanation, as it begs the question. I prefer another explanation, which is that both brothers were in a similar state of very heightened physiological arousal—this is their similarity, and why I noted earlier that their reactions were two sides of the same coin. To one brother, the arousal was frightening, revolting, even disgusting; to the other, the same arousal was fascinating.

Habituation, Opponent Processes, and "Pushing the Envelope" Can Transform the Grotesque Into the Thrilling

I conjecture that a main difference between their two reactions to the arousing situation inheres in their different histories and experiences with the perpetration of serious violence on other people. To grasp this difference, imagine a pair of skydivers, one on her first jump, the other on her 25th. During and after the experience, both feel considerable physiological arousal. When asked about her state of mind, the inexperienced jumper replies, "I was afraid for my life." In response to the same question, the more experienced jumper answers, "exhilarated, a natural high...but I remember my first jump and like her, fear was my main reaction then."

What has happened to this second jumper that she finds an experience to which her brain is designed to react with panic to be thrilling instead? Experience happened. More specifically, through the repeated experience of skydiving, she has awakened what is called an "opponent process"[20]—one that is in *opposition* to the natural process of fearing for one's life while in a freefall. An opponent process, put briefly, is one that, though it starts out weak, becomes amplified and strengthened in reaction to repeated provocative experiences—the opponent process in skydiving is thrill, as it is in many such "daredevil" activities—and as it is, as we will see, in murder. This stands in contrast to the primary process, which starts out strong but fades with repeated familiarity with provocations. In skydiving, the primary process is fear, and everyone feels it on his or her first jump, because our nervous systems evolved to react with immediate panic when the prospect of falling from a height presents itself (even very young babies have this fear reaction, which one can see as they crawl toward a visual cliff, say that of a table, and then rear back when the cliff is perceived). This fear, however, weakens with experience, so that those making their 25th jump hardly notice it. This weakening of the primary process is called *habituation*—or put more colloquially, getting used to something.

People can get used to all kinds of things, and with various consequences. Cesare Beccaria, a leading legal thinker in the 18th century, was concerned that if legal punishments became more and more severe, people would get used to them and thus punishment would lose its deterrent effect. He was worried that, as punishments become more and more harsh, "human minds harden, adjusting themselves, like fluids, to the level of objects around them."[21]

To return to the incident of the two brothers who were, to put it mildly, under the mistaken impression of God's special interest in them, let us imagine that God had commanded this pair to do something more sensible than murder—say, skydiving. Imagine that the one was experienced, and that the other was not. Let's stipulate that both will experience considerable physiological arousal, only natural in the moments leading up to, during, and after jumping from a height of 10,000 feet. Had the brothers been interviewed after their skydiving sortie, one would have reported wanting to blanch, perhaps even doing so by refusing to jump (which happens fairly regularly to novice jumpers); the other, by contrast, jumped with gusto and found the experience thrilling; he might even say "fascinating."

As with skydiving as with murder (at least to an extent). Anyone who has been involved in a killing will report considerable physiological arousal (as long as the individual is not lying, as, of course, interviewed murderers may do). It is an act, to put it chillingly, that is unique in its novelty, and in this sense, it is exciting, not in the way that a trip to Las Vegas is (or rather can be) exciting, but in the way that a harrowing experience is exciting (thus people's attraction to movies in which many people are killed). Anyone who is involved in a killing *for the first time* will report that this arousal was accompanied by an array of mostly negative feelings—things like fear, revulsion, guilt, and disgust (sometimes to the point of nausea or vomiting)—just as anyone who is involved in skydiving reports fear on the first jump. The primary process of killing is fearful revulsion; that for skydiving is fear.

But the opponent process, as we have seen, is different, or at least will be, given repeated subsequent experiences. Skydivers come to see the activity of jumping from a plane—a quite unnatural one if you think about it even for a moment—as exhilarating; killers come to see the activity of killing—also quite unnatural—as exciting and "fascinating." All kinds of people involved in killing are subject to these reactions; they are by no means limited to lawless serial murderers. For instance, in his *Reflections on the Guillotine*, Albert Camus[22] wrote, "The new executioner has guillotine fever. Sometimes he stays at home for days at a time, sitting in a chair, ready to go, his hat on his head, his overcoat on, waiting for a summons from the public prosecutor."[23] That "guillotine fever" is limited to the *new* executioner is telling; more experienced executioners have progressed beyond it.

In *Ecclesiastes*, King Solomon[24] wrote, "The eye never has enough of seeing, nor the ear its fill of hearing...He who loves silver will not be satisfied with silver; Nor he who loves abundance, with increase." People who crave things—whether those things are spicy food, drugs, beautiful shoes, or horrendous violence—can, I suggest, see themselves in these ancient words.

Earlier, I characterized the murderous brother's use of the word "fascinating" to describe aspects of the murder of his sister-in-law and her infant as "obscene" and "evil." Is this what evil is, the opponent process to the natural revulsion to things like killing? In his 1996 book *Evil*, Florida State University psychologist Roy Baumeister has made essentially this argument. He documents, among many other psychological principles and processes, that people who came to relish grotesque murders began as people who were revolted by them.

Serial killers go through a transformation. In the 1981 book *Red Dragon*, the original of his Hannibal Lecter novels, Thomas Harris is aware of this fact when he has Francis Dolarhyde (who idolizes and attempts to emulate Lecter) state, regarding his unfolding murderousness, that it is "a great becoming." This "becoming" involves losing, through habituation, the natural negative reactions to killing, as well as gaining new reactions involving thrill, excitement, and the like. William Faulkner, in remarks to a group of psychiatrists while he was writer-in-residence at the University of Virginia, said, "People do foolhardy, reckless, dangerous things because it makes the glands flow good, makes them feel good."[25]

In his book *Our Culture, What's Left Of It*, Theodore Dalrymple[26] points to an example of just how grotesque murder can become and also implicitly refers to the same process as that noted by Baumeister and Faulkner. The pseudonymous Dalrymple describes "the escalation of appetite that Jeffrey Dahmer experienced, eventually finding sexual release only in congress with the intestines of his increasing number of murdered victims."[27] "Escalation of appetite" is quite right and is another way of saying "opponent process." And, though I do not want to be pedantic, especially about something as gruesome as Dahmer's crimes, Dalrymple's use of the word "only" is accurate too. As Dahmer reached more and more deplorable depths, he found that only more and more depraved things satisfied him. Dahmer exemplified these verses from Baudelaire: "Once we have burned our brains out, we can plunge to Hell or Heaven—any abyss will do—deep in the Unknown to find the *new!*"[28]

Just as someone addicted to heroin or some other drug tends to need more and more of it for the same effect, and just as devoted skydivers search out higher and more interesting dives, serial killers like Dahmer also have to seek out more novelty and intensity in their crimes to achieve the same effects. The dynamic interplay of opponent processes and habituation dictates that, whatever the provocative activity, "pushing the envelope" is necessary to maintain the activity's thrill or excitement.

In context of "pushing the envelope," an article from the March 2010 issue of *Atlantic Monthly* is of interest. The article, entitled "Death Becomes Him," was written by Bruce Falconer about Ludwig Minelli, the leader of a Swiss organization whose business is assisted suicide. In language that I at least find unsettling, Minelli and the agency's employees sometimes refer to their services as "an assist." I trust that it is not just I who find other things about the organization unsettling, like the fact that over 20% of the deaths are among those with a disease that is not terminal or progressive, that "mental disorder" is one of the categories among those the organization "assists," that a 2008 article in the *Journal of Medical Ethics* concluded that "weariness of life" is a reason the organization accepts for its services,[29] or that approximately 60 cremation urns with ashes have been found in Lake Zurich, which some have alleged the organization dumped there.[30]

Given all this, some may question the organization's name, Dignitas. "Dignitas" is a Roman concept that is difficult to translate—"dignity" is not an accurate translation. The concept has to do with one's accrued accolades and self-control. "Pride in the exercise of one's autonomy and the positive consequences thereof, both in self-development and in external accomplishments" is perhaps a reasonable attempt at translation. Although I am not an unalloyed proponent of assisted suicide,[31] I do believe that organizations can conduct themselves in ways that are compatible with this definition of "dignitas" (e.g., the state of Oregon); I see some distance, however, between "dignitas" and Dignitas.

To wit, the *Atlantic Monthly* article describes a man who works for Minelli at Dignitas, who said, remembering his first "assist," that afterward he went dancing: "I could not go to sleep," the man said. "I could only go out and dance." This was true as well regarding the next several deaths with which he was involved. But now, after 200 or so deaths, the worker explained (with what, one seems to detect, is a whiff of regret) that he no longer has this reaction. The man's explanation for his earlier behavior—that is, dancing after involvement with a killing—was that, because he had shared something so profound with another human being as the latter's death, he felt connected to humanity to the extent that he was compelled to dance.

My skepticism of this man's explanation for his behavior is substantial. One puzzles over the matter of why a connection to humanity compels one to dance, as opposed to, say, dropping to one's knees in gratitude and awe, or consoling the family and friends of the deceased, or contributing to a charity. In actual fact, when someone is authentically overcome with the awe, beauty, and the good fortune to be alive and connected to one's fellow man, as was Viktor Frankl on being liberated from Auschwitz, it sounds like this: "One day, a few days after liberation, I walked through the country past flowering meadows, for miles and miles...Larks rose to the sky and I could hear their joyous song. There was nothing but the wide earth and sky and the lark's jubilation and the freedom of space. I stopped, looked around, and up to the sky—and then I went down on my knees."[32] Frankl does not allude to dancing.

I take it as self-evident that anyone who does mention dancing as a reaction to death—and in so doing fails to notice or to care about the "dancing on a gravesite" imagery—deserves skepticism.[33] A more plausible explanation of the Dignitas worker's reactions has to do with the concepts of primary and opponent processes, and of "pushing the envelope." The man's elation in response to death, the opponent process, is something that occurs surprisingly regularly, as we have already seen in the example of serial killing, and as we will see again shortly in the reactions of many people to combat-related killing. But for the elation response to continue, a kind of "pushing the envelope" is required—for skydivers, this means higher or more complex jumps; for heroin users, it means more of the drug; for serial killers, it means more grisly behaviors. But for the man who worked for Dignitas, there was no room for "envelope pushing." The procedures and settings for "assists" were set, with no possibility of novelty. Thus, after the first several deaths, the man's opponent process reaction of needing to dance faded. To use a phrasing from Camus'[34] *Reflections on the Guillotine* that I think is extremely precise, the Dignitas worker had experienced the "regularization of death."[35] He underwent "regularization" in two important senses: first, he got used to death (he habituated and lost the primary reaction to it); second, he lost his opponent process reaction of dancing, because of constraints on "pushing the envelope."

Anyone involved in repeated killing will reference the change in impact over time that results from the push-and-pull of primary processes, opponent processes, and "pushing the envelope." One easily imagines that those such as Jeffrey Dahmer were born deranged and monstrous, but then again, one easily imagines many false things. Interviews with Dahmer's father, Dahmer himself, and others show that, as a young child, he showed little aggression, and even had what some would term a "sweet" disposition.[36] Dahmer's description of his first murder is qualitatively different than his descriptions of his last murders. Although, in manifold ways, he relished his last murders— a fact that, at the end of his life, Dahmer sincerely understood was both unavoidably true and profoundly awful—he remembered his first killing with a mixture of fear, shame, guilt, and disgust.[37]

In *King Lear*, Shakespeare has Gloucester say of a madman and a beggar, "I such a fellow saw, Which made me think a man a worm."[38] Jeffrey Dahmer would be Exhibit A in many people's case for the inherent evil within human nature, for thinking that man can be worm. And yet he was not always thus. He *became* evil, and the process by which it occurred involved getting used to the grisliness of killing while along the way developing, through the operation of opponent processes, an appetite for murder.

This same kind of trajectory can be seen in less evil behaviors. We have already covered the example of skydiving, which, while few view as evil, many view as somewhat hard to identify with. Consider, then, something a little more run of the mill: the ingestion of nicotine. To virtually every novice, nicotine is a noxious substance, causing things like nausea and dizziness. And yet, even despite this early adverse experience, a subset of people goes on to become committed tobacco users, relishing nicotine's effects. The primary process—nausea and the like—faded, and the opponent process—the various rewarding effects of nicotine—became amplified and strengthened with use. This same phenomenon applies to a host of stimuli, ranging from extreme sexual behaviors, to coffee, to alcohol, to spicy foods, really to any provocative stimulus. "He was torn at giving up the thrill. Even a few days away from it had left him feeling restless and gloomy. 'I've just had a large enough mouthful of the real stuff,' he observed, 'to make me perfectly miserable without it.'" Most would guess that the stimulus in question here would be something like a powerful drug like nicotine; in fact, the quote is from the book *The Millionaires' Unit*[39] and is referring to air combat, a topic to which we will return.

For reasons that are not altogether clear, some people are stopped in their tracks by the power of the primary process before the opponent process kicks in and holds sway. Had Jeffrey Dahmer been just a little more disgusted by the first of his murders, or just a little more guilty about it, the rest of that woeful tale may have been quite different. From this perspective, Dahmer becomes a little more human, an example of Harry Stack Sullivan's[40] dictum, "we are all much more simply human than otherwise." And this perspective provides a possible answer to why psychoanalysts were misled to believe that we all have a little murder in our souls. What we all do have in our souls and cells is the propensity to be acted on by the interplay of weakening primary processes and gathering opponent processes.

Genesis got this wrong too. In *Genesis* 4:7, God is speaking to Cain regarding the latter's thoughts about killing his brother Abel. God says, "sin is crouching at your door; it desires to have you, but you must master it." On this view, the urge to murder is lurking in everyone's heart, waiting to spring, like water behind a dam. Freud was persuaded that this view was accurate, perhaps somewhat understandably given that he lived in a society that virtually self-destructed in World War I.[41] Karl Menninger, a follower of Freud's, agreed, and believed that the wish to kill and to die resided in everyone's soul. For example, in his 1938 *Man Against Himself*, Menninger wrote, "The destructive instinct that slumbers within the heart of even the tiny child begins to be apparent as externally directed aggressiveness accompanied by rage from almost the moment of birth."[42] But rattlesnakes, piranha, elk, and the rest of nature belie this view. What is actually there in babies' and everyone else's soul—nature's beneficent default position—is the opposite of a death wish. What is there is the incapacity to let Cain's sin through the door (at least sin of this gravity).

Killing is not there in everyone's heart, but its potentiality is (lest one want to insist that potentiality and presence are the same thing, consider the unpopped popcorn kernel, the seed never planted, or the unfinished dissertation—is there "a little dissertation" in all of our hearts? Some students wish it were so). That the potentiality exists is illustrated by war: while it is true that many who are trained and intend to kill the enemy do not in the end do so, it also clear that many of those who *do* kill in combat, if asked about their potential to kill just months before, would have demurred, believing that killing another was simply not in their constitution. The potential to kill is in humans' constitution, as it is in chimps.' A 2010 report in the journal *Current Biology* summarizes 10 years' worth of researchers' observations of "lethal intergroup aggression" in wild chimpanzees in Uganda.[43] During the 10 years of observation, the researchers directly witnessed 18 instances in which a group of chimps killed another chimp. The attacks were brutal, with some members of the group holding the victim down and others hitting, stomping on, and severely biting the victim. Somewhat disturbingly, the chimps engage in this behavior because it benefits them to do so: it increases the assaultive group's territory and access to food. Some humans kill their own, as do some other primates.

Murderers, especially serial killers, have arrived at a very extreme location along the continuum set up by the interplay of primary and opponent processes. This fact illuminates why it is that one person in a combat unit is more able to kill the enemy than is another in the unit, why only one of two assaultive brothers carried through with murder…and it explains differences between two boys who perpetrated a horrific school shooting.

At Columbine—an incident we will revisit in a later chapter because it is an example, according to this book's framework, of a "glory"-motivated murder-suicide—Eric Harris and Dylan Klebold killed 13 people before turning their guns on themselves. The boys' personalities were quite different, with Klebold being depressed and somewhat of a follower, and Harris being more belligerent, cocky, and callous.[44] On that day, who fired the first shot? The evidence suggests that it was Harris, and further suggests that Klebold panicked as the incident unfolded, requiring Harris to run to his location and reconnect him to the plot.[45] An inescapable fact is that both boys killed others on that day. And yet, would the one have shot had the other not—would Klebold have been able to break that barrier himself had not Harris broken it already?

On this view, Harris *started out* with more aggression-related proclivities—thus started out farther along on the pathway to killing—as compared to Klebold. As we have seen, a major aspect of this kind of "head start" involves previous experience with violence. But even before that, one can be farther along than others toward violence and aggression, due to genetics and, relatedly, to temperament. An important aspect of temperament involves emotionality—some people are intensely emotional, sometimes to the extent of their own detriment (e.g., the workplace tantrum-thrower); others are decidedly *lacking* in emotion, sometimes to the detriment of others (e.g., victims of assaults). One of the main features of the psychopathic personality is a callous, unempathic, and uncaring emotional style.[46] Extreme selfishness is also involved, as it is in a neighboring condition, narcissistic personality disorder.

Consider Fred West in this regard, who, as described above,[47] killed many people before hanging himself in his prison cell. In his suicide note, West suggested that the following be inscribed on his tombstone:

> In loving memory.
> > Fred West Rose West
> > Rest in peace where no shadow falls
> > In perfect peace, he waits for Rose, his wife.

Similar to the tale of the two murderous brothers, there is so much awry with West's suggested epitaph that one struggles to know where to begin. West's wife Rose, for whom he waits "in perfect peace," was herself a psychopathic and narcissistic serial killer and participated in the murder of her and West's own daughter. That West believes that he and his wife—sadistic serial murderers—will be remembered with love and will "rest in peace where no shadow falls," reveals the nearly infinite guiltlessness of the psychopathic mind. This guiltless lack of remorse is a major component of the more general uncaring and callous emotional style shown by psychopaths like the Wests. Another such feature is boundless selfishness. The Wests reportedly explained to some of their victims whom they raped but did not kill that the activity was only natural, implying that their pleasure was an obvious rule of nature—a selfish attitude to say the least. Selfish as well was West's suggestion for his and his wife's epitaph, which is mostly about him. And add in a lack of foresight, also characteristic of psychopaths and also a feature of West's idea for a tombstone inscription: epitaphs are meant to be lasting, a fact that has escaped West's appreciation, in that his suggested inscription will no longer make sense once his wife has died as well.

Behavioral genetics research has left no doubt that part of the reason that an individual ends up with a psychopathic personality is due to genes.[48] The same research has made it clear that non-genetic factors play an essential role too. There are many people with the genetic potential to become killers, but only some do. For every abomination like Fred West, there are others who have the same genetic potential for depravity and yet do not express it. Exactly why this is—beyond things already covered like extent of psychopathic guiltlessness and accelerating familiarity and comfort with violence—remains mysterious, a frontier of scientific research into human nature and the nature of evil.

Examples like those of Fred and Rose West suggest that those who find pleasure, thrill, and elation in killing represent evil in its most unalloyed form. But just as the dynamic between primary and opponent processes can apply to rather mundane activities like the ingestion of spicy food or nicotine, they can affect the attitudes of "mundane" people—"mundane" meant here as a high compliment, as in not a deranged murderer—to killing. It is, I think, essential to understand not only that there are "mundane" people who kill and who have thereby engaged opponent processes about physical violence, but also that there are some who kill and have found it uniquely exhilarating. To be sure, most who find killing in any way pleasurable are deranged, but not all.

For example, in Larry Dewey's 2004 book *War and Redemption* on combat veterans, he states, "The 'adrenaline high' the danger provokes can even be experienced as exciting in a positive way. Some use the words, 'Never have I felt so alive as when others were shooting at me and I at them.' "[49] Even more pointed in this regard is Dewey's description of a veteran who was trained to sneak up on the enemy one on one and strangle him to death; he did so as his unit was trying to take a heavily defended bridge. "He felt a surge of elation as he killed the German and they went on to capture the bridge." Later, according to Dewey, the veteran "wondered how any decent human being could rejoice over killing another with his bare hands."[50]

One might expect that these effects of killing might be limited to incidents that are face to face, or at least at close enough quarters to see the person being killed (e.g., through a rifle scope), but as we have already seen, that is not so. Fighter pilots—or, more precisely, those pilots who overcome the reluctance to kill one another—report some of the same kinds of reactions. In *The Millionaires' Unit*—a history of the birth of American air power preceding and during World War I—Marc Wortman quotes one pilot's view of air combat: "Oh, it's a wonderful, wonderful game…It's glorious."[51] In his 1995 book *On Killing*, Dave Grossman provides similar examples. A fighter pilot stated, "Once you've shot down two or three [planes] the effect is terrific and you'll go on till you're killed. It's love of the sport rather than sense of duty that makes you go on."[52] An American tank commander, in describing his feelings about killing German soldiers, also somewhat from a distance, said, "The excitement was just fantastic…the exhilaration, after all the years of training, the tremendous feeling of lift, of excitement, of exhilaration, it was like the first time you go deer hunting."[53]

This last statement about how killing others was like deer hunting may not inspire much sympathy, perhaps especially among those who do not hunt, many of whom truly cannot understand why people hunt. One plausible reason why people hunt is revealed by an opponent process perspective: people hunt because it is exciting to do so, and moreover, it is "natural" at least in the sense that it does not violate ingrained injunctions about killing one's own. I have a female friend who shot at a troublesome squirrel with a BB gun, at best grazing the squirrel. Decades into her life, this was the first time she had fired a gun of any sort—and she found it "thrilling." This was the point of the story she was trying to tell over dinner one night, but it was hard for her to do, because our professorly companions became fixated on the transgression of firing a weapon at all, and at a squirrel at that (one that lived to trouble the area another day, it should be recalled). The derision our ancestors would have felt about our companions' fixation is hard to overstate.

Perhaps the person who uttered the statement about "the first time you go deer hunting," it might be argued, was a psychopath himself, much as was Fred West. It is difficult to rule this possibility out definitively, but one thing that argues against it is how common such statements are (including, as we have seen, from people who do not seem callous at all, but rather, are suffering decades later because they killed someone in combat), as well as how relatively rare true psychopathy is, mercifully. Attributing the elation of killing to psychopathy also does not square with the diverse array of situations and contexts in which the phenomenon has been observed. Most people who take pleasure in killing are psychopaths, but under extraordinary conditions, experience can instill pleasure in killing. Interviews with Hutus who had killed Tutsis in the Rwandan genocide describe one such extraordinary circumstance.

In this event, which occurred over the course of several months in the mid-1990s, several hundred thousand ethnic Tutsis were murdered by ethnic Hutus; most of the killings were face to face, using machetes. Evidence indicates that many Hutus were, at first, quite reluctant killers, but with experience not only lost their reluctance but came to relish assaulting their fellow countrymen with machetes. One Hutu said, "For me, it became a pleasure to kill. The first time, it's to please the government. After that, I developed a taste for it. I hunted and caught and killed with real enthusiasm...I was very,

very excited when I killed...Yes, I woke every morning excited to go into the bush."[54]

In context of the extreme (and fortunate) difficulty in killing one's own, a question about the Rwandan genocide, incidentally, is not so much how it is that members of one ethnic group came to look forward to killing members of another (though that is an essential enough question), but rather how it is that the killing was so widespread, perpetrated not just by a few, but by many. Recall in this regard the combat veteran who reported, plausibly, that he was the only one in his entire unit to kill the enemy in World War II. One possible explanation comes from Jean Hatzfield's 2005 book *A Time for Machetes*, in which it is documented that people developed a kind of fellowship in killing. A Hutu who had killed several of his Tutsi countrymen said, "In the tumult of the killings, stepping aside is not viable for a person, since that person would then find only his neighbours' backs to talk to about ordinary concerns. Being alone is too risky for us. So the person jumps up at the signal and takes part, even if the price is the bloody work."[55] This same book, it should be emphasized, further documents that within the community of killing, if it can be called a community, a driving force of the mass killing was the giving over of the primary process of revulsion to the opponent process of appetite.

Because many people (understandably and rightly) view the association of "appetite" or "taste" with killing as grotesque, and because of the monstrous examples of some individuals like Jeffrey Dahmer who have embodied this association, it is tempting to view the potential to kill as foreign or alien to one's nature. In one sense, it is, in that, as we have seen, we have a deep-seated reluctance to kill. Nevertheless, it would be wrong, I think, to characterize the attraction to killing as vanishingly rare. In this regard, consider Albert Camus' remarks on executioners in his *Reflections on the Guillotine*: "It will be objected that we are discussing only a few exceptional creatures who make a living out of such degradation. There might be fewer protests if it were known that there are hundreds of men who offer their services as executioner *without pay*."[56]

In the summer of 2008, Scott Johnson was hiding in the woods, dressed in camouflage and in possession of a rifle, near the Wisconsin–Michigan state line. Several teenagers chanced upon the scene, and

Johnson leapt out of his hiding spot. The teenagers fled, and Johnson shot and killed two of them; one was shot in the back, and the other in the back of the head. Johnson then opened fire on a separate group of young people who were lounging near a swimming hole, killing one.[57]

Johnson has offered several different versions of his motives on that day; for instance, he said, "I'm thinking...I got nothing to lose. The only power I have in this life is to take."[58] On another occasion, he implied that his plan was to kill the young people so as to attract police and other emergency responders to the scene, whom he would then target. Still another version was that he wanted to attract police to the scene and threaten them with his weapon, so that they would have to kill him (i.e., "suicide by cop"[59]); in Johnson's words, he wanted to "put police in a position where they would have to put me down."

It is noteworthy how secondary suicide is in Johnson's diverse explanations of his behavior. He mentions it, but only in one of his multiple versions, and even there, the method is indirect and occurs only after Johnson would have presumably perpetrated many killings of police officers (his main goal, in the other versions of his story). Notice, also, the absence of references to any form of virtue—even distorted forms of virtue—in Johnson's remarks. Despite Johnson's occasional references to suicide, the overwhelming preponderance of evidence supports the conclusion that Johnson killed out of a sullen sense of his life being a raw deal and for what he viewed as notoriety. This was not an incident in which a genuine murder-suicide was planned; rather, it was murder plain and simple, consistent with the fact that the incident lacks what are, according to this book's framework, key signatures of murder-suicide—namely, the perversion of virtue following the decision to die by suicide.

Disappointed narcissists are likely to develop paranoia,[60] and this paranoia can lead them to violence—Johnson may have been an example of such processes at play. The "threatened egotism" model of Baumeister and colleagues[61] asserts that an inflated self-concept, combined with a negative evaluation by others, leads to a discrepancy between internal and external appraisals. This causes a state of "threatened egotism" and forces individuals to decide between two things: either they accept the appraisal and lower their self-concept (unlikely for someone with narcissistic personality symptoms), or they reject the appraisal and maintain their self-concept. Maintenance of inflated self-concept, together with rejection of an unfavorable external appraisal, is associated with negative emotions and attitudes (e.g., mistrust, suspicion, anger) toward the source of the threat, and possibly aggression or violence. Though Johnson did not die by suicide and likely did not plan or intend murder-suicide, it is not hard to imagine how processes related to disappointed narcissism may underlie incidents in which murder-suicide is enacted in the name of justice.

Murder has aggrieved our kind for eons. It is no coincidence that it shows up early and often in foundational texts like *Genesis* and Shakespeare, to choose but two prominent examples. It not only aggrieves us, it costs us. In the "Findings" section of the December 2010 *Harper's Magazine,* it is documented that the average economic cost of a U.S. murder is $17.25 million. As costly and grievous as murders are, we have already seen and will see again that murder-suicide is the more so.

Understanding Suicide

IN THE 2006 DOCUMENTARY FILM *THE BRIDGE*, FILMMAKER Eric Steel and his team took footage of the Golden Gate Bridge every day for approximately a year, and in so doing, captured on film the deaths of over 20 people who jumped from the bridge to the waters below.[1] The stories of three people in the film illustrate profound truths about suicidal behavior.

First, there is a girl who looks to be around 20 who is contemplating jumping to her death. She has already climbed over the rail onto a kind of platform from which it is easily possible to jump, and indeed from which many do jump. A photographer is there too, a man who appears to be around 30; he notices the girl, and begins to try to help her. She vaguely waves him away as he, virtually with one hand (he has his camera in his other hand), grabs her by her jacket and hauls her back over the rail, even despite her evident struggles.

The first couple of times I had seen this footage, my main reaction was admiration for the photographer. Both his choice to intervene as a Good Samaritan and his seemingly supernatural strength in securing her safety impressed me. And "Good Samaritan" is clearly apropos here, in that, just as in the Biblical story (which is in the *Gospel of Luke*, Chapter 10), there were passersby on the bridge who did not notice the girl, or, if they did, did nothing to help her. As I watched the clip several more times, however, my positive view of the photographer never changed fundamentally, but some questions did arise in my mind. Did he really have superhuman strength? Did the adrenaline of the situation induce such strength in him, as in stories, which have the feel of urban myth, in which people single-handedly lift cars off people? The girl's jacket was open in the front, and even if it had not been, it is not hard to wriggle out of a jacket that someone grabs from behind and above you, as in this situation. Why didn't the girl wriggle free?

I believe I know the answers to these questions now; in fact they were there in the footage all along and had escaped my notice. As the photographer grabs the girl by the jacket, the viewer's eye is drawn to that point. That point epitomizes the scene, it seems: the struggle of the photographer to prevail and lift the girl over the rail versus the struggle of the girl to wriggle free and to jump. But if one widens one's attention, another crucial detail comes into focus, having to do with the girl's legs. Even as her arms are vaguely resisting the man's help, her legs are actively assisting him in getting her over the bridge's rail, back to safety.

The girl's body is at cross-purposes with itself: her arms and some of her behaviors indicate a desire to die, and her legs and still others of her behaviors (e.g., the lack of vigor with which she tries to wriggle free from her jacket) suggest a desire to live. In fact, the girl is at the bridge, on the other side of the rail, indicating considerable intent to jump…but her legs have not gotten that message. Two contradictory things, such as a desire to die and to live, coexisting in the same mind: this is what psychologists and others mean when they refer to *ambivalence*, and this concept is essential to a comprehensive understanding of the suicidal mind. Even extremely suicidal people can retain ambivalence, and therefore one side of that ambivalence—the desire to live—can be leveraged to prevent suicide even in highly suicidal people. Not in all people at very high risk, alas, but in many.

That even the most intently suicidal person can retain some will to live is vividly illustrated by the experience of Kevin Hines, also chronicled in the film *The Bridge*, the second of the three examples from that film discussed here. Kevin leapt off the Golden Gate Bridge. He did not hesitantly nudge himself over, or step off the ledge; instead, he leapt. This behavioral detail of leaping shows very high intent to die. One might imagine that, for someone so resolved on death to have intently leapt from a very high place, the other side of the ledger—the desire to live—is absent. But one imagines many false things: in mid-air, Mr. Hines changed his mind and was flooded with the urge to survive. Survive he did, and it is even possible that some of his behaviors in mid-air contributed to his survival. He reports, for instance, that he understood that unless his body were in a certain position when he hit the water, his chances for survival were virtually none. And so, he recalls, he worked to get his body in a survivable position during the four or so seconds between jumping and impact.

This anecdote is remarkable on many levels, one of which is that a man profoundly suicidal enough to propel himself off a very high place, with no hesitation whatsoever, can, within a second or so, feel an upwelling of the desire to live. In virtually every single intently suicidal person, the desire to live has not been snuffed out entirely.

Lest you imagine that this anecdote about Mr. Hines is extremely unrepresentative, you would be quite correct in one sense but fundamentally mistaken in another. The anecdote is indeed quite unusual, in that very few people survive a jump from the Golden Gate Bridge; certainly no more than 5% do, and the more accurate figure is probably between 2% and 3%.[2] On the other hand, when the group of interest shifts from all those who jump (very few of whom survive) to all those who have jumped and survived, the representativeness of Mr. Hines' story becomes clear. Many who have jumped and survived reported fear and profound regret at their decision to jump, in mid-air.

This same claim applies to other modes of attempted death by suicide. I am aware of an individual who, in a quite purposeful suicide attempt, ingested a full container of an extremely powerful household cleaning product, more than a third of which was hydrochloric acid.[3] I would suggest that the resolve necessary to do this rivals that necessary to jump from the Golden Gate Bridge. In both cases, nature's warning sirens about pain and fear must have been deafening, and yet both individuals carried on nevertheless. In the case of the person who ingested the cleaner, what was her next behavior after finishing the bottle? The same behavior, I believe, that Mr. Hines would have enacted in mid-air, if only he could have: she called for someone to save her, in this instance 911. Emergency personnel tried to do just that but could not. The extent of the internal damage caused by the cleaner was too great, and she died in the hospital.

A person resolved enough on death to go through something as aversive as drinking an entire container of a powerful cleaner; another resolved enough on death to leap, with no hesitation, from a very high place. Yet both instantly wanted to live. This phenomenon—and its virtual uniformity among those who have survived near-lethal suicide attempts—is extraordinary in itself and is also extraordinarily tragic in one of its implications. It is extraordinary in itself because the desire kicks in, with speed and force, even among the subset of people who not only have decided on their own deaths, and (to take the example of the Golden Gate Bridge) not only have traveled to and walked out onto the bridge, but have resolved on their deaths decidedly enough that they actually jumped. It is hard for me to imagine a clearer demonstration that our instinct for self-preservation will have its say, even under the most unlikely of circumstances. Thus its power, and thus the requirement to address it in any model or theory that purports to explain suicide, the purposeful overcoming of this ancient and ingrained instinct.

Why, then, does the bursting through of this instinct toward self-preservation, even in the most unlikely of situations, imply profound tragedy? Because, as the experience of the person who ingested the cleaner shows, not everyone's wish to live is granted. Given Mr. Hines' experience, and given what happened to the person who ingested the cleaner, I take it as axiomatic that there are people who jump from the Golden Gate Bridge, experience deep regret in mid-air, and do not live to tell about it.

I would like to point out, somewhat in passing, that, although profound tragedy inheres in a clear understanding of cases like that of the person who ingested the cleaner, I have also seen such understanding lead to visible relief among the bereaved. For example, I am aware of a person who was working in a hospital setting as a counselor and who was approached by a patient saying that she was experiencing intense suicidal ideation and needed help. The counselor noted that the patient's mental state seemed somewhat confused. The counselor offered to escort the person to inpatient psychiatry, an offer that was accepted with relief. On the way, the patient collapsed into a coma, from which she never recovered; she died days later. The patient had taken a massive overdose before approaching the counselor for help. The counselor was troubled for years by the incident and was perplexed by and even somewhat angry at the patient's taking an overdose before approaching him, and not mentioning the fact. But, in hearing about the changing of minds that often occurs post-attempt (and in factoring in the confusion caused by the overdose), the counselor concluded that the patient meant him no malice but had simply changed her mind and was confused enough by the overdose's effects that she forgot to mention to him the fact of the overdose.

A medical examiner recently alerted me to a quite different case, but with some similar aspects and a similarly tragic outcome. A young man in the throes of a serious depression decided on death by suicide by asphyxiation, the particular method of which was to place a plastic bag over the head. Which is what he did, but then he changed his mind and made a small rip in the bag, allowing air in. He then changed his mind again, now in favor of death, and placed a second bag over the first—a bag in which he then made a small rip. He was found dead with six bags placed over his head, with only the sixth being unripped. Even very suicidal people change their minds, sometimes many times; unfortunately, of course, not all do.

I noted at the outset of this chapter that there were three people from the film *The Bridge* whose behavior made a very distinct impression on me (actually there were more than three, but the others are not discussed here). The two people already discussed—the girl saved by the photographer and Kevin Hines—both survived. Their stories are quite different, but there is one thing, besides survival, that links their two stories together: namely, both experienced strong pulls toward both death and life, and for both, these conflicting pulls occurred virtually if not literally simultaneously. In a word, they experienced ambivalence.

So did the third of the three people discussed here and depicted in the film. His name was Gene, and unlike the other two (and much like the person who ingested a powerful cleaner), his ambivalence, though considerable, did not save him. Gene jumped to his death from the bridge, an act caught on film by the filmmakers.

Gene's life and death provide deeply important and, I believe, widely underappreciated lessons about the nature of suicidal behavior. After his death, Gene's friends were interviewed in the film, and they say that Gene had talked about suicide for years, probably for approximately 15 years. He had talked about it so frequently and for so long that they gave up worrying about his carrying through long ago—a partly understandable reaction on their part. Their view, given the frequency and chronicity of Gene's talk about suicide, was that he voiced ideas about suicide not because he actually intended to die, but for some other reason, perhaps to blow off steam. Why else, they may have plausibly wondered, would someone talk about something for so long and yet not enact it?

One answer to this question is "ambivalence." In the two instances summarized earlier—the experiences of Kevin Hines and the girl saved by the photographer—ambivalence played an essential role, but it was ambivalence in the moment, with forces against and for life contending with one another contemporaneously. This surely occurs, as these two examples document, and grasping this phenomenon is necessary to a full understanding of suicidal behavior. But what also can occur—and did occur in the life and death of Gene—is that inclinations toward life and toward death can fight it out in someone's mind for years. Gene was holding a very long debate in his mind about suicide. The fact that the debate took so many years suggested to his friends that the debate would be endless, and therefore was not a true debate about death, but rather about something else. His death at the Golden Gate Bridge showed that this was wrong. Gene was genuinely debating death, and although it was a particularly long debate, it was eventually resolved, in favor of catastrophe.

One reason for Gene's long internal debate thus concerned ambivalence. A related explanation has to do with the concept of capability for death. Death is fearsome and daunting enough that many people find themselves incapable of bringing it about even though they genuinely want to, showing that it is quite possible to desire a thing but also to be incapable of arranging for that thing.

There are people, for instance, who would like to travel to India but who cannot because they do not have the means or opportunity. These people may frequently talk of their desire to travel to India, and such talk may go on for years, so much so that others may grow weary of the topic and may form the belief that the wish to go to India is "all talk." And yet, years later, at the instant that enough money and vacation time are saved, off to India they go.

Analogously, there are people whose desire for death is genuine, and thus so is their talk thereof. Such talk may go on for years, so much so that others may grow weary of the topic and may form the belief that the wish for death is "all talk." And yet, years later, when the constraints have come undone, death is enacted.

It is illuminating to ponder the nature of the constraints in these two examples. With regard to travel to India, the barrier is an *external* lack of resources (e.g., money, time); there is no *internal* lack of will or resolve.[4] With regard to death by suicide, the constraint is (mostly) an *internal* abundance of fear. An individual who wishes to travel to India is usually not really ambivalent about it, just unable to fulfill the wish due to external constraints. An individual who desires death *is* ambivalent, because the constraint comes from within, as does the desire. The clash between desire and capability can be viewed as a main reason for the existence of ambivalence in the mind of someone contemplating death.

The lessons Gene's life and death teach us are, first, that the internal conflict between life and death can be enormously variable in terms of time course. The time course can be instantaneous, or virtually so, as in the experiences of Kevin Hines and the girl whose arms seemed to say "death" even as her legs seemed to say "life." Or, it can be very drawn out, on the order even of decades, as in the case of Gene. This variability indicates yet another lesson; namely, that long bouts of indecision do not necessarily indicate insincerity, but instead may indicate incapability. If this incapability is somehow resolved, even if it takes many years, disaster may ensue.

When someone voices suicidal ideation off and on over the course of say, 20 years, what, then, is the proper stance to take toward him or her? I have witnessed mental health professionals take what I deem to be appalling stances toward this complex issue, and these stem from a rote and ungenerous assumption that the person in question is being insincere. The usual comments are along the lines of "if she were really going to kill herself she would have done it already." Even if this were true—and Gene's death shows that it is not, at least not always—the usual disdainful tone with which statements of this sort are uttered is unfortunate. The fact that it is demonstrably *not* always true makes the disdainful tone all the more unseemly. In Eli Robins'[5] comprehensive study of 134 suicide decedents described in the book *The Final Months*, approximately 70% of those who died by suicide openly communicated their intent to others; among these 70%, the average number of suicidal communications was over three.

Let me rush to acknowledge, however, that there are in fact people who voice ideas about suicide over decades and who never attempt suicide. This fact should not produce disdain, because even it does not show that such people are insincere; it could very well be that they are sincere but are incapable of the daunting act of suicide. Nor should this state of affairs really even produce surprise, because there are many health issues like this. For example, there are skin cells that are precancerous and yet, over decades, do not develop into cancer. It would be regrettable if a dermatologist, upon detecting a precancerous cell, said, "oh, let's not worry about it; if it were going to turn into cancer it already would have." It would also be contraindicated to immediately conduct highly invasive surgery. What does the competent dermatologist do instead? Relatively moderate measures like in-office removal of the affected area, and, in a phrase, "watchful waiting"—that is to say, periodic monitoring of the clinical situation, with the determination of what to do next dependent on regularly updated information. If, during ongoing monitoring, an emergency develops, then something like hospitalization or surgery is arranged. The competent mental health professional acts in like fashion with regard to ongoing suicide risk.

Stated differently, from among a group of people with chronic suicidal feelings, we have no way of telling, at a given point in time, who will or will not die.[6] Five years before his death, Gene would have struck a careful mental health professional as at a similar risk level as someone who, though endorsing ongoing suicidal ideation, survived for many subsequent decades. Why this fact produces disdain in many mental health professionals and the corresponding fact produces "watchful waiting" in the dermatologist is, in my opinion, due to the stigmatization of mental disorders and suicidal behavior, which is rampant (even in mental health professionals). We will return to the reasons for this special stigmatization, especially of suicidal behavior, in due course. And, incidentally, consider the possible outcome had Gene been "waitingly watched." His incipient risk may never have progressed to the point of death in the first place, or, if it had, he may have been hospitalized before carrying out his plan for suicide.

I am aware of the death by hanging of a woman who had repeatedly told her husband that she intended to die by suicide. He came home one day to find that she had done just that, by hanging, in their home. The medical examiner spoke with the husband and gently questioned him about his inaction over the years, to which he answered that she had mentioned suicide frequently enough and for so long that he simply did not believe her. She had left a note reminding others that she had said all along that she would die by suicide. There was some anger in the tone of the note, and in fact, some people who die by suicide are angry at loved ones at the time of their deaths. But most are not.[7] More to the present point, the deaths of this woman and of Gene in the film *The Bridge* clearly indicate that people can talk about suicide for years, be dismissed by others as "merely talking," and then die by suicide.

When people claim an intention to do something, they usually do it, and it would be peculiar to dismiss their claim as "all talk." If people repeatedly claim an intention to do something and then repeatedly do not follow through, it is natural to wonder why, but it is also dangerous to answer reflexively. There are two general species of answer to this wonder: insincerity and constraint (either external or internal). That is, the person is not following through either because he or she really does not sincerely intend to (in which case the person actually is "all talk") or because he or she wishes to but cannot (i.e., the person is constrained). With regard to suicidal intentions, a common fault of mental health professionals is to mistake constraint for insincerity. We are not very good at telling the difference between the two (though some are better than others, no doubt), a fact that should produce humility rather than disdain, and should produce as well sadness that people like Gene are dead, not cavalier views on the insincerity of mental patients.

I should also hasten to acknowledge that occasionally people do lie outright about their intention to die by suicide; in so doing, they often reveal misunderstandings about suicide that only the genuinely non-suicidal could harbor. In the September 6, 2010, issue of *The New Yorker*, Carl Elliot described the case of a prominent New Zealand psychiatrist who was convicted of killing his wife; she had been ill (probably from the psychiatrist's past unsuccessful attempts to poison her). In part to cover his tracks, he penned an ersatz suicide note for himself addressed to his wife on the day before the murder, which read, in part, "I'm sorry for being a weakling. I know [your physician] will be back tomorrow and you'll be safe in the medical ward. Please forgive my cowardice. I'm ending my life knowing you will be safe and in good medical care." In the ensuing investigation, the psychiatrist's phone was tapped, and a conversation was recorded between him and his paramour—also a psychiatrist—in which he said, referring to his so-called suicide note, "It's not put on, is it?" Displaying a similar shallowness of understanding, she replies, "no, it's not, but it shows how much you loved your wife and family." "Cowardice" and "being a weakling" occur mostly to the mendaciously suicidal, the genuinely suicidal being rightly daunted by the prospect; these kinds of witless views on weakness and the like do not occur to or are dismissed by competent mental health professionals.

Genuine suicidality and the ambivalence attendant upon it are illustrated well by the examples of Gene, Kevin Hines, and the girl whom the photographer saved. There are some suicidal individuals who are aware that instincts toward life are powerful and difficult to control, and so they take steps to keep these instincts at bay. For example, it is not terribly uncommon—though it is deeply tragic—for those who die by hanging to bind their own hands before their death, so that they will be unable to save themselves.

Hand-binding occurred in the 2009 death of a U.S. Census worker who was found hanged in a remote area of Kentucky,[8] though as we will see, in this particular case, the fact of hand-binding illustrates stigma as well as guarding against self-preservation instincts. The detail of the man's bound hands, and the fact that he was found in a position from which he could have easily stood up before losing consciousness, initially suggested to investigators that he had been killed by someone else. Also consistent with this possibility, the man was found naked with the word "Fed" (as in federal agent) written across his chest and his Census employee ID card taped to his forehead, leading investigators to wonder whether the man had been murdered, perhaps by someone with rabid antigovernment feelings, or perhaps by someone involved in marijuana or moonshining operations (which are fairly common in that area). Initial media reports virtually asserted that this was the case.

In actual fact, the man had stripped down to his socks and used a black felt-tipped pen to write "Fed" on his own chest. He taped his ID card to his head and placed a red cloth into his mouth, which he then taped over with duct tape. He tied a rope over a tree limb and formed a noose, such that the noose was approximately four feet off the ground. The man bound his ankles with the duct tape, and similarly bound his wrists, but loosely. He placed his head through the noose and leaned forward.

Investigators turned up several details that, despite initial assumptions of murder, ultimately led to the conclusion of suicide. The fact that the man was in a position from which he could have simply stood up, investigators realized, is not an uncommon finding in death by suicide by hanging.[9] Another was that tests showed that the letters on his chest had been written from the bottom to the top; that is to say, starting near his waist and ending at his chest. This is the way that one writing on oneself might do, but not the way an assailant writing on a victim would likely do.

Why, if the census worker were intent on suicide, did he attempt to mislead others into thinking that he was killed by an assailant? One motive was financial. The man had two life insurance policies, totaling approximately $600,000. Both policies would pay in the event of homicide or accidental death, but not in the event of suicide or death by natural causes.[10] Suicide for financial gain is not the norm, but it does occur: in India, there have been thousands of deaths by suicide among debt-ridden farmers, and one factor in some of these deaths, it appears, is that the government financially compensates the bereaved families. From the *Harper's Magazine*'s "Harper's Index," March 2011: "Number of suicides last year in one Indian state that a government investigation attributed to unpaid microfinance debts: 54."

A second motive in the choices of the census worker's death had to do with the avoidance of stigma. It is not rare for people to attempt to arrange their suicide so that it resembles a homicide or an accident, in the belief that suicide would stigmatize those left behind. The census worker very likely gathered that his relatives would be more comfortable with his murder than with his suicide, and media interviews of family members conducted after his death was determined to be a suicide are highly consistent with this assumption.

Even though the man, judging by his actions, was intent on deceiving others as to his cause of death, due to factors like stigma and insurance payments, he nevertheless told someone of his impending suicide. He mentioned in passing to a colleague that he had thought of hanging himself near a particular cemetery in rural Kentucky; this is, in fact, what he did, and at that very same location. The colleague did not think the comment was serious and gave it no further thought until he learned of the census worker's death.

In May 2011, an incident occurred that shares some similarities with that involving the Census worker. A man called 911, reported that his home was being burglarized, and hung up. When police officers arrived, they found the man dead from a gunshot wound to the head. Initially, they suspected murder but very soon thought otherwise, as surveillance cameras showed no evidence of anyone coming or going, there was only one set of footprints leading to where the man was found, and the bullet as well as the casing matched the man's own gun. The man had imagined that calling the police and telling them that a robbery was occurring would lead them to conclude that he was murdered, probably with motives similar to those of the Census worker.

These cases exemplify many features of the suicidal mind: ambivalence (which the Census worker anticipated and therefore bound his hands), resolve (which the Census worker showed in not standing up from the position in which he was found), stigma (which both men anticipated and thus staged their deaths to resemble a homicide, which, at least in one case, was also motivated by financial concerns), and the principle (illustrated by the case of the Census worker) that when people talk of suicide, there is at least some risk that they will act.

Learned Fearlessness

There are other essential features of the suicidal mind. One, already alluded to, involves fearlessness of physical pain, physical injury, and death itself—a trait that develops gradually with experience, and once developed, is stable, like a pearl or stalagmite. Without this characteristic, as we have seen, people shy away from death.[11] In his 1678 *Maximes*, François La Rochefoucauld wrote that "On neither the sun, nor death, can a man look fixedly." There is wisdom, I believe, in the comparison of attempting to stare at the sun and to stare down death. It is viscerally difficult to attempt these things, and one's resolve to try is very often gainsaid by instinct.

A 2009 incident that illustrates this principle vividly was caught on security cameras and was covered on news broadcasts in Israel.[12] Though a train was not yet in sight, a woman was dangerously close to the railroad tracks. Redeemingly, and reminiscent of the story of the photographer who saved the girl at the Golden Gate Bridge, some workers noticed the woman and began signaling to her to stand clear. She ignored them, however, and about 20 seconds later, she approached the tracks and kneeled in front of a train barreling toward her. As she looked up at the tons of steel racing toward her, her fear took over, and she threw herself backward an instant before impact would have occurred. For several seconds as the train speeds by, it is not at all clear she is uninjured or even alive, but once the train passes, she gets up, without a scratch on her. She would surely be dead were it not for her fear.

The woman, I believe, would heartily endorse the words of another person who survived a very close call involving setting himself on fire. Interviewed for a radio program, he stated, "I wonder why all the ways I've tried to kill myself haven't worked. I mean, I tried hanging; I used to have a noose tied to my closet pole...but every time I started to lose consciousness, I'd just stand up. I tried to take pills...but that just made me sleepy. And all the times I tried to cut my wrist, I could never cut deep enough. *That's the thing, your body tries to keep you alive no matter what you do"* (italics added).[13] Those who have been through close calls like this have learned like few others that the body will fight for life, even when the mind won't.

People flee from death, even suicidal people. Referring to the end of days, *Revelation* 9:6 reads, "In those days, people will seek death, and will in no way find it. They will desire to die, and death will flee from them." I am very struck by this passage; the context is of course broader—the end of days as opposed to the end of particular lives— but whoever wrote *Revelation* understood that the mere desiring of death is not sufficient to accomplish it.

Our bodies very often will save us. In the preceding chapter, I mentioned a man who changed his mind about suicide after hearing, he believed, the voice of God tell him to turn to snake-handling and other religious activities. People report hearing similar "saving voices" in combat as well. In his 2004 book *War and Redemption*, Larry Dewey reports on more than one combatant who distinctly heard a voice, attributed by the soldiers to God, saying versions of "you will survive this." The religious of course may view this as the actual voice of God—perhaps so. My own view, however, is that these are "safety messages" emanating from the deep brain and being perceived as God's voice.

The conclusion that our bodies and their fear equipment can save us applies as well to a U.S. soldier who was quoted regarding a suicidal crisis. He stated, "we had a cease-fire, and I took a long and healthy look down the barrel of my .45…At fifty feet it shot about six inches to the right, but I'd learned to compensate. It didn't matter anyway, jammed up in the mouth, whether it shot to the right or not…I almost [fired]…and though I wanted to do it, and didn't really have much reason not too, I just couldn't bring myself to pull the trigger. It would have made a god-awful mess in the turret, which my crew would have had to clean up. I told myself later, it's because of the guys. They depend on me—if I were to pop a cap into my forehead I'd probably get replaced by some dumbhead right out of basic training. I could live with being responsible for my own death, but not my crew's. See, don't I sound noble? It sounded better than 'I chickened out.'"[14]

As was noted in Chapter 2, killing is loathsome, and this applies as much to killing oneself as to killing others. But unlike killing others, suicide also involves the fear of one's own death, of being killed. A crucially important fact about suicide is that it combines the loathsomeness of killing with the fear of one's own death. This makes it so daunting that many cannot act on suicidal desires; it is also the reason, in my view, that suicide is particularly stigmatized. It is unique in the degree to which it is stigmatized, and this may be because it is unique in the combining of two very fearsome things: killing and being killed. This compounded or doubled aspect of suicide's impact may explain why it was long and uniquely considered in English jurisprudence a double offense, against God and king, and thus doubly punished: estate confiscated and body disallowed from burial in consecrated ground.[15]

Lest one doubt that suicide is deeply stigmatized, consider the following tale, every detail true, alas. A young man tells family and friends that he intends suicide; the family and friends call police for the latter to do a safety check; the police fail to perform the safety check; the young man kills himself; and two weeks later, his parents receive a bill in the mail for the unperformed safety check. This is beyond bureaucratic ineptitude, even if it happened once; similar things happen all the time though (across society, not just involving the police; as a matter of fact, police officers tend to be above average in their understanding of suicide, largely because many of them have seen more than one suicide death scene).

Is Killing Oneself More Difficult Than Killing Someone Else?

On the logic elucidated above on the difficulties inherent in killing others versus killing oneself, enacting suicide should be more difficult than killing someone else—and as we saw in Chapter 2, this is saying something, because killing someone else is so difficult that the majority of people simply cannot do it. There should be reports, then, of people stating that, although they found killing someone else feasible, suicide, though desired, was a step too far.

This was precisely the claim of Florida felon John Blackwelder,[16] who was in prison for life for committing a series of violent sex crimes. While incarcerated, he developed what, he said, was the sincere desire for suicide—and yet he could not bring himself to die by suicide. Even at this stage of the story, a remarkable claim has emerged: Blackwelder is fully willing to commit—and capable of committing—a series of vicious assaults on others (and who knows what else that escaped the notice of police and prosecutors) but unable to die by suicide.

Blackwelder thus found himself with a dilemma: he wanted to die but felt unable to kill himself. Upon reflection on his situation, Blackwelder lit on a solution, if it can be called that. He decided that he would strangle his cellmate to death, which would then force the state of Florida to execute him. This is exactly what he did, and, as he expected, the state of Florida obliged his wish to die.[17]

This repellant tale, though some of it depends on a quite unreliable source in the felonious Blackwelder, nonetheless corroborates the maxim that of all killing, killing oneself may rest at the very pinnacle of difficulty,[18] because it adds to the loathsomeness of killing the fear of being killed. In his 1957 *Reflections on Hanging*, Arthur Koestler wrote of the death penalty that "it is not a deterrent to the type of person who commits murder because he desires to be hanged; and these cases are not infrequent," which adds some credence to Blackwelder's claims.[19]

Chapter 1's Venn diagram on the interrelations between murder, suicide, and murder-suicide placed murder-suicide fully within the "parent" category of suicide. This denotes that many people capable of murder are incapable of suicide (like the felon Blackwelder); using this same logic, virtually all of those capable of suicide are, largely as a function thereof, capable of murder (as is seen in murder-suicide).

The Desire for Death

To die by suicide, one must have developed fearlessness about physical pain, physical injury, and death. This fearlessness, though necessary, is not sufficient for death by suicide. Fearlessness ensures the capability but does not produce the desire for death. The desire for death arises through a distinct process, composed of two essential elements: the perception that one's death will be worth more than one's life, and the perception that one is deeply alienated from others.[20]

In his *Pensées*, Pascal wrote that happiness "is the motive of every act of every man, including those who go and hang themselves."[21] Far from having anything whatsoever to do with happiness, the prevailing emotion in the moments before death by suicide is abject misery. Even if Pascal would like to have argued that by "happiness" he meant "relief and release from suffering," he still would be mistaken, as, firstly, the act of suicide as we have seen clearly involves suffering, and secondly, relief *per se* is not the foundational issue. People kill themselves not because they have something to die for (pain relief) but because (they feel) they have nothing to live for.

This distinction between reasons to die and reasons to live may seem obscure, but I believe the distinction is not only explicable but essential. If one focuses on reasons to die as a main way to understand suicide, one is immediately drawn (perhaps as Pascal was) to concepts like "emotional pain" and "hopelessness" as explanatory. There is some explanatory appeal to these concepts, it should be admitted;[22] I myself have asserted that the prevailing mindset of the imminently suicidal person is misery, and "emotional pain" and "hopelessness" are key components of misery. There is empirical appeal to these concepts as well in that both have been linked to suicide-related outcomes by respected scientists and scholars, including A. T. Beck (whose work often focuses on hopelessness)[23] and E. Shneidman (whose work often focused on emotional pain).[24]

Here, though, is their Achilles heel. In the United States, the prevalence of major depressive disorder—one form of clinically severe depression—is at least 4%.[25] This rate equates to over 12 million of our fellow Americans suffering from this condition—a condition inherent to which are emotional pain and hopelessness. Viewing these concepts as the driving force behind suicide raises a question: If there are so many with the "reasons to die," why do so few—relatively speaking—attempt suicide (around 750 per day in the United States), much less die by suicide (approximately 95 per day in the United States)? Of course, 750 per day and 95 per day, it should be immediately recognized, are distressingly high numbers, but not "high" in the sense that 12 million is. Put differently, these two concepts of emotional pain and hopelessness are lacking in specificity. They identify a group among whom virtually all suicide attempts and deaths by suicide will occur, but among that group also are vast numbers of people who will neither attempt suicide nor die by suicide.

One preoccupation of my own work over the last 20 years or so has been to propose solutions to this severe specificity problem. My solutions are relevant both to reasons for dying and reasons for living, but I think they are most precisely viewed as a thwarting or frustration of reasons for living. The concepts of "perceived burdensomeness" and "perceived social alienation," already alluded to above, have several advantages, including that each is more delimited and more specific than overarching concepts like emotional pain and hopelessness—and the conjunction between burdensomeness and alienation, which my work proposes is the fundamental cause of serious suicidal ideation, is, by definition, more delimited still. Empirically, numerous studies affirm the connection of these concepts to suicide-related outcomes; in such studies, when the concepts of "burdensomeness" and "alienation" are pitted against emotional pain and hopelessness in their ability to predict suicide-related outcomes, the former concepts win out.[26]

Further still, the reach of the concepts of burdensomeness and alienation outpaces that of emotional pain and hopelessness. By "reach," I mean the scope of suicide-related phenomena, both core and peripheral, that the concepts can explain. As an example of a core suicide-related phenomenon, consider suicidal ideation. The following, taken from a radio interview of a person with a long history of suicidal behavior, including a near-lethal attempt, is quite representative of conversations clinicians have with suicidal patients: "I felt my mind slip back into the same pattern of thinking I'd had when I was fourteen [when he first attempted suicide]. I hate myself. I'm terrible. I'm not good at anything. *There's no point in me hanging around here ruining other people's lives.* I've got to get out of here. I've got to figure out a way to get out of my life" (italics added).[27]

The progression of thought contained in these words is not, in my opinion, coincidental. The progression begins with negative self-views (e.g., "I'm terrible"); had it stopped there, it would have been indicative of quite low self-esteem, perhaps as a part of the clinical picture of major depressive disorder. Or, if the theme had stayed with low self-esteem *per se*—perhaps its roots in the past, or its consequences for the individual's future—a similar conclusion would pertain. But instead, the progression went from "I'm terrible" to (to paraphrase) "I'm so terrible that the effects leak out beyond me and ruin things for everyone." And immediately after this sentiment is expressed, so is frank suicidal ideation. An implication of this anecdote—and one that has been corroborated by empirical studies[28]—is that general expressions of distress (such as low self-esteem, emotional pain, and hopelessness) do not eventuate in suicidal ideation or behavior *unless* they produce perceptions of burdensomeness (as in the anecdote) or alienation. Burdensomeness and alienation represent the final common pathway through which general risk factors affect core suicide-related phenomena, such as suicidal ideation.

Suicidal ideation is an obvious and essential aspect of suicide-related phenomena; by contrast, there are suicide-related phenomena that are more peripheral and yet do belong in the general definitional category. If burdensomeness and alienation are as crucial as I claim, they should display explanatory power even with regard to this periphery, and they should exceed concepts like hopelessness and emotional pain in this regard.

Consider, in this context, Helen Nearing's 1992 book *Loving and Leaving the Good Life*, a memoir describing her and her husband's lives living off the land in Vermont and later in Maine. Her husband lived to the age of 100 and soon after his 100th birthday decided to stop eating. He explained to his wife, "I would like to live as long as I'm useful. If I can be of use, I would like to go on living. If I can't even carry in the wood for you, I might as well go."[29]

It can be debated whether Mr. Nearing's death should be categorized as a conventional death by suicide, and in that sense, his decision to die is more peripheral to the category of suicide-related phenomena as compared to, say, someone who, in the throes of depression, prepares a note explaining his suicide, and dies by a self-inflicted gunshot wound in his home. But two things are not debatable: Mr. Nearing's death contained suicidal elements, and his reason for death had more to do with perceptions of burdensomeness than with things like emotional pain.

In this context, it is interesting to revisit one of the myths that I argued against in the 2010 book *Myths About Suicide*. In particular, the myth "suicide is selfish" is a quite rampant one; it is also quite unfounded. Just as it would be inaccurate to characterize Mr. Nearing's death as selfish, so would it be regarding the vast majority of conventional deaths by suicide. From another angle on this same truth, consider the psychopath. People with psychopathy (a callous, uncaring, deeply irresponsible attitude toward others) are, of all the people with mental disorders, the most selfish. If suicide were about selfishness, it would then follow that psychopaths would have quite high rates of suicide. But they have among the lowest. It was with such individuals in mind that Hervey Cleckley, in his 1941 *The Mask of Sanity*, wrote, "Persons of great dignity and pride may find it necessary to destroy their own lives under circumstances in which those with a shallower scope of feeling can adjust with only moderate emotional damage."[30]

Even more peripheral than Mr. Nearing's death to the concept of suicide, at least in most people's minds, is the intentional, self-caused death of various non-human organisms. Despite assertions to the contrary, this not only occurs but is rather pervasive in nature. "Self-destruct" mechanisms have been described in species as diverse as slime mold, pea aphids, and a particular kind of palm tree, and if the genetic code underlying these mechanisms were translated from guanine/cytosine/adenine/thymine to English, it would read "my death is worth more than my life to my genes." The relevant principle from evolutionary thought is "inclusive fitness,"[31] which asserts that the perpetuation of one's genes is an essential goal of all life, and that it makes no difference as to where those genes reside.[32] One's own survival furthers this goal, because one can live to reproduce another day, but so does the survival of close kin, because one's genes reside in them too. Consistent with this logic, all "self-destruct" mechanisms documented in nature to date are operative only under conditions of inclusive fitness.

The pea aphid—a kind of lice—has evolved not one but two mechanisms of self-sacrifice, one even more astonishing than the other. The relatively less astonishing mechanism is an analog to throwing oneself on a grenade...except for pea aphids, a grenade is not a grenade, but rather parasitization by a wasp. This parasitization is potentially grenade-like in its explosiveness, in that it can wipe out entire pea aphid colonies. But before this can occur, the parasitized pea aphid kills itself, and along with itself, kills the parasite within before the latter can infect the rest of the colony—the mechanism of death being dropping to the ground from plant stems and leaves and thereby sealing its fate as the meal of a predatory ladybug. This saves the colony—and the aphid's genes within the colony—because otherwise wasps would wipe out the entire group.[33]

The more astonishing mechanism of pea aphid self-sacrifice involves not "throwing oneself on a grenade," but rather being the grenade itself. Pea aphids are the suicide bombers of the insect world: they can blow themselves up, and do so under demands of "inclusive fitness." Here again, ladybugs are involved, but now as the direct threat. When a pea aphid is confronted by a ladybug, it can engage a chemical process that results in a small explosion. This explosion has a few consequences, including, on the negative side of the evolutionary register, that it kills the pea aphid, and, on the positive side of that same register, that it kills, injures, or otherwise deters the ladybug and it signals to other aphids to scatter, potentially saving them from predation (this phenomenon has been documented in other insects as well).[34] This can be adaptive to the self-sacrificing aphid, because copies of its own genes exist in the other aphids, which live on and perpetuate the genes. The calculation is that, under certain circumstances, death is worth more than life—a calculation, needless to say, that among pea aphids is not instantiated in thought or in language but in genetically determined behavior.

On this general logic, if escape were available to the individual pea aphid, then that should be the preferred course of action, as opposed to self-sacrifice, because it would allow the pea aphid to live on to reproduce another day. To do so would preserve the individual pea aphid's own life (and thus own genes) *and* would allow the possibility, through reproduction, that more copies of its genes would exist and survive on into the future. And this is precisely what happens: aphids that are mature enough to fly away from the advances of a ladybug do so.[35]

It will not have escaped notice, I trust, that humans blow themselves up too. That suicide bombers are doing so for reasons of inclusive fitness, meant literally, strikes me as unlikely, but what is hard to dispute is that they are doing so according to "death worth more than life" calculations. They believe quite obviously that their deaths will be worth more than their lives to their societies (and in some cases to their martyred souls).

Conventional death by suicide in humans, "quasi-suicide" in humans such as the voluntary, end-of-life self-starvation of Mr. Nearing, not one but two self-destruct mechanisms in pea aphids evolved under pressure of inclusive fitness (not to mention such mechanisms in many other species including even a tree), and suicide terrorism—all are underlain by one version or another of the calculation "my death is worth more than my life." For one concept to exert explanatory power over this extensive a range of phenomena indicates its likely truth. And notice, by contrast, the inability of concepts like hopelessness and emotional pain to illuminate the behavior of suicide terrorists,[36] not to mention that of pea aphids.

Were these self-destruct modules pervasive in nature, one would expect to see them in nature's most abundant form of life, microorganisms. This expectation is met by, for example, slime mold.[37] As part of their reproductive process, slime mold band together in a mass and form a stalk that rises up out of the mass. The stalk is composed of slime mold itself, and in this behavior, they rather resemble acrobats making a human pyramid, or rugby players hoisting one of their teammates above the fray. A capsule of spores forms at the top of the stalk, which opens, releasing the spores. The spores, in turn, keep the cycle going, given adequate environmental conditions, somewhat like seeds in plants and trees.

The mold at the bottom of the stalk are engaging in inclusive fitness-related self-sacrifice. They will not live on, but, if many of the spores germinate, the self-sacrificing mold's genes will live on; its death will have been worth more than its life to the propagation of its genes, a major imperative of life itself. According to an inclusive fitness perspective, mold that are genetically related to one another should be more likely to engage in this behavior than those less related to one another. This was experimentally affirmed by DeAngelo and colleagues.[38]

Are humans an exception to the rule of self-sacrifice in the service of inclusive fitness? In an essential sense, I think the answer to this question is yes, they are an exception (despite the obvious and oft-repeated perils of human exceptionalism). One reason to believe this is that clear examples of self-sacrifice as a means to the end of inclusive fitness are sparse, if not completely absent, in non-human primates. Non-human primates do intentionally self-injure (usually by self-biting), and quite intriguingly, they appear to do so for the same reasons that humans engage in what is called non-suicidal self-injury—namely, for the purpose of self-calming and other forms of mood regulation.[39] Similarly intriguingly, incidentally, non-human primates tend to self-injure the same anatomical sites as do humans—sites that are also the focus of acupuncturists.[40] But, as in humans as in non-human primates, intentional self-injury geared toward mood regulation is distinct from intentional self-injury with the goal of death—a distinction that is too often unappreciated in various clinical and other settings.

Another reason, of course, not to view people's deaths by suicide as instances of inclusive fitness is the appalling implication that suicide decedents' deaths benefit their relatives. Far from it, as many of the bereaved will attest. The suicidal individual *believes* that his or her death is worth more than his or her life, *believes* that the death will remove a burden from others. But believing does not make it so. Suicide decedents are mistaken in their beliefs, and their mistake contributes to their tragic deaths.

Just as perceived burdensomeness and "death-worth-more-than-life" calculations are involved in core suicidal phenomena (e.g., suicide ideation) and in those at the periphery (e.g., suicide terrorism, intentional self-sacrifice in non-human organisms), so is social alienation. Regarding its contributions to core suicide-related phenomena like suicide attempts and death by suicide in humans, indices of alienation like loneliness and social isolation are among the strongest risk factors for suicide of all. I recently learned of a case involving a young man whose main activity in life was fishing. He had become very depressed, though, and had given off many signs that he was seriously considering suicide. The last thing anyone heard him say (and which was not taken particularly seriously) was, "I'm tired of fishing alone." He was found dead by suicide two days later. That loneliness is a powerful risk factor for suicidal behavior was a main argument in John Sym's book *Life's Preservative Against Self-Killing*, which he published in 1637. The first known suicide note, written in Egypt and dated to approximately 2000 B.C., read, "I am laden with misery, and lack a trusty friend."[41]

I regularly receive communications from people who recently have been bereaved by the suicide of a loved one, and on occasion, these communications contain their loved one's suicide note (that this is only occasional is due, in part, to the fact that the majority of people who die by suicide do not leave a note). The notes frequently refer to feeling estranged from others; for example, one expressed the sentiment that the note-writer felt misunderstood and unloved by everyone, with the sole exception of a deceased grandparent, whom the note-writer hoped to see in the afterlife. In this example, the embrace of death is encouraged, in part, by the idea that problems of loneliness and alienation will be solved thereby. Further to this point, the June 2010 "Harper's Index" in *Harper's Magazine* reported that those with unsupportive relatives are less likely than others to fear death.

My colleagues and I recently modeled some of these processes in the laboratory—a study, it should be emphasized given the nature of the work, that was scrutinized and fully approved by our university Institutional Review Board (IRB). We measured fearlessness about death in undergraduates; these same students were then invited to participate, one at a time, in a procedure in our psychological laboratory.

Participants first filled out a brief personality measure, which they believed would be interpreted by the experimenter. An interpretation was indeed forthcoming for two thirds of the participants (the remainder were assigned to a control condition in which no feedback was given). Those who received feedback were randomly assigned to one of two conditions, regardless of their answers to the personality questionnaire. In one condition, participants were told: "You're the type who has rewarding relationships throughout life. You're likely to have a long and stable marriage and have friendships that will last into your later years. The odds are that you'll always have friends and people who care about you."

Participants in the other condition—the social exclusion condition—heard the following feedback: "You're the type who will end up alone later in life. You may have friends and relationships now, but by your mid-20s most of these will have drifted away. You may even marry or have several marriages, but these are likely to be short-lived and not continue into your 30s. Relationships don't last, and when you're past the age where people are constantly forming new relationships, the odds are you'll end up being alone more and more."

Next, the students participated in a competitive reaction time task, ostensibly against an "opponent" in another room, and were instructed to select, from 10 choices, the level of self-administered shock they will receive if they have the slower reaction time. We used selection of higher shock levels as a laboratory-based proxy for self-injury.

Our expectation was that participants in the social exclusion condition would select higher levels of shock if they also scored high in fearlessness of death. This was precisely what we found (intriguingly, we also found that this result was even clearer when data were collected in the spring as opposed to fall/winter; spring is the season in which suicide rates peak, contrary to what many people think).

Social alienation may play a role in the increased number of suicides seen in the U.S. military in recent years, a daily preoccupation of mine as director of the Military Suicide Research Consortium, which the Department of Defense has funded and which I direct at Florida State University. William James wrote, "all the qualities of a man acquire dignity when he knows that the service of the collectivity that owns him needs him...No collectivity is like an army for nourishing such pride."[42] In this light, however, consider the plight of the isolated soldier who feels ostracized from her or his unit: the individual has the usual burden of alienation, exacerbated by the contrast to the camaraderie felt by everyone else. Consider further the situation of the soldier well integrated into the unit, ties forged perhaps by fierce combat in places like Iraq and Afghanistan, and who leaves the military. An individual in this situation may feel understood only by other soldiers, and alienated even in the midst of caring and loving civilian family and friends.

The link between social isolation and suicidal thinking has occurred even in space. In her book *Packing for Mars*, Mary Roach documented the case of a cosmonaut who got so lonely aboard the space station *Mir* that he had thoughts about suicide. The cosmonaut stated, "I wanted to hang myself. Of course, it's impossible because of the weightlessness."[43]

The vital importance of social imbeddedness is easy to observe in nature. Here again, slime mold make their appearance, as they pull together not only for the purposes of reproduction as described above, but also any time they are separated: a video of slime mold re-merging is magical to see, almost as if they are metal shavings being attracted together by a magnet.[44] Geese pull together in a V-formation and thereby reduce energy expenditure by over 50% per bird; one can see a parallel phenomenon in the Tour de France. Small fish pull together and swarm in a swirling, tornadic horde, thereby reducing loss through predation substantially.

Even more pointedly, just as "death-worth-more-than-life" calculations are seen across nature, so are links between social connectedness and death, including self-initiated death. An article on ants infected with a certain fungus in the February 2010 issue of *Current Biology* stated, "Leaving one's group to die in seclusion might be an efficient way of minimizing the risk of infecting kin. Anecdotal observations of moribund individuals deserting from their groups exist for several species, including humans, but have rarely been substantiated by quantitative analysis."[45] The report showed that worker ants of the species *Temnothorax unifasciatus* self-sacrifice under conditions of lethal fungal infection, quite like we have seen in pea aphids for instance. But here, the *mechanism* for self-sacrifice is isolation from nestmates. More specifically, when ants were infected (and thus not only their survival but that of their nestmates—and their genes in their nestmates—were threatened), they left the nest hours or days before death. For an ant, there could be no more certain way to ensure death.[46]

This remarkable ant behavior is reflective of the roles of both social alienation and burdensomeness in self-caused death. Moreover, the phenomenon suggests a specific causal chain in which perceptions of burdensomeness lead to isolation behaviors, which in turn lead to death. Might this same chain apply to death by suicide in people?

I believe the answer to this question is yes, for three reasons. First, it is very common for people to withdraw markedly in the days before their death by suicide. This is often literally the case, much as it is with ants, in that some eventual suicide decedents leave their homes and their families, perhaps go off to a hotel or a remote area, and die there a day or two later. Another common version of this phenomenon involves withdrawal into a bedroom or some other closable space in the home, here again sometimes for days before death by suicide occurs. In Eli Robins' 1981 book *The Final Months*, which details the cases of 134 deaths by suicide, a very common feature of the decedents was withdrawal, sometimes even to the point of muteness even in response to direct questioning. Yet another version of this involves not actual physical withdrawal but psychological withdrawal—that is to say, the person is physically there but otherwise "not there," withdrawn into one's self. It is important to note that this particular phenomenon has received very little empirical scrutiny; nevertheless, I have certainly observed it in people who have gone on to make lethal suicide attempts. My impression of the phenomenon is that it includes a "thousand-yard" stare—there is a look in the eyes that conveys the impression of a distant, faraway gaze. This, combined with the remoteness of psychological withdrawal, and with other acute warning signs for suicide, represents an ominous clinical picture.

Second, and highly relatedly, some consensus has emerged in the field of scientific and clinical work on suicidal behavior around the list of the top several acute warning signs for death by suicide.[47] Social isolation is one of them (along with talking about/planning suicide, insomnia, nightmares, and agitation). It is useful to distinguish social isolation from ongoing, temperamental shyness. The former represents a marked change in functioning, from an individual who was more or less engaged with others to one who has drastically cut others off through withdrawal; the latter represents an enduring personality style of some social discomfort, but nevertheless ongoing connection to and interest in others.

Third, in understanding the relative rarity of suicide notes (for most deaths by suicide, there is no note), it is interesting to consider the alienated state of mind of the person about to die by suicide. Should one feel like a tremendous burden on loved ones, that feeling in itself may be the main motive to withdraw from them—as we have seen, this same process has been observed in ants, for example. Moreover, this may explain why it is not rare for people to plan and die by suicide without telling anyone, including close intimates; to unburden themselves about suicidal ideation may, they feel, represent even more of a burden than already exists (they feel) to loved ones. A related phenomenon is that many suicide decedents take active steps to spare their families the miserable details of death scenes, by choosing locations in which they are likely to be discovered by strangers—often authorities—or by alerting emergency services as the last act before death.

Phenomena Beyond the Definitional Boundary of Suicide Per Se

The foregoing sketches a reasonably clear picture, I hope, of what suicide *is*. I at least have learned much over the years from pondering what a thing is in its essence, versus what it is *not*. This can be especially illuminating when the focus is on phenomena sitting just opposite one another across a definitional boundary. What are some things that lie just beyond the definitional limits of death by suicide, or of murder-suicide?

Consider, in this regard, Timothy Treadwell, subject of the enthralling and tragic 2005 documentary *Grizzly Man*. As the film documents, Treadwell and his girlfriend Amie Huguenard were killed by a grizzly bear in the Alaska wilderness in October 2003. In the years prior to that, Treadwell—a passionate advocate for protection of the bears and their habitat—became very close to the bears and would approach them fearlessly and touch and even frolic with them. There was little question that this was dangerous behavior even before his death; his and Huguenard's deaths removed any doubt at all about that. Indeed, Treadwell was told this frequently, and in these conversations, it would not surprise me in the least had the people warning Treadwell used words like "death wish" and "suicidal" to describe what he was doing.

But would the use of such words be accurate—was Treadwell's death a suicide? After all, he willingly subjected himself to lethal conditions. Moreover, could the incident be described as a murder-suicide, in that Treadwell knowingly exposed Huguenard to extreme danger, leading to her death, and then he himself died in the same manner?

For two reasons, I believe that Treadwell's and Huguenard's deaths should not be categorized as suicide or murder-suicide. The first reason has to do with the important concept of *intent*. Genuine suicide is characterized by intent to die. Although it is true that such intent may not be unalloyed—it may be and often is tempered by ambivalence—suicide nonetheless involves an intent to die that is demonstrably "greater than zero" (i.e., is present in some degree, and cannot be said to be absent). There is no evidence at all that Treadwell intended his death; on the contrary, he had a joy in and commitment to his activities with bears, and his intent (as unwise as it may have been) was to be with them, not die by them. Second, according to the framework developed in this book, genuine murder-suicide is defined as an event in which someone decides on his or her own to die by suicide, and then from there, reasons via an appeal to virtues such as justice and mercy that at least one other person should die too. None of these elements fits Treadwell's and Huguenard's situation: as already noted, Treadwell did not intend suicide—this alone rules out murder-suicide. But furthermore, he certainly did not intend Huguenard's death, and I believe, would be much more horrified by the fact that a grizzly had killed her than that one had killed him. These unfortunate deaths should be understood as *accidents*; the fact that Treadwell's unwise behavior toward bears is a major factor in causing the accidents does not change the essential character of the event as a tragic accident.

The death of a young man described in Jon Krakauer's 1996 book *Into the Wild* can be understood similarly. Christopher McCandless hitchhiked to Alaska and then walked alone into the wilderness of Alaska. He lived off the land there for many weeks, successfully at first, but then he became ill and had trouble finding enough food to sustain himself. He was found dead there a few weeks later, having starved to death. Investigators were at first puzzled by many aspects of McCandless' death, including that he was found within just miles of places that could have provided him food and medical care.

Krakauer's detailed investigation of McCandless' life and death indicates the tragedy was caused by McCandless, but quite unintentionally: he ingested seeds that, unbeknownst to him, contained a mold that poisoned him. The poisoning is not acute, and so McCandless probably did not notice it initially; instead, the poison prevents absorption of essential nutrients, thus leading to severe fatigue (making the search for food difficult even if it were to be absorbed), malnutrition, and eventually death through starvation. Some have viewed McCandless' behavior as suicidal: he intentionally went into a very unforgiving environment and starved to death there, despite the fact that help was relatively accessible. Krakauer's work, however, shows that this represents a distorted view of the incident. McCandless did well in the wilderness until he was accidentally poisoned; his accessing of nearby resources was prevented by the seasonal flooding of a river, his severe fatigue, and his lack of knowledge of a way over the river within walking distance. As with Treadwell, it is easy to question McCandless' judgment—but that is a different matter than attributing a death wish. Neither man intended to die; both died accidentally.

In suicide *qua* suicide (i.e., involving no murder), the state of mind is characterized by profound social alienation and the view that one's death will be worth more than one's life. Consider the following description: "He felt as though he were wandering in the forests of the sea bottom, lost in a monstrous world in which he himself was the monster. He was alone. The past was dead and the future was unimaginable. What certainty had he that a single human creature now living was on his side?" This passage could easily have come from a clinical (if literary) description from a progress note or psychological report on a suicidal person. But it did not; it is a passage from *1984*, in which the experience of the main character Winston Smith is described.[48] As uncannily perceptive as some fiction writers are (including Orwell certainly), we need not rely on fiction for depictions of the suicidal mind (indeed, it is generally a mistake to do so, because even giants of literature, like Shakespeare and Dostoevsky, regularly miss the mark in their portrayals of suicide).

In the January 2011 issue of *Harper's Magazine*, Clancy Martin described his experiences with alcoholism and suicidal behavior, and in so doing, captured the suicidal state of mind very accurately. He wrote, "the reason [for suicide] is the conviction that you deserve your loneliness, that no one needs to be cast out more than you do." This same mental state, perhaps surprisingly, characterizes those who enact murder-suicide; it is why they have decided on suicide in the first place. Interestingly, as we will see in subsequent chapters, the type of murder-suicide explains differences in "death-worth-more-than-life" calculations. In incidents motivated by mercy or duty, the calculation is clearly interpersonal in its emphasis (e.g., "my death and others' death is the right thing to do by them"). In murder-suicides spurred by justice or glory, the calculation has an overlay of grandiosity (e.g., "I will mete out justice" or "their deaths are worth my glory"). The cases of glory- and justice-motivated murder-suicides are of interest for a variety of reasons, including that they represent a nuance of the rule I articulated in the 2010 book *Myths About Suicide*. The rule is "death by suicide is not an essentially selfish act;" murder-suicides associated with glory and justice certainly seem an exception to the rule, but it is the murder part that is inherently selfish, not the suicide part.

In conventional death by suicide, the virtues discussed in this book are operative to a degree, and they are less distorted than they are in murder-suicide (though still distorted, and the distorting agent, I would contend, is, in every case, mental disorders). For example, when a person truly believes that he or she is a burden on others, takes steps to make his or her death less of a massive blow to others (e.g., ensuring discovery by authorities, not by relatives), and kills himself or herself but harms no others, the actual virtues of duty and mercy can be discerned somewhat, certainly to a greater degree than they are visible in murder-suicide incidents involving perverted versions of mercy or duty. As another example, when a person truly believes that he or she has wronged others to the degree of deserving death and kills himself or herself but harms no others, the virtue of justice, though distorted, is easier to see than it is in murder-suicides involving distorted appeals to virtue. But virtue—or rather its per-version—is involved nevertheless.

Because it involves both killing *and* one's own death—each of which in its own right is deeply emotional, not to mention their combina-tion in one act—and because it is spurred by conditions that them-selves are stigmatized, suicide is a delicate subject, regardless of the audience. It is challenging to contain one's reactions when someone not only misunderstands the phenomenon but bases the misunder-standing on prejudice (the usual basis in this domain). One tempering thought is that the misunderstanding and the prejudice are in part caused by the same thing, fear. People *should* be afraid of suicide—it is fearsome not to mention miserable—but that is not the same thing as saying they should be ignorant about it.

As afraid as people should be about suicide, as fearsome and daunting as it is, murder-suicide is worse still; it trumps even suicide, which is saying something, by adding to it the often-vicious murder of innocent people. To connect this atrocity to virtue in any way is thus more than delicate. I am doing it nevertheless, because I think it is true. Truth can be hard and even awful, but its opposite—illusion and delusion—easily exceeds it in the production of misery, as the falsehoods of 20th-century despots, among many others, amply showed. Even if awful it is true, as the subsequent chapters will show, that murder-suicide involves an appeal to virtue, though to a deeply perverted version of it. Facing this truth may point the way to intervention and prevention, and thus to a reduction of human suffering.

Understanding Virtue

"Can it be denied, but that the moral principle, which…directs virtuous and praiseworthy actions, is natural or innate?"—William Bartram, in his 1791 *The Travels of William Bartram*[1]

IN THEIR *CHARACTER STRENGTHS AND VIRTUES: A HANDBOOK and Classification*, Peterson and Seligman catalogued numerous virtuous qualities.[2] They view virtues as "universal, perhaps grounded in biology through an evolutionary process that selected for these aspects of excellence as means of solving the important tasks necessary for survival of the species,"[3] and point out that virtues like justice, humanity (cf. mercy), courage (cf. glory), and temperance (cf. duty) have consistently emerged in historical surveys. Furthermore, they demonstrate that two virtues are emphasized in *all* religious-philosophical traditions, including Confucianism, Aristotelianism, Tao, Buddhism, Hinduism, and the Abrahamic religions. These two are justice and humanity (cf. mercy). Intriguingly, these two are also the two leading perverted virtues in murder-suicide.

There is a plausible enough belief in many circles that last words have not just a certain truth but a profundity. This is not always true, as demonstrated by the often concrete and mundane character of suicide notes; when they are left, which is relatively rare, they often contain instructions about insurance, bills, and matters like where car keys are. But the mind of the person about to die by suicide is in a highly unusual state, one that is unrepresentative of others who are about to die. We should perhaps look elsewhere, then, for the themes of last words of those at the doorstep of death.

In his 2010 book *Last Words of the Executed*, Robert Elder provides one such source. Unsurprisingly, there is considerable variety in the words and sentiments of those on their way to the execution chamber. However, and of considerable interest in light of the theme of this book, the two main categories are penitence (cf. mercy) and vengeance (cf. justice). As an example of the former, a man executed in Texas in 2006 said to his victims' families, "I want to ask if it is in your heart to forgive me…I just ask you to forgive me and ask the Lord to forgive me…You did not deserve this. I deserve what I am getting."[4] As examples of the latter, Richard Snell said to the then-Governor of Arkansas, "look over your shoulder; justice is coming. I wouldn't trade places with you or any of your cronies. Hell has victories."[5] After having spat at a priest, a convicted murderer in Colorado told the warden "I hate your guts," and went on to remark that he looked forward to seeing all his friends in hell.[6]

All religious-philosophical traditions emphasize justice and mercy; the majority of last words on death row (and not just there) contain expressions of justice and mercy; and the two leading perverted virtues in murder-suicide are justice and mercy. This leads me to wonder if the virtues perverted in murder-suicide represent an essential list of virtue in general.

The situation of the perpetrator-to-be of a murder-suicide is, for all its atrocity, unique in its philosophical vantage point. Why would murder-suicide perhaps represent a special lens into human nature itself? As awful as it is to do so, think of it. You are not psychotic. Your life problems suddenly do not concern you, because you will soon be on the other side of the veil of life from them. You are not merely focused on the reasons life should be taken or spared, but consumed with them. The perpetrator of murder-suicide is in a unique position as a philosopher of life and death. Of course, he turns out to be a very poor philosopher indeed, because of perverted logic. But the mistake, as profound as it is, is in the distortion of logic, not in the identification of core virtue. In this latter activity, in the delineation of what are essential virtues, I want to broach the possibility that the perpetrator-to-be of a murder-suicide is eagle-eyed, though I do not want to lose sight of the fact that the conclusions drawn from accurately identified virtues can be inaccurate, and in the case of the murder-suicide perpetrator, appallingly so.

"[T]hou shalt give life for life, Eye for eye, tooth for tooth, hand for hand, foot for foot, Burning for burning, wound for wound, stripe for stripe" (*Exodus* 21:23–25). These words from *Exodus* are, in one sense, ancient—they were probably written around 3,000 years ago. But if, as Peterson and Seligman suggest in their handbook on virtue, virtue is biologically geared toward solving common problems in human life, prominent analogs of human virtue should be apparent in non-human animals, particularly non-human primates, suggesting an even more ancient link. Characteristically incisive, Charles Darwin remarked, "the difference in mind between man and the higher animal, great as it is, certainly is one of degree and not of kind."[7]

A premise of John Vaillant's 2010 book *The Tiger* is that tigers have a marked sense of justice, and that a violation of one particular tiger's sense of justice caused the deaths of two people in the Russian Far East. The book chronicles how a poacher who killed tiger cubs was in turn painstakingly stalked and killed by a vengeful tiger. Interviewed about a similar tiger, a hunter recounted, "we once took some of a tiger's kill…We didn't take it all because you can't take everything…you have to share. But when we came to check the next day, the tiger hadn't touched what we left for him. After that, we couldn't kill anything: the tiger destroyed our traps and scared off the animals…That tiger wouldn't let us hunt for an entire year…the tiger is such an unusual animal: very powerful, very smart, and very vengeful."[8]

In fact, recent research involving monkeys suggests that a sense of justice may have evolved in non-human primates. In work that might have been entitled "Not the Grapes of Wrath but of Justice," but what was adeptly enough entitled "Monkeys reject unequal pay," researchers taught monkeys to trade tokens for food.[9] Under usual circumstances, the monkeys were happy to exchange a token for a piece of cucumber, which they view as appetizing (but not as appetizing as a grape). But, if a monkey saw another monkey get a prized grape instead of a piece of cucumber, the first monkey seemed offended, and either refused to trade at all or rejected the cucumber reward. Some even responded by throwing the token or cucumber completely out of the cage. A monkey who saw another monkey get a grape for nothing (without trading a token) seemed even more incensed. The researchers believe that this sense of a fair deal is probably an innate ability that evolved in a primate ancestor that humans and monkeys share; a sense of fairness is required to live in large, complex groups, and thus can be viewed as adaptive in an evolutionary context.[10] Compared to justice as a concept in hominids' minds, the words from *Exodus* are very recent.

Mercy is very likely evolutionarily ancient as well, judging by the fact that it exists in many mammalian species, including rats. Rats work hard to rescue a trapped cagemate—they take mercy—and they will do so even though they find the trap scary and they get no obvious reward for their work. In fact, when given the choice between opening a container containing chocolate (which is very prized among rats) and opening a container with a trapped cagemate, rats often free the cagemate first (and then share the chocolate).[11]

The Interpersonal Nature of (Some) Virtues

An assumption of the research on grapes and monkeys as well as that on merciful rats—and one that is compatible with Peterson and Seligman's statement on virtue as biologically evolved to solve problems in daily life—is that justice and mercy evolved and survive because they facilitate social life. They are thus *interpersonal* virtues, by which I mean they are not just relevant to but partly definitive of social relationships. Stemming as they do from the social brain, it stands to reason that they would be interpersonal in emphasis; moreover, the other two virtues highlighted in this book's framework—duty and glory—also have clear social or interpersonal essences. These four virtues all have evident interpersonal aspects and, it will be argued here, wield explanatory power with regard to all cases of murder-suicide.[12]

Three of the four—justice, duty, and glory—are easy to detect in the following passage: "We the People of the United States, in Order to form a more perfect Union, establish Justice, insure domestic Tranquility, provide for the common defense, promote the general Welfare, and secure the Blessings of Liberty to ourselves and our Posterity, do ordain and establish this Constitution for the United States of America." Mercy is a little harder to detect, unsurprisingly given the aims and context of the document in question, but nevertheless can be vaguely discerned in the reference to "domestic tranquility" and "the general welfare." This is a virtuous document indeed, focused on the interpersonal matter of the political relations between individuals and the attendant responsibilities, and its inclusion of the four interpersonal virtues emphasized here is consistent with the view that they are core virtues.

These four virtues, I am arguing, are distorted to the extreme in cases of murder-suicide. It is worth noting, however, that they can be warped in a less extreme and thus less disastrous (though still pernicious) manner. In his 2008 book *Not With a Bang but a Whimper*, Theodore Dalrymple complained of recent cultural trends, involving the "elevation of emotion over principle, of inclination over duty, of rights over responsibilities, of ego over the claims of others."[13] He is not writing about abominations like murder-suicide, but rather about moral slippage. Justice can deteriorate into moralistic self-righteousness; mercy, into maudlin and shallow emotional displays of concern for others; duty, into "what just feels right;" and glory, into unmerited demands for standing and even for adulation. In each of these cases, the deterioration of virtue into diluted versions of itself requires, in a phrase, moral laziness.

In his profoundly moving "I've been to the mountaintop" speech, Martin Luther King, Jr., articulated this same understanding, by referring to the parable of the Good Samaritan: "and so the first question that the priest asked, the first question that the Levite asked was, 'If I stop to help this man, what will happen to me?'" The priest engaged in an abrogation of responsibility and duty. By contrast, King continues: "But then the Good Samaritan came by, and he reversed the question: 'If I do not stop to help this man, what will happen to him?'" An embrace of duty. And notice that, in reversing the question from rights to responsibility, from selfishness to virtue, the Good Samaritan uses half the number of first-person pronouns than does the priest (and that his only usage is "I help"). This detail is reflective of a more general truth—that self-focused, narcissistic people use more such pronouns than others;[14] in fact, an effective aspect of the psychotherapy for narcissistic personality disorder is to teach the mantra, to be used in interpersonal situations one after the other, "this is not about me, this is not about me...."[15] We will encounter this reversal from self- to other-focus again later in this chapter.

The deterioration from full-throated virtue to much paler versions represents an attenuation, the wearing down of virtue. Much as mountains can erode, so can virtue. Erosion, however, is different than perversion—mountains break up, but retain their character as rock. What I am arguing in this book is that the processes underlying murder-suicide do *not* represent a wearing down of virtue, are *not* the consequences of the kind of laziness that transmutes mercy, for example, into maudlin vapidity.

Rather, and somewhat ironically, the perpetrators of murder-suicide, far from indulging in mental laziness, are resolute and in some ways clear-eyed about the essence of virtue. They pervert virtue not by misunderstanding its essence but by woefully misunderstanding its application. In his *A Mathematician's Apology*, referred to at the outset of this book, G. H. Hardy wrote, "Ambition is a noble passion which may legitimately take many forms; there was *something* noble in the ambition of Attila or Napoleon."[16] Hardy leaves it unsaid (perhaps judging that it goes without saying) that there was much ignoble in their behavior as well.

In the 18th century, Adam Ferguson wrote, "Freedom is not, as the origin of the name may seem to imply, an exemption from all restraints, but rather the most effectual applications of every just restraint to all members of a free society, whether they be magistrates or subjects."[17] One factor that accounts for the process of perversion in murder-suicide is a defect in empathy, a fervor for virtue without restraint, and without the leavening effects of emotional understanding of others' perspectives. Understanding others' views, in turn, reins in impulse and instills self-control. In his January 1776 pamphlet *Common Sense*, writing at about the same time as Ferguson, Thomas Paine stated, "Society is produced by our wants and government by our wickedness." The wickedness that is murder-suicide stems from ungoverned thought processes transforming virtue into atrocity. It is this kind of extreme and distorted virtue that I believe George Orwell had in mind in *1984* as he had Winston Smith, kneeling face to face with Julia, say, "I hate purity, I hate goodness. I don't want any virtue to exist anywhere."[18] Winston is railing against the perverted virtue of Big Brother ("freedom is slavery, ignorance is strength"), not the old verities of love and loyalty that he shared, in temporary and doomed fashion, with Julia.

The Derangement of Empathy in Murder-Suicide

The role of empathy in murder-suicide can differ depending on the perverted virtue in question. In incidents involving the perversion of justice and glory, empathy is essentially inactive. The perpetrator feels no empathy in perverted justice scenarios, because he views his victims as "other,"[19] as those who have violated basic human principle and are thus undeserving of empathy. The perpetrator feels little empathy in perverted glory scenarios, because victims are viewed as largely anonymous and incidental to the larger purpose of glory. There is callousness of feeling at play in both scenarios.

By contrast, in murder-suicides perverting the virtues of mercy and duty, empathy is very active, perhaps even overactive. In perverted mercy scenarios, the perpetrator anticipatorily feels the acute future suffering of his victims, and acts to spare them from that suffering. In perverted duty scenarios, a similar dynamic is operative, but additionally, the perpetrator feels the burden that he believes would be left to others in the event that he spares the victim and kills himself (e.g., caring for an incapacitated spouse). Far from callousness, there is a swamp of feeling at play in murder-suicides perverting the virtues of mercy and duty.

These considerations suggest that, from among the four virtues of mercy, duty, justice, and glory, a conceptual clustering is possible, with mercy and duty forming one cluster and justice and glory another. Across the four virtues perverted in murder-suicide incidents, empathy is deranged, but the way in which it is deranged differs for the two clusters. In the justice–glory cluster, empathy is underactive or absent, with callousness as a result. In the mercy–duty cluster, empathy is overwrought, with the effect of making atrocity seem caring in the mind of the perpetrator.

For Thomas Aquinas, a core virtue is "misericordia," feeling others' pain as acutely as one feels one's own, because, he believed, this facilitated the dissolving of barriers between people.[20] I believe this *can* dissolve barriers, but also, that if overdone, can create them as well. This is not hard to observe in the mental health profession, for which many believe, reasonably enough, that an adequate ability to empathize is a job requirement. But many in the mental health field confuse emoting with empathy; they lose sight of the fact that there must be a non-emotional aspect to empathy for it to be accurate and thus helpful. This non-emotional component might be called "perspective-taking;" swamps of emotion are just as likely to impede as to encourage accurate perspective-taking, and the latter, in turn, is necessary for genuine empathic understanding. According to the framework developed in this book, and expanded upon later in the chapters on the perversions of mercy and duty, murder-suicide perpetrators in the perverted mercy–duty cluster are engrossed in a swamp of emotion, the fog of which prevents them discerning what is right from what is woeful.

It is interesting to ponder the extreme fervor of the murder-suicide perpetrator in the context of a social psychological theory called Terror Management Theory.[21] Terror Management Theory takes the ideas articulated in Ernest Becker's 1973 book *The Denial of Death*, elaborates their conceptual basis, and, crucially, puts these claims to rigorous empirical tests. The theory asserts that an important motivator for various forms of human behavior involves regulating the deep fear that people feel regarding their own mortality. When people are reminded of their mortality, they react by embracing things they feel will live on (e.g., the ideals of their own in-group, such as their religion or country).

It is worth noting, in passing, how different this conceptualization is from the psychoanalytic notion of a death instinct. The postulation of a death instinct indicates that we are driven toward death, that we in some way desire it. This view—in addition to being rather implausible on its face and contradictory to Darwin's magisterial work—has caused decades of misunderstanding in the psychoanalytic corpus on things like death, aggression, and suicide. To his credit, Ernest Becker, who won the Pulitzer Prize for his 1973 book *The Denial of Death* and who was far from unsympathetic to psychoanalysis, saw this clearly. He wrote, "Freud's torturous formulations on the death instinct can now securely be relegated to the dust bin of history. They are of interest only as the ingenious efforts of a dedicated prophet to maintain intellectually intact his basic dogma."[22] Sympathetic to psychoanalysis or not, it is rare to find such a clear-eyed assessment, particularly by someone writing almost four decades ago.

In contrast to the psychoanalytic claim for a death instinct, the terror management view is that, far from wanting death, we are terrorized by it, so much so that it guides, either consciously or not, most of what we do. The experimental paradigm for testing this conceptual framework involves participants experiencing either something that reminds them of death or something that reminds them of something else unpleasant (e.g., dental pain). True to the expectations of the framework, those exposed to a "death prime" become more prejudiced, more fervent about their in-group.

As applied to murder-suicide, the perpetrator is not merely mindful of death (as are the participants in terror management experiments) but is intent on causing his own as well as that of at least one other person. Therefore, according to the terror management conceptualization, the press to embrace cherished ideals should be at a fever pitch for the imminent perpetrator of a murder-suicide. A participant in a terror management experiment is asked, as a reminder of death, to write a half-page essay on what death will be like, and this experience, evidence shows, makes the participant subtly though detectably more loyal to and invested in cherished values. This loyalty and investment can be negatively or positively valenced, depending on the individual and the context: if negative, it may be expressed as hatred toward an out-group; if positive, the cherishing of virtue.

The perpetrator of murder-suicide needs no reminder of death—he is already preoccupied by it—and thus the effects on his state of mind ought to be far from subtle. In his mindset can be observed both the negative and the (distorted) positive valencing of cherished value that can occur, on a much reduced scale, in terror management experiments. The negative aspect of the murder-suicide perpetrator's attitude needs little elaboration; the positive, if it can be called that, involves the preoccupation with (if perversion of) virtues like justice and mercy. Far from being slightly more invested in core values, the murder-suicide perpetrator has values like justice or mercy so much on his mind that he can see little else. The imminent perpetrator of a murder-suicide is, in a sense, blinded by his emphasis on what he thinks is justice, mercy, glory, or duty, so much so that he cannot clearly see the appalling horror of what he is about to do. So preoccupied with virtue that he will kill for it, the murder-suicide perpetrator perverts virtue into evil. It was phenomena like these that I believe psychiatrist D. L. Thompson had in mind in 1949 when, in an address at a meeting of the American Psychiatric Association in Montreal, he said, "Everything spiritual and valuable has a gross and undesirable malady very similar to it."[23]

Virtue is implicated in the unfolding thought processes in murder-suicide; more precisely, virtue that is severely *warped* and also *interpersonal* in essence is involved. The process of warping—or to put it in the terms used in this book's title and thesis, perverting—has already been elucidated, and subsequent chapters will further draw this point out.

To return to the topic of the interpersonal nature of virtue, it is interesting to consider further that (1) most virtues are interpersonal in essence—not surprising given the gregariousness of human nature; (2) those that are not interpersonal are nevertheless quite important in the course of human affairs; and (3) these latter, non-interpersonal virtues are, at least according to the framework developed here, not involved in murder-suicide.

What would be an example of a non-interpersonal virtue? Consider freedom and autonomy in this regard. There is little doubt that they should be viewed as essential virtues, as history attests in such examples as the U.S. Revolution. An enduring symbol of autonomy in U.S. history is the Gadsden flag, with its coiled rattlesnake and the words DONT TREAD ON ME inscribed underneath.[24] The sentiment of the flag is not particularly interpersonal in emphasis; in fact, it is hard to hit on a less interpersonal symbol than the rattlesnake. The flag continues to serve as an emblem of fierce autonomy, most recently adopted by those in the Tea Party. The sacrifice of wide togetherness for individual independence is unlikely what the framers of U.S. founding documents had in mind with symbols like the Gadsden flag. One of the documents in question, of course, begins "We the people..." and continues from there to exude a feeling of social harmony for all. The flag also saw a resurgence in the wake of the 9/11 attacks, and there, the sentiment was essentially what the framers intended, along the lines of "let's all pull together to protect all of our freedoms."

In his work on moral systems, psychologist Jonathan Haidt has come to similar conclusions about the nature of virtue. Specifically, in some work (e.g., the book *The Righteous Mind*), Haidt includes liberty as a core virtue, but in other work, he excludes it.[25] There are contexts in which freedom, though core, is not as important as other virtues. My argument is that murder-suicide represents one such context: as expanded upon in a later chapter, when the virtue of self-control (cf. liberty, freedom, and autonomy) is perverted in the course of violence, such violence does not constitute genuine murder-suicide, but rather some "neighboring" form of violence.

Intriguingly, Haidt and Joseph emphasize five moral dimensions—care, fairness, loyalty, authority, and purity—and write of them, "four of our proposed five foundations (all but purity) appear to involve psychological 'building blocks' that are present in other primates."[26] I agree with these authors that this confers foundational status on these four virtues. These four correspond well to the four emphasized in the present book—mercy (cf. care), justice (cf. fairness), duty (cf. authority), and glory (cf. loyalty). The overlap is so plain as to be self-explanatory, except for the last one, glory–loyalty. Consider, however, that Haidt and Johnson point to emotions and associated virtues of loyalty that contain elements related to glory or heroism, namely group pride and self-sacrifice. The framework for understanding virtue espoused in the current book thus converges with accounts emanating from various scholarly traditions.

This framework emphasizes interpersonal virtue, but I reiterate that there are important non-interpersonal virtues too (though they are not implicated in murder-suicide), such as autonomy. That the latter is a virtue can be seen in an account of human motivation called Self-Determination Theory (which, importantly, also focuses on social connection as an important source of thriving).[27] The theory asserts that one's autonomy is so important that full health and thriving are not possible in its absence. To experience autonomy, one has to experience that the self is regulating the self; one has to feel that one's perspective is understood, that choices for one's decisions are ample, and that any restriction on choice is well explained and understandable.

It is striking how often this motive is evoked in numerous activities of human affairs, and how extremely rarely it is invoked as a motive for murder-suicide. Occasionally, as we will see in the chapter on the perversion of justice, murder-suicide perpetrators have a "take-things-into-my-own-hands" attitude, which has notes of autonomy. However, the primary emphasis in their minds, the reason to take things into their own hands, is to deliver vengeful justice. Themes of justice have overwhelmed them, so much so that they can think of little else. This, in turn, means that they cannot generate options and alternatives; their choice is restricted, and thus, by definition according to self-determination theory, their autonomy is low.

Wishes of autonomy and self-control are sometimes attributed to suicide decedents, mostly wrongly I believe. It is true that some patients state that having the option to die makes them feel more in control, but an often-overlooked word in this phrasing is "option," meaning that death would be one of many choices. That is not the signature state of mind of someone about to die by suicide; the latter sees no options other than death. This is yet another misunderstanding about suicide that I dispute in the 2010 book *Myths About Suicide*.

Suicide and its subspecies murder-suicide are not primarily about autonomy, nor, in the case of murder-suicide, is it primarily about any non-interpersonal motive. As we have already seen and as will be delved into in more detail in a later chapter, there is a death-related phenomenon that, on the surface, resembles murder-suicide but upon detailed analysis is not. That phenomenon is when someone plans a murder as well as an escape and life after the escape. In the course of perpetrating the murder, events transpire that thwart the plan to escape and to live on, catastrophically enough that the person then decides on suicide. One could make the argument that a virtue is perverted here; namely, the virtue of autonomy or self-control inherent in thinking along the lines of "I choose to die by suicide rather than facing up to the crime I have committed." But I do not view these instances as genuine murder-suicides because suicide is not primary in these cases, and relatedly, because of the lack of contingency between suicide and murder in these cases. Moreover, I suggest that the virtues in question differ in these cases (i.e., autonomy or self-control) versus genuine murder-suicide, in which the perverted virtues are interpersonal.

In speaking of interpersonal virtues, I do not mean collectivist virtues. Consider, in this context, the words of Austrian economist F. A. Hayek from his 1944 book *The Road to Serfdom*: "It is more than doubtful that an…approach toward collectivism has raised our moral standards, or whether the change has not rather been in the opposite direction…It may even be that the passion for collective action is a way in which we now without compunction collectively indulge in that selfishness which as individuals we had learnt a little to restrain."[28]

The implication of this view for the current framework is that a collectivist approach to these interpersonal virtues undermines them. Something of a paradox thus emerges, in that for interpersonal virtues to function properly, the approach to them must be individu-alistic, in the sense that individuals are taking it as their responsi-bility to honor and act on the virtues. Ironically, there is a sense in which the perversion of virtue inherent in murder-suicide takes a collectivist approach; the perpetrator of a murder-suicide often would endorse thoughts like "what I have decided to do is better for society as a whole." This is particularly so in the minds of those perverting duty and mercy; they are very mindful of the need to kill in order for things to be optimized for everyone else.

Their "collective" view has disastrously freed them from restraint, the kind of personal and disciplined restraint that Hayek believed was essential to free democracy and economy, and which he felt was subverted by collectivism. In *King Lear*, the King advises one of his daughters, "Mend your speech a little, lest you mar your fortunes" (Act I, Scene 1). Lear was wrong about the daughter in question but right as a general matter: the future smiles on the self-disciplined. The famous "marshmallow" experiments showed this empirically.[29] Young children are brought into a laboratory, are seated at a plain table, and are presented with a marshmallow. They are told that they can eat the one marshmallow right away, or if they wait for a lit-tle while until the experimenter returns, they will receive a second marshmallow. Children who were able to exert self-control, as evi-denced by waiting and receiving a second treat, had overall better outcomes as adults than children who could not wait.[30]

This chapter has drawn on the Peterson and Seligman[31] handbook of virtues, as well as on other foundational texts such as the Bible, to elucidate the properties of the virtues (and their perversion) explored throughout this book. The Biblical perspective may be particularly intriguing, in that some incidents of murder-suicide are clearly Old Testament "eye-for-an-eye" events (e.g., killings perverting the virtue of justice), others have New Testament overtones (e.g., those involving distorted mercy), and others span the Old and New Testament sensibilities (e.g., at Virginia Tech, Cho exacted revenge and in so doing viewed himself as Christ-like). This book's next sec-tion delves into the perversion of the specific virtues of mercy, jus-tice, duty, and glory as the *sine qua non* of genuine murder-suicide.

Section 2

Understanding Murder-Suicide as a Perversion of Virtue

A Perversion of Mercy

"I love him who makes his virtue his addiction and his catastrophe: for his virtue's sake he wants to live on and to live not longer." — Friedrich Nietzsche, *Thus Spoke Zarathustra*[1]

"...the exercise of liberty requires virtue if it is not to turn into a nightmare."—Theodore Dalrymple, *Life at the Bottom*, p. 123

A POTENTIAL ADVANTAGE OF THE CONCEPTUAL FRAMEWORK proposed for murder-suicide in this book is that it produces a simple and yet, I contend, valid and penetrating typology for murder-suicide. Typologies of murder-suicide have been proposed in the past, but they can be viewed as problematic, in that they lack parsimony and also describe surface features better than they do motives. This well-known framework was proposed by Marzuk and colleagues:[2]

I. Spousal or consortial
   Perpetrator
      (a) Spouse
      (b) Consort
   Type of homicide
      (a) Uxoricidal (Spouse killing)
      (b) Consortial (Killing of lover)

II. Familial
   Perpetrator
      (a) Mother
      (b) Father
      (c) Child (<16 years)
      (d) Other family members
   Type of homicide
      (a) Neonaticide (Child < 24 hours)
      (b) Infanticide (Child > 1 day, < year)
      (c) Pedicide (Child > 1 year, <16 years)
      (d) Adult family members
III. Extrafamilial
   Class
      (a) Amorous jealousy
      (b) Mercy killing
      (c) Altruistic or extended suicide
      (d) Family, financial or social stressors
      (e) Retaliation
      (f) Other
      (g) Unspecified

This approach has some benefits (e.g., careful consideration of relationship[s] between perpetrator and victim[s]), but it is not particularly succinct. Most of its energy is expended in describing relationships among those involved, but motives are also touched upon in the last section on "Class." The motives proposed by these researchers bear some similarities to those proposed here (e.g., mercy, retaliation), but motives like glory and duty are not specifically included. Additionally, whereas the current book's framework strives to categorize all murder-suicides within it (and in so doing strives to combine parsimony with reach), the approach outlined above allocates some incidents to "other" and "unspecified" subtypes.

In another attempt at typology, Guileyardo and colleagues[3] focused only on murder-suicides in which parents killed their children and then themselves. They listed 16 subtypes:

1. Altruism
2. Euthanasia
3. Acute psychosis
4. Postpartum mental disorder

5. Unwanted child
6. Unwanted pregnancy
7. Angry impulse
8. Spouse revenge
9. Sexual abuse
10. Munchausen-by-proxy
11. Violent older child
12. Negligence and neglect
13. Sadism and punishment
14. Drug and alcohol abuse
15. Seizure disorder
16. Innocent bystander

Here, as with the previous framework, parsimony gives way somewhat to comprehensiveness. Because the list was developed only for a specific form of murder-suicide (i.e., when parents kill children and then themselves, like the Lupoe tragedy), other lists would have to be developed to cover other forms of murder-suicide. The list contains a mix of motives (e.g., altruism, revenge), mental and other disorders (e.g., seizure disorder), and distal precursors (e.g., sexual abuse). The list contains motives that do not apply to murder-suicide or are implicated vanishingly rarely (e.g., sadism; drug and alcohol abuse) and contains elements that are not directly relevant to murder-suicide *per se* (e.g., innocent bystander, which is not murder; unpremeditated killing, also often not considered murder).

The taxonomy proposed in the present effort attempts to avoid these pitfalls by arguing that all murder-suicides fit within four categories, categories defined by perversions of mercy, justice, glory, and duty. Of these four, the two most common involve perversions of justice and mercy, an assertion corroborated by a useful study by Steve Stack.[4] In an analysis of murder-suicide incidents in the Chicago area, Stack reported that the likelihood of an individual's suicide, given that the person had killed someone else, was highest in those who killed ex-lovers (mostly perversions of justice according to the current framework), followed closely by those who had killed their own children (mostly perversions of mercy, again according to the current framework).

Two additional categories involving the perversion of self-control and of fate are included as well, but not as categories of genuine murder-suicide. Rather, these are neighboring phenomena, with some similarities to true murder-suicide (i.e., a suicide preceded by someone else's death) but with enough differences in parameters like underlying thought process and motive to place them outside the definitional boundary.

In this section of the book, this chapter and Chapters 6 through 8 will explore in depth the four fundamental virtues—mercy, justice, duty, and glory—that are perverted in the psychological processes occurring in the minds of murder-suicide perpetrators. Chapter 9 will examine the neighboring phenomena of the perversions of self-control and fate and will explain why, although these categories appear to be murder-suicides on the surface, they really are not.

> ...charity is more perfect than faith and hope which, without charity, are not perfect. So charity is the mother and root of all virtue.[5]

This quote from Thomas Aquinas assigns a pride of place to mercy (or to use his term, charity). There is wisdom in this view, at least regarding the interpersonal, other-directed virtues, because without mercy, the other virtues can be immoderate, even to the degree that they lose their essential quality as virtues. For example, justice, in the absence of at least some mercy, can be cruel. Glory, without the leavening effects of mercy, can become self-glorifying and in the process lose the true character of heroic glory.

A potential quibble with Aquinas' statement is that much the same could be said about at least one other virtue: justice. Virtues like glory, duty, and mercy, absent a sense of what is fair and just, can be transformed into things that are really not virtuous at all. It is not hard to imagine scenarios in which an individual feels he is doing the glorious or dutiful thing, but which everyone else views with horror because it is so lacking in basic fairness. Throughout this chapter and the three that follow we will repeatedly encounter exactly this pattern.

Taking together Aquinas' assertion as well as this one counterpoint, the perversions of mercy—the focus of this chapter—and of justice—the focus of the next—can be viewed as foundational in murder-suicide. Even if in instances in which glory or duty is perverted and leads to tragedy, some undertones of the perversion of mercy or of justice can usually be discerned. If even a small amount of true justice or mercy is added to a situation that perverts glory or duty, the tragedy may be averted. The reverse is not as true: if glory or duty is added to the mix of an unfolding mercy- or justice-related murder-suicide, the process may not be stopped and may even be accelerated (e.g., situations, like the Virginia Tech incident, in which perverted glory accelerates the main process, which was a perversion of justice).

The foundational roles of mercy and justice square neatly with three other facts. First, overall, the majority of murder-suicide incidents involve the perversion of either mercy or justice;[6] those involving the perversion of glory and duty are relatively rare, and, when they occur, they often include significant undertones of either mercy (common with duty-related incidents) or justice (common with glory-related incidents). Second, from the standpoint of virtue in general (apart from its role in murder-suicide), many thinkers over the centuries have developed philosophical or religious viewpoints that can be viewed as boiling down to mercy and justice (e.g., Jesus, Martin Luther King, Gandhi). In the remainder of this chapter, we will delve into the role that the perversion of one of these foundational virtues—mercy—plays in the mental process of the individual who has decided to perpetrate a murder-suicide.

The Nature of Mercy

What is mercy? It is charitable, compassionate, and caring. It contains elements of control, power, and initiative too, as can be discerned in the phrase "to take mercy." Pity is a neighboring concept, and in pity, the element of control is clearer still. Both aspects of the virtue of mercy, charity and control, can be seen in its perversion in murder-suicide. As described earlier, a case in point is the Lupoe tragedy. The parents took control of what they viewed as an ordeal, and in their view, delivered compassion in killing.

In his 2002 book *The Exact Location of the Soul*, Richard Selzer relates an anecdote involving the father of modern surgery, Ambroise Paré.[7] Paré accompanied French soldiers in war, and in one particular instance, encountered three soldiers in a barn who were gravely wounded. The soldiers were beyond help, and Paré could do no more than look at them in sympathy. An experienced soldier chanced upon the scene and asked Paré if anything could be done. Paré shook his head to indicate the hopelessness of the situation, whereupon the solider, according to Paré's memoirs, "gently, efficiently and without ill will," cut each of the dying soldiers' throats. Paré cried out in horror, to which the man replied, "I pray God that if ever I come to be in that condition, someone will do the same for me." Selzer concludes his description of this affair with the question, "Was this an act of villainy, or mercy?"

The soldier did not perpetrate murder-suicide, and thus it would be reasonable to question the relevance of this incident to the phenomenon of murder-suicide. Nevertheless, this chapter will make the case that, just as the soldier viewed the circumstances as necessitating that he take lethal actions, so too does the perpetrator of murder-suicide in perversions of mercy. Each believes he is acting in a way that is merciful, even if awful.

There are differences between the two as well, needless to say. First, the experienced soldier's actions did not stem from his first deciding on his own death. I consider such a decision as a *sine qua non* of genuine murder-suicide. Second, the soldier had a clear-eyed view of the entire, miserable situation. He did not misperceive his comrades' future fate; he understood unstintingly that death would come and that forestalling it would mean substantially greater suffering. By contrast, the perpetrator of the murder-suicide—more specifically the murder-suicide involving the perversion of mercy— profoundly misunderstands the situation's contours. He imagines his victims are in the same awful ordeal as the wounded soldiers; if this were true, mercy-based action may be defensible, as it may have been in the case of the soldier who decided to take lethal action. But, of course, it is not true that victims of murder-suicide are fated for ongoing and needless misery. That the perpetrator thinks they are and that this thought causes their deaths underscores the profundity of murder-suicide's tragedy.

Perverted Mercy in Murder-Suicide

But might some victims of murder-suicide be in actual and genuine misery, and therefore welcome their deaths? In covering recent murder-suicides among elderly married couples in the Atlanta area, an *Atlanta Journal-Constitution* reporter echoed the question about the experienced soldier: "Were these deaths the result of depression, some level of domestic abuse, or were they the actions of a benevolent, merciful spouse?"[8]

The daughter of one couple in their 80s inclined toward the latter answer. Her father had carried out a very carefully thought-through plan to kill his wife—who had dementia—and himself; the daughter viewed the deaths as "mercy killings." As happens in some murder-suicides, there may have been an additional motive at play: duty. The daughter said of her father and referring to the onset of dementia, "I think he was afraid [that] what was happening to her…was happening to him." That is, the man may have felt that, since he would soon become as incapacitated as his wife, and thus be unable to care for them both, he would save others the obligation. He may well have believed that that was the dutiful (and merciful) thing to do. In a letter he left behind, the man stated, "I believe that everyone concerned will get along with me and [my wife] out of the picture."

The same *Atlanta Journal-Constitution* article noted a different perspective on these deaths. A representative from the Georgia Commission on Family Violence, far from viewing the deaths as merciful or dutiful, saw them as one person taking power over another. The representative stated, "I'm very troubled by the whole language of 'mercy killings,' because I don't think I feel comfortable with someone else determining when you should die…[C]omplicated lives…[do] not excuse murdering someone." One intended contribution of this book is to show that both perspectives are correct: of course murder is wrong; but, from the perspective of the perpetrator, it is not murder but rather the consequences of a serious adherence to the dictates of virtue.

A psychiatrist interviewed for the same article hit on two important issues in stating, "Often times, when people are thinking about suicide, they are feeling hopeless and helpless and see no way out of their situation." First, this assertion assigns primacy to suicide in murder-suicide, rightly I believe. Second, in the phrase "see no way out of their situation," the psychiatrist is touching on the initial steps of the underlying psychological process that culminates in murder-suicide. That is, the perpetrator of a murder-suicide drastically misperceives the initial setting conditions of a given situation, by, for example, far overestimating the amount of future suffering his victims will experience if they are not killed. It is here that the perpetrator "sees no other way." Murder-suicide expert Donna Cohen, interviewed for the same article, stated, "These are acts driven by…a sense that there is nothing else they can do." Once this initial assumption is set, the appeal to virtue dictates the rest of the awful story, according to the framework advanced in this book.

In his 1957 book *Reflections on Hanging*, Arthur Koestler says that charity is the combination of humility and imagination, a thought-provoking definition.[9] The perpetrator of murder-suicide is lacking in both humility and imagination—the lack of imagination referring to the same process that the psychiatrist in the story above and Professor Cohen refer to in "sees no other way" and "nothing else they can do." In perverting the virtue of mercy, murder-suicide perpetrators leave out both humility and imagination; either one would stave off their urge to die and to kill.

I believe this would have applied to the Lupoe parents, who, as described in the opening passages of the book, killed their children before killing themselves. They believed they were doing the merciful thing; if someone had understood the unfolding tragedy and gotten through to the parents, persuading them that the future for them and their children, though possibly difficult, would not be disastrously painful, this profound tragedy may have been averted.

"[T]hough…I have all faith, so that I could remove mountains, and have not charity, I am nothing. And though I bestow all my goods to feed the poor, and have not charity, it profiteth me nothing." This verse (*1 Corinthians* 13:2–3) harkens back to the quotation earlier in this chapter from Thomas Aquinas (indeed it may have been his inspiration); the verse not only assigns a kind of primacy to mercy in the hierarchy of virtues, but it also understands that great and powerful strivings can be for naught. In fact, as murder-suicides involving the perversion of mercy show, they can be for far worse than naught.

"Worse than naught" certainly characterizes an incident that occurred in the San Diego area in May 2011—one with similarities to the Lupoe tragedy. Two parents, Alfredo and Gina Pimienta, decided to die together and, because they had decided thus, reasoned that it was the virtuous thing to do to take their two daughters, ages 17 and 7, with them.[10] Like the Lupoes, the family was having serious financial problems; the license for the business they ran was set to expire in days at the time of the tragedy. Like the Lupoes, the parents left a note explaining their rationale for what they had decided.

An important detail in this incident involves the behavior of the father in the days leading up to the deaths. A neighbor described him as pacing up and down the street, and also as being uncommunicative, to the point of completely ignoring neighbors' small talk. Significantly, these represented recent changes as compared to Mr. Pimienta's usual comportment.

Mr. Pimienta's behavior in the days leading up to the tragedy is very consistent with the behavior of someone contemplating suicide. In the timeframe before suicide, agitation—inner turmoil (often located in the midsection) combined with extreme physical restlessness—is regularly noted; pacing is a behavioral indicator of agitation. Also in the immediate timeframe preceding death by suicide, extreme forms of social withdrawal are a common feature. Socializing takes many forms—we talk together, have meals with one another, have drinks with each other, have sex with each other. Many suicide decedents stop doing these things altogether in the days before their death—they eat so little that they lose a noticeable amount of weight; they talk so little that they can become virtually mute even in response to direct questioning. On the points of drinking alcohol and sex, people who regularly enjoyed these activities often cease engaging in them in the timeframe before death by suicide.[11] Mr. Pimienta's uncommunicativeness with his neighbors is consistent with this scenario of marked social withdrawal preceding serious suicidal behavior. Given that the evidence indicates that Mrs. Pimienta was a participant in the incident and not a victim, I conjecture that she too was suicidally depressed. For those who are severely depressed at one point in time, odds are that they have experienced depression earlier, and this may have been the case for both Mr. and Mrs. Pimienta, whose lives included many hardships, including the death of an infant years before their own deaths.

The Pimientas' deaths very probably started out as an agreement between the parents that the two of them would die by suicide. Once that was decided, they asked a question—a question that is reasonable enough and that I believe virtually all people about to die by suicide contemplate to at least some extent: What will happen to loved ones—in the case of the Pimientas, their daughters? Those who die by suicide and who do not first perpetrate murder answer this question, tragically, with "everyone will be better off." They are mistaken in that view, but nevertheless, it is their view. Had the Pimientas come to this same conclusion, I believe they would be dead but their daughters would have been spared.

But their answer was different. Theirs was along the lines of "our daughters most certainly will not be better off; they will be catastrophically worse off. To spare them this miserable and certain future, it is the virtuous thing to do—the merciful thing to do—to take them with us." Here, too, the fact that the Pimientas were horribly mistaken in their logic does not change the fact that that was indeed their logic, and this distorted logic—the perversion of virtue—was a key process in the family's deaths, just as it is, I argue, in all deaths in murder-suicide incidents.

At the beginning of the book, I quoted the inscription on Lydia Beadle's headstone, made on the occasion of her death in 1782, which reads, "Fell by the hands of William Beadle/an infatuated Man who closed the/horrid sacrifice of his Wife/& Children with his own destruction." In this incident, like in those involving the Lupoe and Pimienta families, an entire family was killed. The inscription blames William Beadle and his "infatuation" for the deaths; if he alone were to blame, and considering that he killed both his wife and his children, a likely motive would have been perverted mercy (by contrast, if he had killed just his wife and himself but spared his children, the likely motive would have been perverted justice, as most such murder-suicides involve vengeance as a primary motive). His "infatuation" may have involved a belief in some form of oncoming doom and woe, which he deemed more agonizing than death itself; in this scenario, he chose death for his family and for himself to avoid suffering what he thought would be worse than death. Another possibility, however, is that the headstone's inscription misreports the incident (those who wrote the inscription, it should be remembered, were probably Lydia Beadle's relatives). The inscription absolves her from blame—quite possibly accurately. But incidents like those involving the Lupoe and Pimienta families show that, in situations in which an entire family dies, both parents can be involved as perpetrators.

When this occurs, as the evidence indicates it did in the Lupoe and Pimienta incidents and possibly in the 1782 Beadle incident, the suicide part of the murder-suicide equation involves a suicide pact. The pact is between two people (in these examples, spouses) who mutually agree that they intend to die by suicide. As we will see again shortly, a pact by itself is not a murder-suicide; if, for example, the Lupoes had decided to enact their own deaths but not their children's, a murder-suicide would not have occurred, but a suicide pact would have.

In an earlier chapter, I presented anecdotal evidence for the possibility that suicide is an inherently more fearsome thing even than killing someone else (itself very daunting). There should therefore be people who found it possible to kill someone else but could not enact their own deaths, even though desired. In the earlier discussion, I mentioned the Florida felon who reportedly killed his cellmate in order to induce the state to execute him (which it later did). The principle that suicide is more difficult even than killing someone else emerged in an incident in New York in 2010, relevant to the perversion of mercy.

A mother administered an overdose of drugs to her severely autistic son, who died as a result. She claimed that she intended murder-suicide but survived the overdose she herself took. In a note prepared before the incident, the mother wrote, "I can't bear to watch my son live this life and worry that I will be taken from him or he will be taken from me...It's impossible to live knowing you can't protect your only child from unbearable torment...I hear about parents with children like mine who jump off bridges with their adult children rather than face the prospect of leaving them alone in the world."

The phrasing "protect from unbearable torment" and "leaving them alone in the world" is a succinct description of how perpetrators of murder-suicide who pervert mercy think of their actions; like the mother in this case, they believe that their own deaths will inevitably lead to such acute suffering in their loved one that the latter's death is not only indicated, but is the virtuous thing to bring about.

The tragedy involving the mother and her autistic child illustrates two other important principles. First, as alluded to already, killing others, as against our nature as it is, may be easier than suicide. In this case, the mother was able to perpetrate a killing but not her own death.[12] Second, killing, as we have seen, is gendered. That is, men kill themselves and kill others far more frequently than do women. It stands to reason, then, that should a woman plan to enact murder-suicide, the likelihood that she back away from full completion, either to begin with or after the murder is perpetrated, is greater than the corresponding likelihood for a man. To my knowledge, there is no systematic study testing this expectation, but my anecdotal impression of media reports certainly corroborates this viewpoint (including the Kimura case, discussed later in this chapter).

Incidents like this one, and like those involving the Pimienta and Lupoe families, seem starkly different from those involving suicide bombers (which, though quite debatable, can be argued are murder-suicides). However, in his 2005 book *Landscapes of the Jihad* and his 2008 book *The Terrorist in Search of Humanity*, Faisal Devji argues that there is a crucial similarity. In the latter book, he asserts that the main motive is often not perceived injustice or reaction against oppression, but rather "pity for the plight of others, the same abstract and vicarious emotion that characterizes the actions of pacifists or human rights campaigners."[13] Part of Devji's argument derives from analysis of speeches given by terrorist leaders like Osama bin Laden and Ayman al-Zawahiri, who use, according to Devji, "the language of humanitarianism" and who, again according to Devji, model their actions on Western military intervention for humanitarian relief (e.g., in Bosnia).

The framework developed in this book is not fully compatible with this view, however. In murder-suicide scenarios that clearly involve mercy, like the tragic cases of the Lupoe and Pimienta families, the perpetrator believes he is showing mercy to those killed. In the scenarios analyzed by Devji, the mercy (if it can be called that) is on behalf not of those killed but of those avenged. It is not mercy fundamentally; what motivates these crimes in suicide terrorism is perverted justice, and feelings of charity and humanitarianism, though possibly discernible, are secondary.

In murder-suicides in which parents kill their children and then themselves, the horror is multi-determined, but one source of it is to imagine the awful confusion and terror of the children. There are other instances in which the virtue of mercy is involved (and perverted) in which the victim is at least a somewhat willing participant—indeed, the example noted above of the couple in their 80s may have been one such case. Many such incidents involve older people (often married to one another), and relatively few involve parents and children,[14] but an exception may have occurred near Dallas in 2010. The mayor of Coppell, Texas, killed her 19-year-old daughter and then herself. The father of the family had died approximately two years before; both women had had great difficulty coming to terms with his death, both emotionally and financially. One of the notes left by the mother read, "O grace of God, please forgive me and have mercy on my eternal soul. My sweet, sweet [daughter] had grown completely inconsolable. She had learned to hide her feelings from her friends, but the two of us were lost, alone and afraid. She just kept on asking, 'Why won't God just let me die.' We hadn't slept at all and neither one of us could stop crying when we were together."[15] Her use of the term "had"—as in "she *had* learned to hide her feelings" and "*had* grown inconsolable"—suggests that she may have killed her daughter before writing this note.

This sad tale illustrates three important points. First, insomnia often is a precursor to death by suicide (including the subset of suicides that are murder-suicides). Second, examples like this push up against the definitional boundary between murder-suicide versus a suicide pact. In the latter, no murder is committed; rather, two or more people have decided to simultaneously and usually by the same method die by suicide. Furthermore, the thought process in a suicide pact differs from that in a genuine murder-suicide. As we have seen, in murder-suicide, there is, in the mind of the perpetrator, a logical contingency between the suicide and the murder—a thought process along the lines of "because I am dying it logically implies that, via an appeal to virtue, someone else dies too." By contrast, in suicide pacts, the logical contingency is absent—the line of thought is not "because you are dying I will die too" but rather "we have both decided to die together." The tragedy described above involving the mother and her 19-year-old daughter has some of the features of a suicide pact, in that both women, it appears, were depressed and suicidal, discussed death, and did in fact die together. However, the evidence in the case places the incident on the murder-suicide side of the boundary between suicide pact and murder-suicide, in that it shows that the mother killed her daughter before killing herself. In so doing, the virtue of mercy was likely on her mind (indeed she mentioned the word in the note quoted above, although in a different context).

Third, and more tragic still, it is possible that the mother in this case misinterpreted her daughter's desire to die. The daughter, according to the note quoted above, frequently said, "Why won't God just let me die." Patients who say things like this often also articulate thoughts like "I wish I were dead" and "I'd be better off gone."

It is true that these statements have a suicidal character, but the nature of that character deserves further consideration. There is a continuum of suicidality, which runs from rather mild all the way up to extremely lethal. The mildest form includes thoughts not of one's own death but of death in general (e.g., preoccupation with funerals, cemeteries, dead bodies). Somewhat more severe—but still relatively mild—are thoughts not of killing oneself but of being dead oneself. This is precisely the kind of ideation that the daughter evinced when she stated things like "Why won't God just let me die." The rest of the continuum is as follows: thoughts of killing oneself without intent or plan to do so; intent and plan to die by suicide absent suicidal behavior; non-fatal suicide attempt using relatively non-lethal means (e.g., mild overdose; superficial cuts); non-fatal suicide attempt using relatively lethal means (e.g., surviving a self-inflicted gunshot wound[16]); and, lastly, death by suicide.

It is a very tragic possibility that the mother and daughter were at very different points along this continuum of suicidality. The mother, by definition, was at the most severe end of the spectrum—her death by suicide makes that clear. Her daughter, however, may have been at the other end of the range, regularly talking about her own death but not intently and genuinely suicidal. Talking about one's death but not intending it is a common presentation of major depressive disorder (which if left untreated can progress to a more severe form in which a person talks about death and very much intends it). This seeming paradox of desiring death but not intending it is resolved by the fearsome and daunting qualities of death, emphasized earlier in this book. The mother may have mistaken her daughter's relatively mild suicidal ideation for genuine intent to die by suicide; this misinterpretation (if it occurred) would have been facilitated by the mother's state of mind—gravely and suicidally ill with major depressive disorder, which would have affected her powers of reason and logic, and might have led her to assume that all depressed people felt as she did, welcoming of death.

In *The Merchant of Venice*, Shakespeare wrote, "The quality of mercy is not strain'd, It droppeth as the gentle rain from heaven Upon the place beneath. It is twice blest: It blesseth him that gives and him that takes" (Act IV, Scene 1). As was his unmistakable wont, Shakespeare has captured many truths with parsimony. True mercy is not forced; it requires a mutuality and reciprocity between participants, who understand one another and who are in harmony about their needs and resources. Mercy-related murder-suicide incidents pervert this character of mercy.

An incident that occurred in Staten Island in late July 2010 likely involved the perversion of mercy and furthermore illustrates how the conceptualization developed in this book may be of practical use to, for example, police investigating death scenes. This particular scene involved the deaths of a mother in her 30s and her four children, who ranged in age from two to fourteen.[17] They died at their home, which had been set on fire. Initial reports focused on the 14-year-old boy as the perpetrator, because two of his three siblings had had their throats cut before the blaze, a razor was found near his body, and the boy had been in trouble for many things, including firesetting. These factors reasonably enough focused suspicion on the boy, but there was reason for skepticism of the idea that the boy had killed his mother and his siblings and then himself. The basis for skepticism was due to a few facts: (a) suicide is extremely rare in children aged 14 and below (though, alas, it does occasionally occur); (b) in the very rare instances in which a 14-year-old does die by suicide, the chances that the child decides to first kill others approach zero; and (c) in the few instances in which a murder-suicide involves a teenage perpetrator, the motive is usually a perversion of the virtue of heroic glory—as we will see, this was the motive for the two teenage killers who killed students and others at Columbine before killing themselves. There was little at the burned-out scene in Staten Island that suggested any kind of attempt by the 14-year-old at glory. None of these considerations rules out the child as the perpetrator, but it would immediately suggest to investigators that they should take a hard look at alternative scenarios.

A more plausible explanation might be that the family was killed by an assailant, who attempted to cover his tracks by setting the house on fire. But investigators could find no evidence of a break-in, and interviews with neighbors and relatives revealed no suspects who had been in conflict with the family or hanging around the neighborhood with no explanation. Moreover, a fragment of a note was found, reading "…am sorry…" The note's handwriting matched known samples of the mother's handwriting.

The mother, subsequent investigation showed, was the perpetrator. The awful truth is that the Staten Island mother knifed her three eldest children to death and then set the fire. She died from the effects of the fire, as did her youngest child. In all likelihood, she had decided on her own death and believed that the effects of her own death on the futures of her children would be worse than their deaths, leading her to conclude that taking their lives was the merciful thing to do.

It is somewhat perplexing that all of the children except one died of knife wounds. Why kill three of the four children using one method and a fourth using another? A definitive answer is lost to history, but plausible speculations are that she coldly calculated that the youngest would die in the fire, whereas the oldest three may have been able to escape the house had she not killed them first, that she blanched at the prospect of killing a child so young by knife wound (even though she had not hesitated with her oldest three), or some combination of the two.

Another incident in the same area and also involving a mother and her children likely involved the perversion of mercy and also illustrated a basic and tragic principle regarding death by suicide. The mother drove her van with her four children into a body of water, intending that they all drown. All of them did, with the exception of the eldest child, a 10-year-old boy, who was able to extricate himself from the car and swim to shore. He reported that, as the car was going under, his mother changed her mind and frantically tried to undo what she had wrought. She failed in this, and she and her other children perished.[18]

This sad tale shows not only the potentially horrible effects of the perversion of the virtue of mercy, but also the deeply fearsome nature of the prospect of death. Even someone as intent on murder-suicide as to planfully gather her children into a car, drive to a body of water, and drive the five of them to their deaths—even she flinched at the last moment. This is a regular feature of any kind of suicide. I have already described the woman who ingested an entire bottle of a very powerful household cleaner containing substantial amounts of hydrochloric acid. This behavior shows very high intent to die indeed. And yet she too flinched; after ingesting the cleaner, she changed her mind about death and called 911. Her flinch was too late to save her life, as was the flinch of the mother to spare her and three of her children's lives.

The deaths of two women in the life of poet Ted Hughes illustrate the difference between suicide and murder-suicide (and the perversion of mercy in the latter case). Both women, Sylvia Plath and Assia Wevill, died by suicide by sealing off a room and opening gas vents. Plath made certain her children would not be affected by the gas, showing that mercy toward others need not be—in fact usually is not—perverted in suicide. In contrast, Wevill made certain that her four-year-old daughter would be affected by the gas. Wevill placed a mattress in the kitchen, sealed the doors and windows, drank a mixture of liquor and sleeping pills, and lay down on the mattress with her daughter.[19]

Wevill did not kill her daughter out of anger or spite. On the contrary, the child meant everything to her, and her suicide note makes it plain that she felt killing the child was the merciful thing to do. The note and other sources indicate that Wevill was certain that the child would be put up for adoption, was too old for anyone to actually adopt, and so would grow up alone as a foster child. Like the Lupoes, Wevill's profound misunderstanding was not of the logic of mercy, but of the facts of first principles. She badly overestimated the future misery of her daughter in foster care, sincerely believing that death would be preferable to such suffering. The case can be made that death is preferable to some forms of suffering; we have already seen, for example, that this fact is a basis for Oregon's Death With Dignity law, and that a similar calculation applied in the anecdote of the soldier putting comrades out of their misery. What sets apart these examples from those that are perversions of mercy is the misunderstanding— the extreme exaggeration—of future misery and suffering.

Interestingly, Wevill's biographers misclassified her murder-suicide as involving duty rather than mercy. This is somewhat understandable, as Wevill's journal contained the line, "Execute yourself and your little self efficiently," penned three days before her death. Her biographers stated, "Her murderous act was thus the outcome of a distorted over-responsibility."[20] This is not so; if it were, her journals and notes would have indicated that she was killing the child so as to remove the responsibility of her care from others (e.g., Hughes, the father). But she cared more about the child than she did about herself or Hughes, which is why she killed her. This logic seems impenetrable to most, but not to Wevill, who, like the Lupoes, linked it to an act of mercy.

An incident with similar undertones occurred in southern California in 1985. Fumiko Kimura drowned her two children (ages six months and four years) and attempted to drown herself, but she was saved.[21] The precipitant for this tragedy was Ms. Kimura's learning that her husband had had a mistress for years. Subsequent investigation revealed that Ms. Kimura saw this as a great shame on her and her children, so much so that, in her view, death would be preferable to their living on in shame. In part because she had killed more than one person, prosecutors considered the death penalty. Many members of the Japanese community in southern California petitioned on Ms. Kimura's behalf, arguing that, in a Japanese cultural context, her actions would not constitute murder but instead *oyako-shinju* or "parent–child suicide." According to Japanese law and tradition, *oyako-shinju* represents a form of involuntary manslaughter.

Indeed, Ms. Kimura's lawyers attempted a "cultural defense" (i.e., exoneration of wrongdoing if the illegal act would have been culturally acceptable in the defendant's country of origin). This defense was not successful; instead; the Court gave Ms. Kimura a relatively light sentence (i.e., one year in prison and five years' probation) because it was convinced that she was seriously mentally ill at the time of the incident. The framework developed in this book might recommend a similar decision: Ms. Kimura decided to die, and reasoned further that it would be unmerciful to her children to live on under family shame. Her reasoning was badly distorted by grave mental illness. This tragedy is a relatively clear example of a mercy-related murder and (attempted) suicide, and this is so irrespective of cultural factors. Virtues like mercy are universal; my argument in this book is that the perversion of such virtues typifies murder-suicides, and that this process, too, is universal, discernible in one way or another in murder-suicides occurring in different cultures, societies, and countries.

Mercy can be invoked in incidents in which people first kill not other people but instead their animals before enacting their suicide. As we will see in a future chapter, duty can also be invoked in such incidents. In early 2010 in upstate New York, a dairy farmer pinned a note to his barn stating that whoever finds the note should not enter the barn but should alert the police. The fact that this note was there shows forethought on the part of the farmer, not to mention consideration, because the scene behind the barn door was very graphic. After placing the note on the door, the farmer closed it, and then shot to death half of his approximately 100 cows. He then turned the gun on himself.

On first examination, this incident seems beyond explanation. Why would the farmer decide to kill any of his cows? Why, having decided to kill some number of them, settle on half? The answers to this mystery, it turns out, involve mercy (and to a degree, duty). The farmer only killed those particular cows that required twice-daily milking; should his body have lain for days undiscovered—a distinct possibility given that the man was isolated and ran the farm essentially by himself—the suffering of these cows over those days would be very acute. The half of his cattle that could go for days with relatively little discomfort, the farmer spared. This pattern of evidence suggests that, far from the man killing cows in a fit of rage or psychosis, he had decided on his own death, and then reasoned that, given his death, the merciful act would be to kill those cows who would, as a consequence of his death, suffer enormously.[22]

A news article on this tragedy related that, based on interviews with fellow farmers, the farmer in this incident "was most likely concerned that the cows would not have been cared for after his death." This statement refers, in all likelihood, to the farmer's concern for the cows' suffering in the days after his death—a concern underlain by a sense of mercy—but it could also refer to the long-term duty of placing and caring for the cows—a concern with a foundation in a sense of duty. As we will see in a later chapter, it is not rare for distorted versions of mercy and duty to blend in incidents involving murder-suicide as well as those involving killing animals before killing oneself.[23]

This chapter has considered the nature of the virtue of mercy, as well as the consequences of its perversion in instances of murder-suicide (and suicide preceded by the killing of animals). Mercy, if not perverted, can be redemptive. In his 2004 book *War and Redemption*, Larry Dewey quoted a combat veteran of the Vietnam War: "Mercy is the opposite of vengeance. A Vietcong woman tries to lead you to your death in an ambush. When you have the chance, you could exact justice. Instead, you are merciful and spare her. Mercy is not imposing vengeful or retributive justice when you have the opportunity.

Mercy is inconsistent with the hate frequently generated by war. Hate and bitterness have to be let go for mercy to have a place."[24] Mercy usually preempts vitriolic forms of vengeful justice. In this chapter, however, we have seen that mercy, if perverted, can lead to horror; mercy can be the seat for hateful behavior if terribly distorted. In the next chapter, we will see what happens when hate and bitterness run amok, pervert justice, and result in disaster.

A Perversion of Justice

"You can have vengeance, or peace, but you can't have both." —
Former President Hoover to President Truman in 1946, on the proper
attitude toward post-war Germany[1]

IN HIS 1997 BOOK *VIOLENCE: REFLECTIONS ON A NATIONAL Epidemic,* researcher James Gilligan writes that "all violence is an attempt to achieve justice, or what the violent person perceives as justice for himself."[2] We have already seen in the last chapter on the perversion of mercy, as we will see in subsequent chapters too, that this statement overreaches somewhat: not all violence is about justice; people kill in the name of other virtues too. But a lot of it is about justice, as Gilligan claims, and as will be seen in this chapter. Gilligan's statement is notable for another reason; in his remark on what the violent person *perceives* to be justice, he alludes to the theme of this book. Violence in the form of murder-suicide is about a misperception—a perversion—of virtues like justice.

The Nature of the Virtue of Justice

Justice is, in essence, a solemn virtue, one that virtually always requires decorum and is rarely openly celebratory. This is easy to see, for example, in the comportment of the vast majority of judges, bailiffs, lawyers, and jury members in court proceedings where justice is being decided and delivered. The atmosphere is—or should be—formal.

This sense of decorum and solemnity was plain to see on the face of President Obama in photos of him watching events culminating in the death of Osama bin Laden in 2011; the same could be said of others who were with him in the White House's Situation Room. There was, it should be acknowledged, applause when the transmission "Geronimo EKIA" was received (EKIA means "enemy killed in action," and Geronimo was the code name given to bin Laden[3]). But this was the applause of relief, not of celebratory gloating. Relief was understandable—the people in that room had ordered the SEALs very much into harm's way, and they were seeing an extremely dangerous, sensitive, and intricately planned mission succeed. In *The Odyssey*, after killing people he thought deserved it, Odysseus said, "To glory over slain men is no piety."[4] There was no glorying over slain men in the Situation Room.

Outside of the Situation Room—on college campuses for example—celebratory cheering did occur, including the chant "Nah-nah-nah, nah-nah-nah, hey-hey-hey, goodbye!" Personally, this chant makes me cringe and seems unseemly even in its usual environs, the dwindling moments of a decided sports contest in which the soon-to-be victorious side of the crowd taunts the other side. To hear it on the occasion of someone's death—even an evil person's death—is as inappropriate as if it occurred at a funeral or execution. Youth is no excuse for the cheapening of heroism or of the pathos of justice delivered expertly and quite rightly. Many, by contrast, immediately and intuitively grasped the moment's significance, understanding the virtue of justice, with its primitive vengefulness leavened by reflective decorum.

Revolutionary War hero Francis Marion, who, in arguing against a piece of post-war legislation in the South Carolina senate that would have provided him with a lot of personal protection against lawsuits, said, "If I have given any occasion for complaint, I am ready to answer in property and person. If I have wronged any man I am willing to make him restitution. If, in a single instance, in the course of my command, I have done that which I cannot fully justify, Justice requires that I should suffer."[5] Marion believed that any failure of duty on his part required not just his acknowledgement but his own suffering—a far cry from those who are preoccupied by their rights (not their duties) and are quick to call for others' suffering if they believe their rights have been disrespected. The perpetrators of murder-suicide have much more in common with the latter than they do with paragons of honor like Francis Marion.

Marion's perspective is based on his own sense of obligation and duty (which, as we will see in a later chapter, can also be perverted in instances of murder-suicide). His words include eight first-person references (i.e., "I," "my") and only two third-person references (i.e., "any man," "him"). This can be an indicator of narcissism; Marion is, in a sense, self-focused, but his words are far from selfish. Virtues like justice and mercy are, it is true, interpersonal in essence; however, what is also quite true is that they require a self-focused, responsible attitude. Over 2,000 years ago, Marcus Seneca endorsed this view in saying, "It is a denial of justice not to stretch out a helping hand to the fallen; that is the common right of humanity."[6] The impulse here is interpersonal—like the Good Samaritan, to help humanity—but the impulse cannot be properly discharged unless contained within a framework of personal responsibility.

The Perversion of Justice in Murder-Suicide

The impulse toward justice in murder-suicide is improperly discharged, to put it mildly and somewhat clinically. However, consistent with this book's theme, strivings for justice can be discerned through the fog of murder-suicide. "He who desires to inflict rational punishment does not retaliate for a past wrong which cannot be undone; he has regard to the future, and is desirous that the man who is punished, and he who sees him punished, may be deterred from doing wrong again. He punishes for the sake of prevention." A justice-motivated murder-suicide perpetrator might have said this; it captures his view that the continuation of an injustice (e.g., a relationship between his ex and someone new) should be prevented; if he feels shamed by, for example, his ex's new relationship, he is further motivated to undo the injustice of his name being sullied after his death, in perpetuity. This latter aspect has to do with defending one's honor, an aspect of justice to which I will return (honor is also relevant to the virtues of duty and glory). The words above, however, are not those of someone who enacted a murder-suicide; they are the words of Plato.[7]

Under conditions of perceived injustice, emotions run hot, and the willingness to contain them is affected by how likely people think it is that justice will be served, sooner or later. In his 2009 book *American Homicide*,[8] Randolph Roth points out that there is a remarkably close correlation between the U.S. murder rate and indices such as distrust in the government and how corrupt people think government is. The higher the distrust and perceptions of corruption, the higher the murder rate. This is, of course, merely a correlation, and there may be no causal connection at all between these perceptions and the murder rate. But it is tempting to suspect that when a general atmosphere of injustice is perceived (e.g., corruption), people tend to take things into their own hands more, in part through violence.

In early August 2010, Omar Thornton referred specifically to taking justice into one's own hands. Thornton was disgruntled at his workplace, claiming that the atmosphere was racist and that he was being singled out for scrutiny because he was African-American. His supervisors' view was different: he was being scrutinized not because of his race, but because he had been caught on video stealing from the company. A meeting was called to discuss the stealing incident, but the meeting did not occur. Instead, Thornton started shooting, and in the process killed eight employees at the worksite and injured two others before turning his weapon on himself. This incident has all the markings of a justice-related murder-suicide; for instance, because Thornton had been disgruntled and troubled for years leading up to the fateful day, there is evidence of a long process of deliberation and planning leading up to the tragedy. His having a gun on his person that day is further corroboration of premeditation.

Even clearer are Thornton's own words. After he had killed and injured his fellow employees, and before killing himself, he called 911 and was recorded saying the following: "You probably want to know the reason why I shot this place up. This place is a racist place. They're treating me bad over here. And treat all other black employees bad over here, too. So I took it into my own hands and handled the problem. I wish I could have got more of the people."[9]

This horrible incident illustrates several aspects of justice-motivated murder-suicide. First and foremost, it shows the very grave toll that can be associated with murder-suicide: nine dead and two wounded, and this is not to mention the waves of shock and sadness that will affect the families and that worksite for years and not to mention costs to that business, to insurance companies, to the local area's law enforcement resources, and so on. Second, this workplace shooting shows how the view of justice held by the perpetrator has more to do with his own rights being trampled on than with any sense of larger duty or obligation. That is, his perception of being treated badly at the workplace, of his rights being trampled, is primary, and there is no sense of duty or obligation regarding the rights of others (for example, the right not to be gunned down at work). Third, the perpetrator is so certain in his sense of justice that the only thing he is remorseful about is that he was not able to kill even more people. Finally, in the killer's own words, he took things into his own hands, reflective not only of the certainty in the sense of justice, but also of a more general deranged mindset of the deeply aggrieved: that in a perceived atmosphere of betrayal and corruption, the self is the only sure source of justice.

In a letter to John Adams' wife Abigail, Thomas Jefferson wrote, "The spirit of resistance to government is so valuable on certain occasions, that I wish it to be always kept alive. It will often be exercised when wrong, but better so than not to be exercised at all. I like a little rebellion now and then."[10] The occasion was Shays' Rebellion, and at the time that he wrote the letter from Paris, Jefferson was unaware that the rebellion had involved the deaths of several people. This awareness, however, probably would not have deterred him, as he later wrote in another letter "What signify a few lives lost in a generation or two? The tree of liberty must from time to time be refreshed with the blood of patriots and tyrants."[11]

In these sentiments, Jefferson shows a clear if somewhat ruthless understanding of justice; he sees the problem that, if rebels take things into their own hands, justice can be served (e.g., the American Revolution).[12] He also understands that things can go horribly wrong, as things did in Oklahoma City due to the atrocity of Timothy McVeigh, who, when apprehended, was wearing a T-shirt that read "The tree of liberty must from time to time be refreshed with the blood of patriots and tyrants."[13] Indeed, McVeigh's crime can be viewed as a murder-suicide, on the assumption that he certainly understood that his own death would result sooner or later (as it in fact did when he was executed) and that he was depressed (and probably had suicidal ideas) in the timeframe before he developed his horrific plan. When viewed this way, McVeigh's would be an unusual murder-suicide in numerous ways, including that it perverted three of the four virtues emphasized in the present framework (e.g., justice, duty, and glory). As we will see, McVeigh's crime was a primary inspiration for a murder-suicide that primarily perverted glory—the goal of the two teenagers who perpetrated the Columbine incident was to "outdo" McVeigh.

What differentiates rebellions that go down in history as laudable, and events that are awful crimes? One difference is their consensual nature. In successful rebellions like the American Revolution, there was wide (though not total) consensus among many sectors of colonial society that revolution was just. Action occurred after debate and reflection. In other instances—including murder-suicides—an individual (or perhaps two individuals, as at Columbine) believes that the action is justified and understands that his belief would be disdained by others (if known). There is no public scrutiny, no consensus, and thus no opportunity for "our better angels,"[14] in Lincoln's immortal words, to have their say. True justice has a public and open character, even if sometimes subversive; perversions of justice are virtually always private and thus immune to the leavening effects of empathy and of the trial by fire of public debate and opinion.

Justice is ancient and primitive. We have already seen that our primate cousins understand it, as evidenced, for example, by when a prized grape is obtained without due effort. Without the leavening effects of empathy and care for humanity, justice is not only ancient and primitive, it can be barbaric. Consider, in this context, the actions of a group who call themselves, in a historical reference that seems unearned, the Minutemen. As described by William Powers in the November 2010 issue of *Atlantic Monthly*, this group regularly destroys water stations in the desert set up for illegal immigrants by a group called Humane Borders (a more plausible eponym). In so doing, the Minutemen, so called, have almost certainly caused at least one death. They evidently view these as just deaths; perpetrators of murder-suicide hold the same view toward the deaths of their victims.

As do murderers toward the deaths of theirs. In *Reflections on the Guillotine*, Albert Camus wrote, "the murderer for the most part considers himself innocent when he commits his crime. Before being judged, the criminal acquits *himself*. He feels he is—if not entirely within his rights—at least extenuated by circumstances. He does not reflect; he does not foresee; or if he does, it is only to foresee that he will be pardoned—altogether or in part."[15] Characteristically, Camus is largely on target here; the only passage with which to quibble is that the murderer "does not reflect…does not foresee." Killing being as hard as it is, it is likely that it usually requires more foresight than Camus allows. And murder-suicide, because it begins with suicide and emanates to murder, clearly requires reflection, as, I argue, do all suicides.

In this context, it is interesting to ponder whether revenge-motivated suicides represent paler versions of justice-related murder-suicides. That is, might someone who plans suicide in such a way that the impact on those left behind will be particularly woeful have justice in mind, much as does the justice-motivated perpetrator who ensures negative impact on others by first killing them before enacting suicide? In both cases, suicide is primary—has been decided on first—and then, from there, a thought process occurs along the lines of "as long as I am going to die, it seems right and just to me that they know my wrath." In both cases, the individual aggresses against others. It is possible that these are neighboring phenomena, and that the vengeful suicide decedent would transform into the murder-suicide perpetrator if his sense of injustice were more aggravated, and especially if killing were not so hard to do.

I rush to emphasize that most suicides are not vengeful in nature, whereas many murder-suicides are—another difference between suicide *per se* and murder-suicide. As I spell out in detail in the 2010 book *Myths About Suicide*, revenge is a relatively rare aspect of suicide *qua* suicide. This fact can be quite clearly seen, for example, in Eli Robins' 1981 book *The Final Months*,[16] which explores in detail the mental state of 134 people who died by suicide in the St. Louis area in a given year. Of the 134, less than 10% met the following descriptors regarding the timeframe preceding death: "threatened someone" and "seeming to feel like hurting someone."

A death by suicide occurred in southern California in 2011 that might well have endangered others. The death occurred in a parked car; the decedent, a woman in her 20s, had set off a chemical reaction within the car that produced highly toxic fumes.[17] In most deaths of this kind, the lethal agent is hydrogen sulfide gas. The fumes killed the young woman in this case; they were toxic enough that they might have been the cause of death of someone who chanced upon the car and opened it in an effort to help—the gas can be so toxic that one breath can prove lethal.

Indeed, in the United States since 2008, over 70 such deaths have been documented, and in well over 50 of the cases, first responders—usually law enforcement or other emergency workers, sometimes civilians—have been injured by the fumes. The injuries to date have been minor, but in a June 2011 *New York Times* piece, a fire chief noted that those who open a car containing fumes are knocked "right to the ground," unless they have extensive protective gear. Without such gear (and even with it, depending on the location of the car), the proper procedure is to leave the victim in the car until the hazard is cleared, a process that can take several hours and which a police chief quoted in the piece characterized as "heart wrenching." A reason that it can be important to wait hours even if protective gear is available is that the released gas can harm people over a wide area; if the car is in a populated region, release of the fumes would endanger many. In documented cases in Japan, such incidents have led to the evacuation of entire neighborhoods. In a January 2011 incident in Massachusetts, a woman was injured by fumes that leaked through her ceiling from an upstairs apartment in which her neighbor had died by suicide by mixing chemicals that produced lethal fumes. In Japan, a young girl's death by a similar method sickened dozens of her neighbors.[18]

When incidents like this occur, people might see the decedent as particularly spiteful, callously and needlessly causing the injuries or even deaths of others. As noted already and as will be returned to later, spite and revenge usually do not characterize the state of mind of the suicidal individual, even in cases in which others are harmed. Usually, in such cases, the decedent was so focused on his or her own death that he or she did not fully think through all of the consequences for others postmortem.

And, frequently, as was the case with the woman who died from toxic fumes in her car in California, suicide decedents take active steps to lessen the traumatic impact on those who might discover them. For instance, it is not unusual for people to call 911 and report their own deaths just before they kill themselves, so that emergency responders will know what to expect and so that they and not family members will discover the scene. Or, for similar reasons, they may choose a very remote area for the scene of their deaths. In the case of the woman in the car, she placed a note in the car's window which read, "Danger! Chemicals inside! Call 911."

Interestingly, the 10% of suicides in Eli Robins'[19] study that seemed to have a vengeful quality were accounted for, in substantial part, by instances of murder-suicide or attempted murder followed by suicide. One such instance described by Robins is a justice-motivated incident and also illustrates an essential property, alluded to in earlier chapters, about phenomena related to murder-suicide. A man, aware that his wife was seeing another man, said to his wife one night, "I'm going to settle this once and for all. I'm going to bring him here."[20] He found the man at a local tavern and said, "We'll settle things peaceably. If my wife tells you she doesn't want to see you anymore, will you leave? If she chooses you, I will leave."[21] The man at the tavern agreed, and rather predictably, a severe argument ensued at the house, during which the husband suddenly pulled a knife and stabbed his wife in the back. The other man fled, but the husband chased him down in the front yard, where he stabbed him six times. Both the wife and the other man survived their wounds. Their assailant died by suicide.

In earlier chapters, I emphasized the premeditated nature of murder-suicide incidents (or attempted ones). This example seems an exception to that rule...until one learns that the man had been contemplating his death by suicide for many months, and in expressing this to his wife, did so in menacing ways. For example, as Robins reports, "He had several times held a knife to his bared chest and whispered to her, 'I wonder how it would feel.' "[22] He said the same thing to her on a separate occasion when he had tied a noose and put his head through the noose. After his death, a note was found referring to his troubles with his wife, stating he planned suicide, and asking forgiveness for what he planned to do. This incident, when examined in detail, conforms to the rule that the perpetrators of murder-suicide (or, as in this case, attempted murder followed by suicide) deliberate on their plan well in advance, often for months.

It is in part because of examples like this one that many people believe that suicide is primarily about revenge against others. There were menacing elements to this man's death, it is true, but the vast majority of suicides *qua* suicides are not vengeful (and many have elements that, if anything, are the opposite of vengeful). The misunderstanding that suicide is primarily about revenge has arisen in part due to the influence of psychoanalytic thought, which contended that suicide is really aggression toward someone else, but self-directed. This is a misreading. I have already noted the fact that many suicide decedents take active steps to make their death scenes less, not more, difficult on their loved ones. Consider also that, in the minds of suicide decedents, the mental calculation is along the lines of "everyone will be better off when I'm gone."[23] This is a profoundly tragic miscalculation, but it is what suicide decedents believe, and, although there is sadness and indeed misery in the belief, there is not anger and certainly not revenge.

This perspective, I believe, would have been helpful to a writer who, in the April 2011 issue of the *New Yorker*, wrote of his friend and fellow writer, David Foster Wallace, who died by suicide at his home, by hanging. His body was discovered by his wife; as in the death of the Census worker described earlier, Wallace had bound his hands. In Wallace's case, the hand-binding was about one thing only: his premeditated understanding that self-preservation would kick in in the moments before he lost consciousness, and that he may not be able to resist the urge toward life. The writer stated of Wallace, "To deserve the death sentence he'd passed on himself, the execution of the sentence had to be deeply injurious to someone. To prove once and for all that he truly didn't deserve to be loved, it was necessary to betray as hideously as possible those who loved him best, by killing himself at home and making them firsthand witnesses to his act." In other passages, the writer described suicide as a "last grand score" and as involving "displaced homicidal impulses." The writer has more access to the details of Wallace's life and death than I do—and was plainly devastated by his death—but in all of this, I nevertheless think he is wide of the mark. Suicide decedents, in the moments before their death, are not under the impression that they are enacting a "grand score," and usually mean no malice, much less homicidal malice, to those who will be bereaved. Wallace was profoundly depressed and likely intended nothing like injury to others or a last grand act; rather, he intended death because he thought, tragically, that it would be best for everyone. That he badly miscalculated is a reflection of Wallace's grave mental disorder (i.e., major depressive disorder, severe, recurrent, documented from when Wallace was in his late teens), not of revenge toward others or a grand last act.

There are a fair number of laws that have to do with defending or restoring one's honor, laws on libel for example. That this is so should come as no surprise in a species such as ours in which social standing is a key aspect of virtually every area of life, as it is for our non-human primate cousins for whom social hierarchy could not be more important. The focus on honor and reputation illuminates many human behaviors that are otherwise hard to explain. I delve into this topic in some detail in the 2011 book *Lonely at the Top*, which explores male loneliness and its many woeful consequences. Honor and reputation represent winnable resources, especially among men; anything that is winnable is also losable. In this context, consider the following work on people's attitudes toward the attainment of manhood versus of womanhood. The study asked undergraduates their opinions of statements like "A boy must earn his right to be called a man" and "All boys do not grow up to become real men."[24] Keep in mind the respondents were undergraduates in the 21st century, both women and men, and so should be relatively enlightened and flexible about gender role issues. These students tended to agree with the statements about the need for boys to earn their right to become men. Interestingly, when the very same statements were used, except that the wording was changed to be about girls and women—for instance, "A girl must earn her right to be called a woman"—the students tended to disagree. For females, womanhood is conferred automatically; for males, manhood must be earned. And if mere status as a man must be earned, then status as wealthy or influential, all the more so. This has the effect of fixating many men's attention on their honor, a losable resource.[25]

Which is why they can do silly or appalling things in honor's name. It is silly for men to strut and talk trash to one another in pickup basketball...until you understand that honor can be at stake. It is appalling for "honor" killings to occur; they are indefensible, but they show the lengths people will go to preserve honor and reputation.

In *Great Expectations* Charles Dickens wrote, "In the little world in which children have their existence, whosoever brings them up, there is nothing so finely perceived and so finely felt, as injustice."[26]

The aggrieved child becomes the aggrieved adult—or when it comes to murder-suicide, the aggrieved man, usually. It is, I believe, no coincidence that virtually all honor-related incidents of physical violence are perpetrated by men, as are virtually all justice-related murder-suicides.

As alluded to already, a sense of justice and fairness has very likely characterized the primate mind for eons. The "Monkeys reject unequal pay" study points to the ancient roots of justice—monkeys who got cucumber and saw another monkey get a grape instead became offended, some so much so that they threw the cucumber completely out of the cage (which feeling, as we will see later, was likely generated by a brain region called the right temporoparietal junction).[27] A sense of fairness is required to live in large, complex groups, and thus can be viewed as adaptive in an evolutionary context.

The emphasis on a "fair deal" is important, because it is the aspect of justice that is most implicated in murder-suicide. In Peterson and Seligman's[28] "virtue handbook," justice is viewed as having several facets, including leadership, responsibility, teamwork, and fairness. Above the other facets, it is the sense of fairness that perpetrators of murder-suicide pervert. In their minds, it is simply not fair that certain others go on living when they themselves will die.

Vengeful justice requires a kind of bloodlust, even when it is justified. In this context, Larry Dewey's[29] book *War and Redemption* provides an example. A World War II vet described how he carried out battlefield justice with a samurai sword he stole from an enemy prison guard who was extremely cruel to everyone; he had the sword with him years later in group therapy at the VA. He had hacked the guard to death with the sword. Then he chased down a factory manager where he as a POW was forced to work, and he killed him similarly. He said, "Both men's blood is on this sword. I never got it off. I never tried. Their blood is on me too, and I don't know how I can face God. They deserved everything I did to them, but even though the cease-fire hadn't been signed the war was really over, and I had no right to do it."[30] This example shows someone in the throes of enacting justice—a justice that seems as true and consuming as anything. This same state of mind affects the perpetrator of many murder-suicides, though with far less true justice, and with far less remorse.

Fiction can be an inaccurate lens through which to understand reality, because it is, well, fiction. Even undeniably great writers—Dostoevsky, for example—have misunderstood death by suicide, and at least one—Shakespeare—has misconstrued murder-suicide. Even so, and characteristically, Shakespeare gets much right along the way. In *Othello*, the eponymous main character kills Desdemona for her infidelity and then, discovering Iago's deception and his mistake, kills himself (Act V, Scene 2).

A murder has occurred, as has a suicide, both in one of the world's most famous works of literature. This, I believe, is one major source for the misunderstanding of murder-suicide—more people read *Othello* than read all books on suicide prevention combined (and a fair number of the latter are guilty of propagating the same myths, to boot). As the foregoing has shown, Shakespeare has dramatized not a genuine murder-suicide (with suicide as primary and murder stemming from the decision to die by suicide via an appeal to perverted virtue, according to the current framework) but rather a murder that, due to an unexpected turn, is followed by a suicide. In this, the account is much like that of the case of the "Santa Claus" killer, who intended murder, enacted it, and had planned on escape, but an unexpected turn led to the decision to die by suicide.

In his 2001 book *Life at the Bottom*, the pseudonymous Theodore Dalrymple wrote, "Jealousy has always been a feature of the relations between men and women: *Othello*, written four centuries ago, is still instantly comprehensible to us. But I meet at least five Othellos and five Desdemonas a week, and this is something new, if the psychiatric textbooks printed a few years ago were right in claiming that jealousy of the obsessive sort was a rare condition. Far from being rare, it is nowadays almost the norm, especially among underclass men, whose fragile sense of self-worth derives solely from possession of a woman and is poised permanently on the brink of humiliation at the prospect of losing this one prop in life."[31] Dalrymple's remarks apply beyond the underclass, and beyond those whose only possession is a mate, as many cases in this chapter have shown.

George Zinkhan III was another case in point. A University of Georgia business professor, he appeared to use the perversion of justice in deciding to kill his estranged wife, her new partner, another person, and then himself.[32]

In the spring of 2009, in front of many witnesses, Zinkhan killed the three people in downtown Athens, Georgia, and then disappeared. In the days after the killings, there was much speculation in the media about Zinkhan's whereabouts, with two leading accounts being that he had fled the country or that he was camping and hiding in the woods. In support of the first theory, it was noted that Zinkhan's passport was missing and thus presumed to be on him, and that he had lived and worked in the Netherlands for part of every year for the last several years. He even had plane tickets for a trip to the Netherlands. In support of the second theory about hiding in the woods, Zinkhan was an avid and experienced hiker, and people were aware of the case of Eric Rudolph, who did in fact hide out in the woods and elsewhere for years after committing a series of bombings, including the one in Atlanta's Olympic Park, which Rudolph intended as anti-abortion and anti-gay statements.

Several facts suggested a different scenario, however: (a) Zinkhan was accustomed to the lifestyle of a professor (a business professor to boot, with the attendant higher average salary), and, even though he was an experienced hiker, I have yet to meet the professor of any type who I think could try to survive in the woods for the long term, à la Eric Rudolph, nor have I met the professor who even imagined that he or she could do this, even though I have seen other examples of professors' self-deception, some of them quite breath-taking; (b) the prospect of leaving the country undetected, and then supporting himself abroad under an assumed identity, is also something that Zinkhan likely viewed, correctly, as nearly impossible; (c) Zinkhan seemed a proud man—his meticulous grooming in photos suggests this, as does the fact that he named his son after himself (as his own father had done; Zinkhan was George Zinkhan III and his son is named George Zinkhan IV); (d) Zinkhan killed his estranged wife and her new partner (as well as someone else who was at the scene); virtually all such killings are perpetrated by someone who feels wronged not only by the victims, but wronged more generally.

A proud man has committed three murders with numerous eyewitnesses present, and he feels wronged. He may well have planned death on his own terms, but, because he felt wronged, did not want to make things easy on people, including investigators. This adds up to a suicide in a place that he knew better than others and that would allow concealment of his body. This last detail has at least one precedent: in early 2009, a man's skeleton was discovered in the woods in Germany. The man had climbed a tree, tied himself to the tree, tied a gun to his wrist, and then died by self-inflicted gunshot wound. He had left a note telling family and others not to bother looking for him, because he would never be found. He was nearly right—his body was not discovered until 30 years after his death, which had occurred in the late 1970s.[33]

In fact, Zinkhan's body was discovered in the woods around 10 days after the murders. He died by self-inflicted gunshot wound in a pit that he had dug; before he died, he pulled a platform over the pit, a platform that had been prepared in advance to look like the ground around it. Cadaver dogs found the pit; investigators said that they would never have found it otherwise.

Zinkhan's thinking is, to my knowledge, lost to history, because he did not leave a note or journal or tell others what he had planned. But it is likely the same line of thinking that other perpetrators of murder-suicide based on perverted justice use, and it is along the lines of "I am the one who was wronged, and if I am to die, then surely it is just that those who wronged me, and thus caused all this in the first place, should die too."

As in the Zinkhan case, a common pattern in justice-motivated murder-suicides is that a jilted man seeks vengeance not only on the woman who jilted him, but also on her new boyfriend or husband. In these instances, it is as if the perpetrator concludes that the new boyfriend or husband is a co-conspirator, equally or almost equally guilty and deserving of death as the woman. Of course, in relationship breakups in general (not just those leading to murder-suicide, but all of them), it is not always the case that the jilted person "indicts" the other person along with the ex-partner. The focus of anger can be squarely and only on the ex-partner. It therefore stands to reason that, in instances of justice-motivated murder-suicides, there should be occasions in which a person focuses his revenge just on the ex and not on anyone else, even if the ex is in a new relationship.

Indeed, one such incident occurred in February 2010 near Orlando. A man in his 60s met a young woman at a Hooters restaurant, where she worked. About a year later, the man shot the young woman as she was on her way to work, and then died by self-inflicted gun-shot wound.[34] In the intervening year, the man had quickly grown attached to the young woman, frequently showing up unexpectedly wherever she happened to be, not only at work but also at her home and places like the beach. At first, the man's interest seemed reasonably harmless, and the young woman gave him her email address at his request. His interest, however, grew worrisome to the young woman, and, when he tried to hug her at her place of employment, she fended him off. This incident upset the man very much, and he began sending angry emails such as "I know I will never get an honest answer from a cheating little whore like you, but there is always hope. I sincerely pray that someday Brent sees the light."

Brent was the woman's new boyfriend, and in this email, it is evident that the man is incensed at the young woman but holds Brent blameless, and indeed hopes that Brent will be spared the supposedly evil effects of the young woman. In fact, the man sent letters to Brent himself disparaging the young woman and advising Brent to protect himself from her. In the murder-suicide, Brent was not targeted.

A harrowing case in which the probable paramour was most definitely targeted occurred in Brazil in late 2010. A man and a woman were married, and the ceremony itself went off without incident. At the reception following the wedding, however, the bridegroom announced to the guests that he had a "surprise" for everyone. He then extracted a gun, killed his bride, his best man, and then himself.[35] An investigator later commented that the incident was very likely premeditated, given the bridegroom's announcement to the attendees, as well as the fact that he had stowed a gun in his father's truck. Investigators indicated that the bridegroom believed his wife-to-be and his best man were having an affair. In despair, the bridegroom decided on suicide, and thereafter decided on justice and revenge (as he saw them) to occur at the wedding reception. Indeed, one can speculate that the bridegroom may have viewed the reception as a particularly appropriate scene for his plan—what better place, he might have thought, for the deaths of the people who betrayed him with the knowledge in their minds that they were, in days, to be his bride and best man?

This incident was clearly premeditated, as was an incident I heard described, in very vivid and compelling terms, by someone who was caught up in the midst of an unfolding murder-suicide incident. The individual attended a conference and participated in a panel on murder-suicide.[36] All in attendance, certainly including myself, were enthralled by her story, which she told through sobs. She and her new boyfriend loved one another but experienced many hardships, including a constant need for money as well as the badly deteriorated relationship between the boyfriend and his ex-wife. He told his girlfriend to hold on a while longer, that everything would be resolved on a particular spring day (not a trivial detail in that suicides, including murder-suicides, tend to occur in the spring). This resolution, he implied somewhat vaguely, would involve the culmination of a financial deal he had been working on diligently. On the day in question, much to the woman's horror, three events transpired: (1) the man murdered his ex-wife; (2) he then killed himself; and (3) a large check arrived in the mail, made out to her—the man had arranged to cash out a life insurance policy, with his girlfriend as beneficiary. The amount of premeditation in this incident hardly needs pointing out.

In this instance, the basis for vengeance has emerged from within a long-term, intimate (and terminated) relationship. Occasionally, there are murder-suicides that have some similar qualities but in which the perpetrator does not know the victims well. One such incident occurred at an exercise club in the Pittsburgh area. A man walked into the club, turned off the club's lights, and started shooting, mostly in a direction where he knew several young women were. Three women were killed and ten other people were injured before the man killed himself.[37]

On a blog that the man kept in the weeks and months before the incident, he posed the question about his unfolding plans for murder, "Why do this?? To young girls?" That he posed this question weeks and months in advance of the incident is a clear indicator of the premeditated nature of the event.

His answer to his own question of "why" involved his frustration that he could not find a woman who found him attractive; at other places in the blog, the man, aged 48, complained that he had not had sex in well over a decade. My answer is that he perverted justice. He was deeply lonely and depressed and as a consequence began to ponder suicide. But it seemed to him very unjust that the women who both aroused and thwarted his desire—who, in his view, taunted and rejected him—should live on in impunity. Like other murder-suicide perpetrators who pervert the virtue of justice, he took things into his own hands and meted out to the women what he sincerely believed was their just due.

The man planned this incident for months. Furthermore, he had at one point attempted to enact his plan but backed out, and later berated himself in his blog for lack of the requisite resolve. As pointed out in an earlier chapter, suicide of all forms requires fearlessness of physical harm, death, and killing. George Orwell understood this fact, and alluded to in it *1984*: "it needed desperate courage to kill yourself in a world where firearms, or any quick and certain poison, were completely unprocurable."[38] In addition to the Pittsburgh killer's escalating resolve about his horrible plan, he showed another feature of the suicidal mind: severe loneliness.

There are parallels between the Pittsburgh incident and the horror that befell the Virginia Tech campus at the hands of Seung-Hui Cho. The latter also did not really know his victims, and killed them out of a conviction that it was just to do so, that their behavior merited death. Within the category of murder-suicides perverting justice, there are two potential subcategories corresponding to whether the perpetrator intimately knew his victims or not. The more common form is when the victim is intimately known—often an ex-wife or ex-girlfriend—and in these incidents, the overall number of victims tends to be relatively low, usually just the ex herself, occasionally her current romantic interest.

The less common form is when the victims are not well known by the perpetrator. The killer is usually motivated by a depersonalized form of perverted justice—in Cho's case, justice in response to the supposed debauchery of his fellow students and relatedly because of his profound alienation from them; in the case of the Pittsburgh exercise club perpetrator, justice in response to the supposed fickle exclusivity of the young women. In these latter kinds of tragedy, the number of victims tends to be high, as a general rule.

There are exceptions to this rule, however. In "depersonalized" incidents like what occurred at the exercise club in Pittsburgh and at Virginia Tech, it is interesting to consider the degree of depersonalization. That is, although it is true that neither killer knew his victims well, there was at least some tenuous connection to them: membership and frequent attendance at the same exercise club in the example of the Pittsburgh incident; enrollment or employment at Virginia Tech in the example of the murder-suicide perpetrated by Cho. I am aware of one incident, however, in which the degree of depersonalization was total, or nearly so.

In California in March of 2010, men in separate cars had some kind of dispute, which escalated to the point that their cars crashed into one another. One man then got out of his car, approached the other, and shot him to death; a woman in the passenger seat of the latter's car was uninjured. The man then turned the gun on himself. Investigators later learned that there was no prior connection between the two men.[39] This incident not only violates the rule that murder-suicides involving strangers tend to have high numbers of victims, it also raises the question of what the main motive was in this specific case. To my knowledge, the man did not record his motive, but my speculation is that he was very preoccupied about having been wronged in numerous and diverse ways, including by inconsiderate drivers. He had decided on suicide (and perhaps for this purpose had his gun with him in his car), but may have believed that it would be unjust for him to die and for those who had variously wronged him to live on. The last person to have crossed him was the one he chose as his victim—a perversion of justice (with some fateful undertones as well, in that the victim, though not exactly chosen at random, was singled out for relatively arbitrary reasons).

This latter case was as "depersonalized" as justice-motivated murder-suicides ever get; most such incidents, it should be recalled, are very personal, in that they usually involve perpetrators and victims who were in an intimate relationship. In discussing murder-suicides in which a man kills a current or former romantic interest, Donna Cohen, one of the world's foremost authorities on murder-suicide, stated, "The perpetrator is extremely attached" to the victim with "a strong sense of control…Usually what precipitates the act is a belief that there's something imminent that is going to take away that control."[40] This is an apt description of many murder-suicide scenarios, but cases like the Pittsburgh exercise club killings and Virginia Tech show that it is limited, in two ways. First, it is not always the case that the perpetrator is attached to victims; indeed, he may not know them well. Second, an emphasis on control minimizes the primacy of suicide as well as misattributes the essential motive—there are justice-related murder-suicides in which control is not primary; there are, in my view, no "control"-related suicides that are not primarily due to perversions of either glory, duty, mercy, or justice.

In the same piece, Professor Cohen points out that murder-suicide perpetrators experience "significant mental health problems," and also that they have planned the murder-suicide "for a long period." These comments are highly consistent with the present emphasis on suicide—which is spurred by mental disorders, and which involves a considerable amount of planning—as primary in murder-suicide.

The incident in Pittsburgh had some unusual features, especially in that the perpetrator did not know his victims well, but it was similar to the vast majority of murder-suicides, in that a male perpetrator attacked female victims. The reverse pattern does occasionally occur, as illustrated by the death of football star Steve McNair. McNair was involved in an extramarital affair with a younger woman, who, a day or two before the incident in question, told a friend, "my life is a ball of shit, I should just end it."[41] Here again, as we have seen throughout the book, suicide is primary in the thinking of those who go on to perpetrate murder-suicide. Part of the woman's distress was due to her belief that McNair had initiated a second affair with another young woman. Her reasoning may have been that McNair should not go unpunished since his behavior spurred her death. She decided to become the instrument of his punishment as her second-to-last act on this earth.

In mid-2011, a commercial airliner had to return to its point of origin, escorted by two F-16 fighter jets, badly inconveniencing approximately 150 passengers and costing the particular airline in question considerably in terms of rescheduling, customer relations, fuel (which the airliner dumped to lighten weight for landing), and the like.[42] The cause of the incident? A passenger reclined his seat, displeasing the man in back of him, who slapped him on the head. This, in turn, led to a fistfight, requiring the physical intervention of fellow passengers and flight attendants, as well as causing the plane to turn back.

In both passengers, a region in their brains called the right temporoparietal junction was likely very active. This area is involved in the production of moral judgments, and both men were morally judgmental toward the other. Researchers have demonstrated the fact of this brain area's role in forming moral views, using two approaches, one more satisfying than the other. First, when people are hooked up to brain imaging equipment and are exposed to material on moral beliefs and intentions, the right temporoparietal region is activated.[43] As interesting as that is, it would be more satisfying still to somehow manipulate the activity of that brain area, and demonstrate expected consequences on moral judgments. Researchers did exactly this,[44] using a tightly focused magnetic field to temporarily disable or to "turn off" specific brain areas. For half of the participants, the field was directed at the right temporoparietal junction; for the other half, the field was focused on a different brain region, one thought not to be involved in moral judgments.

The participants read brief scenarios. In some scenarios, a person accidentally killed someone else; in other scenarios, a person intended to kill someone else but failed in the attempt. The participants were asked to rate how excusable they found the person's behavior, on a scale ranging from "not at all" to "completely." Regardless of condition, everyone rated intentional attempted murder as less excusable than accidental killing. However, those whose right temporoparietal junctions were disabled by the magnetic field were more lenient toward attempted murder—less judgmental—than were others.

This brain region can thus be viewed as one anatomical seat of our sense of justice.[45] When the right temporoparietal junction is active (i.e., with lots of blood flow and not shut down by something like a magnetic field), judgments of justice are relatively harsh. In justice-motivated murder-suicides, the right temporoparietal junction is very likely quite active, perhaps even overactive. It is interesting to speculate whether, in someone contemplating murder-suicide involving the perversion of justice, a magnetic field focused on the right temporoparietal junction might diminish the intent to kill. Given that this brain region is likely involved in other kinds of moral judgments as well, a similar intervention could potentially prevent murder-suicides perverting other virtues too.

In the opening chapter, the woeful tale of the "Santa Claus" killer was told. This man was out for vengeance and justice, and so, like the participants in the experiment described above whose right temporoparietal regions were not debilitated, this brain region in the "Santa Claus" killer was probably extremely active. But his case was not really a genuine murder-suicide. The same brain region was very likely quite active in the Virginia Tech killer, who clearly did perpetrate a murder-suicide, and whose motive (so he thought) was justice, but with undertones of glory.

This has been a persistently misunderstood aspect of Seung-Hui Cho's mindset as he perpetrated 32 murders at Virginia Tech before killing himself. The incident has been compared to Columbine, which was misunderstood as involving social misfits and as being about justice when really, both killers fit in reasonably well socially, and in their minds, it was about glory. The comparison is ironic, because the Virginia Tech incident actually was perpetrated by a social misfit and it actually was about justice (as Cho saw it). Cho was a very isolated young man, with essentially no close friends and no romantic attachments. He left behind a suicide note in his Virginia Tech dorm room that complained about his peers as "rich kids" and "deceitful charlatans," whom Cho felt regularly engaged in "debauchery."

On the day of the shootings, Cho killed two people in a dorm, then returned to his own dorm room. He changed clothes and picked up a package he had already prepared, addressed to NBC News. He mailed the package and then continued the rampage, killing 30 more people in a building containing classrooms—a building the main doors of which Cho had chained shut before he started shooting.[46]

The killings perpetrated by Cho at Virginia Tech became international news and have been etched in people's memories, because, among other reasons, of the very high death toll. There are other incidents, much less well publicized, that have highly similar attributes.

Rick Rodriguez was raised in a cult called The Family, in which, it is alleged, children are sexually abused. Rodriguez left the cult in adulthood and attempted to adapt to his new life, marrying and finding work as an electrician. The marriage fizzled, and Rodriguez began ruminating about his abusive childhood experiences. He arranged to meet a former female member of the group who, he recalled, had been involved in Rodriguez' own sexual abuse as a child. He invited the woman to his apartment, where he stabbed her to death. A short while later he died by self-inflicted gunshot wound. In the weeks and days leading up to the murder-suicide, much like Cho, Rodriguez repeatedly documented his state of mind on videotape. A *New York Times* article described a passage of the tape as follows: "he said he saw himself as a vigilante avenging children like him and his sisters who had been subject to rapes and beatings. 'There's this need that I have,' he said. 'It's not a want. It's a need for revenge. It's a need for justice...'"[47]

A Perversion of Duty

"Let integrity and uprightness preserve me; for I wait on thee." —
Psalms 25:21

IT IS 146 B.C., AND ROME IS ABOUT TO DESTROY CARTHAGE.
The Carthaginian commander is Hasdrubal, whose wife's final
words—"wretch" and "traitor"—are scornful toward her husband;
he has fled to the Romans, leaving behind his family and troops. She
and his troops demean Hasdrubal, because he has abrogated his duty.
In the final siege, Hasdrubal's wife does what she deems the dutiful thing: She kills her children, places their bodies into the flames
engulfing Carthage, and then leaps into the flames herself.[1]

The Nature of the Virtue of Duty

Duty involves the honorable discharge of one's perceived responsibilities to others. It usually involves loyalty, decorum, dignity,
obligation, and honor. It is enacted with some sense of solemnity
whether or not the duty in question is difficult or even distaste-
ful. In this sense of solemnity and seriousness, even in the face of
misery, tragedy, and conflict, duty shares elements with the virtue
of justice. Duty is the opposite of that which is described, accurately in my view, by Theodore Dalrymple in his 2001 book *Life at*

the Bottom: "in the modern climate, after all, rights always trump duties."[2] To exercise rights without observing duty leads to entitlement and perversions.

Consider, in this context, the rights and duties of service members aboard the U.S.S. *Carl Vinson* in early May 2011, who, according to news reports, buried the body of Osama bin Laden at sea. In doing so, they at least attempted to be mindful of Islamic sensibilities; for example, the body was cleansed before burial, and, also in accord with Islamic custom, the burial took place within 24 hours of death. Religious scripture was read aloud and translated into Arabic.[3] It seems quite likely that at least a few of the individuals involved believed they had the right to be disrespectful to the body and memory of bin Laden. But they had the duty to be respectful, and they let duty trump rights, to their and all of their fellow countrymen's credit. It will not be hard for many readers, especially those in the United States, to recall incidents—for instance in the streets of Mogadishu—in which people, full of self-righteousness but neglectful of the principle of duty (and duty's bedfellows decorum and dignity), mistreated the dead.[4]

The Perversion of the Virtue of Duty in Murder-Suicide

In murder-suicide involving duty, the virtue is perverted in that perpetrators believe they are discharging their responsibilities by killing another, usually another who is highly dependent on the perpetrator (e.g., a young child, a very ill adult). This book asserts that each of the four virtues perverted in the process of murder-suicide is a particularly interpersonal virtue. In this context, it is interesting to consider the interpersonal target in cases of the perversion of duty, particularly as compared to a closely related phenomenon: Murder-suicides involving the perversion of mercy.

In emphasizing duty, the perpetrator of the murder-suicide is particularly mindful of those who are left behind (e.g., relatives, society at large). In his mind, he is discharging a duty so that a burdensome obligation does not fall to others who survive and would inherit the obligation. The perpetrator in these kinds of incidents is thinking about survivors (as well as about the victim). By contrast, in murder-suicides involving the perversion of mercy, the perpetrator is focused solely on the victim—the goal, in his mind, is to be merciful to the victim by not leaving her behind to suffer an even worse fate.

One might argue that duty-related murder-suicides are really a subtype of mercy-related incidents. It is true that both types involve a perpetrator under the belief that he is doing right by "taking care" of the victim. As noted earlier, the biographers of Assia Wevill (who was in a relationship with poet Ted Hughes after his wife Sylvia Plath died) ran into this issue and misunderstood the murder-suicide involving Wevill and her daughter as involving duty when really it involved mercy. The essential difference, however, between perversions of mercy and of duty in murder-suicides is that, in the mind of the perpetrator, he is "doing right" by survivors in duty-related incidents and "doing right" by the victim(s) in mercy-related incidents.

Duty-related incidents occur most commonly perhaps in older, married adults, in which one spouse is ill and the other is the caretaker. The caretaker may decide to end his own life, and reason that the only way that he can carry out his responsibility or duty to his spouse is to kill her first. This prevents, he reasons, the transfer of his own obligation onto others. In such scenarios, mercy is not in the forefront; the motive is not primarily mercy for the victim, but rather duty toward others.

As we have seen already, although most murder-suicides represent the perversion of a single virtue, it is occasionally the case that a secondary virtue is also involved. In incidents involving the perversion of justice, for example, undertones of perverted glory can be detected; this was true in the case of the Virginia Tech killer, who killed primarily out of his deranged sense of justice, but in so doing, portrayed his actions as heroic, on par with those of Jesus. In cases like these, there is a perverted virtue that is primary, accounting for substantially more than a half of the motivation, and a secondary perverted virtue, accounting for the rest. When, by contrast, the perversion of duty is implicated and is blended with a second perverted virtue, that virtue is virtually always mercy, and it can be difficult to assign primacy to one or the other.

A case described in Eli Robins' 1981 book *The Final Months*, about suicide decedents in the St. Louis area, is illustrative of this dilemma. A hard-working pharmacist met and married a local girl, and during the first years of their marriage, she developed a serious illness that required surgery. The surgery seemed reasonably successful, but nevertheless, the woman became more and more incapacitated, to the degree that she was house-ridden. During this time, she also became severely obese, having gained a few times her original body weight.

In the last six months of their lives, the man developed agitated depression. Robins described that "at work he paced back and forth, waving his arms."[5] As alluded to earlier, agitation can be an ominous warning sign for imminent suicidal behavior—as can insomnia, which the man also experienced. These manifestations are clinically relevant in monitoring for the possibility of unfolding disaster, a point to which I will return in the chapter on clinical applications.

Robins wrote of the day of the murder-suicide "he went home and that evening he killed his wife, hitting her several times in the head with a hatchet as she lay in bed."[6] He then ingested a lethal dose of poison. Robins interviewed someone who knew the couple, who stated that the man had killed his wife "because he felt she could not take care of herself without him"—a reasonably clear attribution to the perversion of duty. But the informant continued that the man "believed his wife had an abdominal malignancy and might have killed her out of mercy."[7]

This tragic incident is instructive in at least three ways. First, it is an example of how, in some murder-suicides, the perversions of mercy and of duty can be simultaneously and equally implicated as motives. Other incidents can involve blended motives (e.g., justice and glory), but only in deaths combining the perversion of duty and mercy is it difficult to tell which is primary. Second, this man's profile looks much more like that of a suicide decedent (which of course he was) than it does that of a murderer (which he also was). Like most suicide decedents, in the time frame leading up to his death the man was agitated (e.g., "nervous, tense, and irritable" in Robins' words) and sleepless. He had also mentioned to his wife the idea of suicide. It is very likely that the man had decided on his own death by suicide, and only after that, through a perversion of the virtues of duty and mercy, decided on killing his wife. Third, his method of suicide, poisoning, is not surprising given his decades-long career as a pharmacist. What is somewhat surprising is his choice of method in killing his wife. The evidence from Robins' case description does not address this issue one way or another, but I speculate that the man had been pondering his and thus his wife's deaths for months (his mention of suicide to his wife occurred about a year before the incident) and that he had tried to develop a fail-safe way to poison his wife, and, in feeling unsure of this plan (or having tried it and it having failed), resorted to a second, more certain method. This method, though more certain, was less familiar to him, and thus required many months of deliberation and thought in order to work up the resolve to enact.

This last example involved one spouse perverting his sense of duty and mercy towards another, with murder and then suicide as a result. It is as just as common, perhaps even more so, for such cases to involve parents and children. It is treacherous to ponder whether one kind of killing is more tragic than another, but murder-suicides involving parents and children certainly would be candidates for the apogee of horror. One such incident occurred in Minnesota, involving a man in his sixties and his adult son, age 45, who was severely autistic. The man and his son rented out an area of a family's house, and according to the family, the man was concerned that his son would be taken from him and placed in a state facility. The man evidently concluded that that state of affairs would be worse than death for both his son and himself. He wrote a note to the family to call 911 and inform the authorities that he and his son were in the garage, where they were later found, deceased, with gunshot wounds.[8] A member of the family stated that the father "was a good man and a good father, he thought he had no other choice, he had to take [his son]." Mercy seemed to preoccupy the man's mind in this incident, though undertones of duty can be discerned as well.

There is some research from evolutionary psychology that bears on scenarios like this one. This research focuses on deaths in which there is a father/stepfather perpetrator and a child victim. Two essential results are as follows: (1) stepparents are dozens of times more likely to kill their children than are biological parents (predictable based on an evolutionary account); (2) however, a perpetrator's subsequent suicide is much more likely if he is the biological father of the victim than if he is the victim's stepfather (mothers/stepmothers are not examined because of the rarity both of female perpetrators but also of children living with their stepmothers).[9]

In my view (and in Daly and Wilson's as well; see footnote 9), the essential variable here is *care*. That is, on average, genetic fathers care more for their offspring than do non-genetic fathers, and so usually do not harm them. In the rare event that they do, Daly and Wilson's data show that it is regularly in the context of their own suicides, and the motives usually involve things like mercy and duty, very compatible with the current framework.

Care, whether motivated by mercy or duty, can be perverted, and I believe this is an apt view of the murder-suicide involving the man and his adult autistic son. A news article describing this incident was posted to the Internet, and the site allowed for reader commentary. The vast range of opinions as reflected in the comments is illuminating. At one end of the range, a typical view was "while the son may have been on the more severe end of the autism spectrum he should have at least had a chance to live out his life. His father did a very selfish thing." At the other end of the range, a representative opinion was "...I think the father did a noble thing, he ended his son's suffering."

Viewpoints like these two are the very ones that animate one of this book's central theses. Murder-suicides are, on the one hand, selfish by definition, because taking someone else's life, not in self-defense and without sanction of a court of law or a declaration of war, is indisputably selfish. On the other hand, from the perspective of the murder-suicide perpetrator, the motive can involve self-centeredness (especially in cases of justice- and glory-motivated incidents), but the main point is something more than selfishness—it is the enactment of a highly distorted form of virtue. Both reader comments are thus correct, because what the father did was self-centered and at the same time, he believed he was doing the right thing, indeed, perhaps he believed, the noble thing. One's reaction to the deed will depend, in large measure, on which aspect one focuses on, the murder or the (perverted) virtue. We have seen this same dynamic already, for example, in the case of Rick Rodriguez, who had been raised in an allegedly sexually abusive cult, and in adulthood, tracked down one of his accused abusers, murdered her, and then killed himself. Even though the person he murdered did not inspire much sympathy, she was nevertheless a person with rights; to take the decision to end her life at knifepoint and to enact that decision requires extreme self-certainty, a form of selfishness, and was wrong. In Rodriguez' mind, by contrast, it was not only right, it was a supremely just act. It is interesting to note, in passing, that there are incidents like that involving Rodriguez and that involving the father and his autistic son, to which at least some people respond with sympathy (even though a murder has clearly been perpetrated), and there are others (e.g., the Virginia Tech tragedy) that inspire none at all or very little. This is the case even though all such events, at their core, represent the perversion of one or more of the four virtues of justice, mercy, glory, or duty.

Matthew 5:7 reads, "Blessed are the merciful: for they shall obtain mercy." The perpetrators of murder-suicide, when they pervert the virtues of mercy and duty, are under the impression that what they are doing is the saving of their loved ones, but also, of themselves. They want mercy for their loved ones—they feel it is their duty to provide it—but mercy from what? The answer, I believe, is from what they perceive to be an intolerably cruel world: cruel to themselves, thus their decision on suicide; and cruel alike to their loved ones, thus their decision to perpetrate murder.

The cases of the father and his autistic son, and also that described by Eli Robins of the pharmacist who killed his wife and then poisoned himself, show that perverted versions of duty and mercy can blend in some cases of murder-suicide. However, there is a phenomenon that I believe shows that incidents involving duty and mercy usually represent distinct subtypes, and this is the fact that pets are sometimes victims in some incidents.

Consider the death of a California state official who was having a severe conflict at her workplace.[10] In May 2005, she was supposed to attend a meeting to discuss the matter, but did not show up, and instead sent a long e-mail. The e-mail was not explicit about suicide, but contained passages such as "I cannot take any more...of the humiliation I have had to endure for the past year." To their credit, those who received the e-mail understood that she might be at risk, but there were delays in sending help, due in part to the fact that the woman lived 75 miles away. Authorities reached her house two hours after her e-mail was sent. There, in the front yard of the house, they discovered the woman's two dogs, both dead from gunshot wounds, and the woman herself, also shot, but still alive. She was airlifted to a hospital, where she died less than an hour after she was found. It was later discovered that she had been preparing for suicide for days at least—her possessions were packed up and labeled, and she had left labels differentiating her computer and other personal possessions from those owned by her workplace. A lengthy suicide note was also found.

Duty was important to this woman, as evidenced, for example, by her packing and labeling items that belonged to her workplace separately from those that belonged to her personally. Evidence for her sense of duty is also revealed in her choice to kill her dogs. Why do that? It almost certainly was not about anger or contempt. It is possible that it was about mercy, the notion being that the dogs would not fare well in her absence. But dogs fare reasonably well under most circumstances. The woman had a dutiful personality; the preponderance of the evidence in her case points to distorted duty as the motive in her decision to kill her pets. That is, it was her responsibility—her duty—to care for her dogs, and, she may have believed, an abrogation of her duty to leave their care to others. She may have felt, in her very distraught state of mind, that in killing her dogs she would both meet her responsibility and not burden others with it. In the chapter on the perversion of mercy, we saw an incident with some parallels to this one, in which a dairy farmer killed many of his cows before killing himself, in that case out of a sense of distorted mercy.

Killing one's animals before killing oneself is a phenomenon that is on the definitional fringe of murder-suicide. Plainly, there are differences between incidents involving the murder of people and the killing of animals, and it is not my point to argue otherwise. Rather, I suggest that any powerful framework for the understanding of a given phenomenon should ideally not only illuminate that core phenomenon (i.e., murder-suicide *per se*) but should burn brightly enough that it also sheds light on neighboring phenomena (e.g., incidents involving killing animals and then death by suicide). The current framework, I would argue, achieves both things. It does so by providing a coherent and plausible view of, for example, the relationship between murder-suicides and suicides preceded by killing animals, and furthermore, it does so by explicating core murder-suicide subtypes—such as those involving the perversion of heroic glory, the topic of the next chapter.

A Perversion of Heroic Glory

"People will die because of me. It will be a day that will be remembered forever."—Eric Harris, Columbine shooter, on audiotape the morning of the massacre

"The urge to heroism is natural, and to admit it honest." —Ernest Becker, *The Denial of Death*, 1973, p. 4

"…for every heroic act measures itself by its contempt of some external good. But it finds its own success at last…." —Ralph Waldo Emerson, *Essays, First Series*, 1841

The Nature of Heroism and Glory

Implicit in the Emerson quote above is the idea that, at the time of a potentially heroic act, not everyone will see it as heroic or even good, but the incipient hero will see it that way. In May 2011, U.S. Special Forces killed Osama bin Laden. The Navy SEAL who took the fatal shot views the act, I assume and many will agree, as heroic. Even in this example, in which the case for heroism is not particularly hard to make, not everyone sees it that way. The SEAL must have, in Emerson's phrase, had "contempt for the external good" of "thou shalt not kill," and in that contempt, found success (at least success as measured by American public opinion and military mission).

To take a starkly different example, on the morning of the crime he perpetrated at Columbine High School, Eric Harris would have endorsed Emerson's quote too, believing that what he had planned was heroic and glorious and would find "its own success at last;" indeed, in Harris' words, "remembered forever." Virtually everyone views the shootings at Columbine, Virginia Tech, Northern Illinois, and Binghamton with horror, but the perpetrators of these acts saw them differently—they believed they were doing something of value, and in this belief, they are similar to the Navy SEAL who killed bin Laden. The perpetrators of incidents like Columbine perverted the virtue of heroism; the Navy SEAL embodied it. What differentiates horror from true heroism is less the virtue itself than the circumstances and assumptions in which the virtue is embedded—a major theme of this book.

The Perversion of Heroism and Glory in Murder-Suicide

The shootings at Columbine High School in Colorado illustrate the grave toll inflicted by these kinds of murder-suicides and also illustrate some of the misunderstandings that can crop up around them. In terms of the toll, 15 people lost their lives at Columbine (including shooters Eric Harris and Dylan Klebold, who killed 13 people before killing themselves), many were injured, the school itself was badly damaged, and the students, teachers, staff, and the community at large were psychologically affected for years after the incident.

In terms of misunderstandings, the media largely misperceived the shooters' motives.[1] Interestingly, in light of the framework proposed in this book, the media mistook a "glory-motivated" incident for one motivated by justice. In the days and weeks after the tragedy, it was reported that the two shooters were social outcasts who had been bullied and otherwise victimized by particular subgroups of other students, especially athletes. In the incident, so the reporting said, athletes were singled out for revenge—a perversion of justice. In early 2011, well over 10 years after the incident, I heard an expert on bullying give a compassionate and rousing plea that our society needs to do better in combating the problem of bullying…and in the process repeated the notion that the Columbine shooters did what they did because they were bullied. However, as made very clear in Dave Cullen's 2009 book on the incident, *Columbine*, this is not what happened at all.[2]

The two boys were not social misfits; they were not bullied (in fact, if anything, they bullied younger students);[3] none of those killed were singled out because they were athletes; and, as the journals and videotapes the boys left behind demonstrate in disturbing detail, their motive was a perverted version of glory and had very little to do with justice. Their goal was to exceed Timothy McVeigh (who was responsible for 168 deaths in the Oklahoma City bombing), and they probably would have if their bombs had not malfunctioned. Their goal was to be remembered forever—perverted glory.[4]

U.S. President Theodore Roosevelt said, "Far better is it to dare mighty things, to win glorious triumphs...than to take up ranks with those poor spirits who neither enjoy much nor suffer much, for they live in that gray twilight that knows neither victory nor defeat."[5] William James, writing at about the same time as Roosevelt made his statement, remarked that "mankind's common instinct for reality...has always held the world to be essentially a theatre for heroism."[6] James' words, supported by those of Roosevelt, suggest that heroic glory may be the pinnacle of human virtue, that all other virtues and the rest of human nature to boot are accounted for by a striving for heroism. This is a lofty claim, but one that has been made more than once, including by thinkers in evolutionary theory, who have claimed that behaviors like heroic altruism, generosity, and the like are, in reality, attempts to appear heroic and thus to attract mates and resources. Even if heroism is not the ultimate virtue, a solid case can be made that it is among the handful of core human virtues, and thus, according to the framework advanced here, regularly perverted in instances of murder-suicide.

The perpetrators of Columbine would have identified with and recognized themselves in Roosevelt's and James' words; neither Roosevelt nor James, by contrast and to put it mildly, would have recognized the boys' plans and actions as examples of their words. The boys understood the virtue extolled by Roosevelt and James, but perverted its application.

An important fact about the Columbine shooters involves their suicidality. The evidence suggests that the boys' suicidality formed first, well before plans for the shooting. This was particularly clear for Dylan Klebold, whose journals indicate that he expected to be dead by suicide months before the Columbine tragedy. It was clear as well for Eric Harris, who graphically faked his suicide approximately three years before the shootings, and who fantasized about a world without people (including without him).[7] As different as these boys were, not just from everyone else but from each other—and Cullen's[8] *Columbine* shows convincingly that they were different indeed from each other—suicide came first for both of them; homicide came later, and developed as a function of their perverted views of glory.

Suicide is part of the "first principles" assumptions that perpetrators of murder-suicide make. In the case of the Lupoe family, who killed their children and then themselves in a perversion of mercy, their logic about their children's future flowed from the primary decision that the Lupoes themselves would not be around to fend for the children, because the Lupoes had decided on suicide—the note they left makes this clear. In the case of George Zinkhan, who killed his ex and others in a perversion of justice, the documentation is less clear, but in other similar cases in which a note and other data were available, the logic is along the lines of "since I will die, it is only just that they do too."

An underappreciated aspect of many school shootings is the primacy of suicide. It is quite understandable that this element would be under-emphasized, as people's hearts break at the senseless murders. Because of this, people tend to attribute primacy to the murder part of the murder-suicide equation, but this, I believe, is mistaken.

Consider, for example, Steve Kazmierczak, who killed five people and himself at Northern Illinois University in early 2008. In a piece in *Esquire* magazine (August 2008 issue), David Vann documents Kazmierczak's long history of suicidal ideation and attempts. In April of 1997—11 years before the incident at NIU—Kazmierczak ingested 40 Ambien tablets and cut his wrists. Seven months later, after an argument with his mother, he overdosed on 50 Depakote. In early 1998, he was admitted multiple times to an inpatient psychiatric unit for suicidal thoughts. Also in that year, he ingested 120 Depakote, usually a lethal dose, but he survived. This is a quite severe history of suicidal behavior, including at least one attempt that was very close to proving lethal. It is worth noting, incidentally, the escalating nature of Kazmierczak's suicidal behavior—40 Ambien, 50 Depakote, 120 Depakote. "Pushing the envelope," as was pointed out in the chapters on murder and suicide, characterizes people who go on to kill others and/or themselves. The gravity of Kazmierczak's suicide history, and its clear antecedence to what occurred at NIU, are compatible with the argument made here that in murder-suicide, suicide comes first.

Although it is controversial, this same perspective may apply to suicide bombers. Many have viewed their intent, reasonably enough, as political in emphasis, not much involving personal issues. A very plausible view of the psychology of the suicide terrorist runs along the lines of "it is virtuous that I use my death for the glory of my society and for revenge and justice too, and my own death is incidental to that." Here, suicide is secondary, which contradicts this book's framework.

There are at least three ways to resolve this contradiction. First, this book's conceptualization may be mistaken; more specifically, the claim that suicide is always primary in murder-suicide may be incorrect.[9] Second, it could be argued that suicide terrorism is not a true form of murder-suicide (a very plausible and, in my view, probably correct standpoint). Third, perhaps suicide is, after all, primary in suicide terrorism.

A new line of scholarship has made exactly this latter point. There is evidence that many suicide terrorists struggle with depression, develop suicidal wishes, and channel their suicidality into terrorism. Merari and colleagues[10] found that, compared to the organizers of suicide terrorism and to another control sample, would-be suicide terrorists had lower ego strength and more avoidant and dependent personality features. More than half of the would-be terrorists had clear depressive tendencies, and close to half had clear suicidal tendencies.[11] In a compatible account, social psychologist Arie Kruglanski stated, "Terrorists feel that through suicide, their lives will achieve tremendous significance. They will become heroes, martyrs. In many cases, their decision is a response to a great loss of significance, which can occur through humiliation, discrimination, or personal problems that have nothing to do with the conflict in which their group is engaged."[12] According to this viewpoint, the logic of the suicide terrorist is very similar to that of the murder-suicide perpetrator: "I have decided on suicide, but as long as I am to die, it is it is dutiful, just, and glorious that I kill others on behalf of my people." Here, suicide terrorism is personal and only incidentally political.

It is a feature of penetrating frameworks that they explain core phenomena as well as neighboring phenomena. They may also link together in compelling ways phenomena that heretofore seemed disparate. The current conceptual approach, I contend, does just this, by illuminating some potential underlying similarities between murder-suicide and suicide terrorism.

In his Nobel speech, William Faulkner said, "It is [the writer's] privilege to help man endure by lifting his heart, by reminding him of the courage and honor and hope and pride and compassion and pity and sacrifice which have been the glory of his past." Notice, in this, that glory derives from, and cannot be gained without, the other virtues like honor and pity. Murder-suicide can involve the perversion of glory; the perverting process includes thinking that glory, unleavened by other virtues and by empathy, is all.

The Neighboring but Distinct Categories of Perverting Self-Control and Fate

The Perversion of Self-Control

"A man without self-control is like a city broken into and left without walls."—*Proverbs 26*

As described already, in December 2008, Bruce Pardo, dressed in a Santa Claus suit, went on a shooting rampage, killing his ex-wife and several others. He also doused the house in which this occurred with accelerant and set it ablaze. His body was later discovered approximately 25 miles from the scene; he had died from a self-inflicted gunshot wound.[1]

The description of this incident thus far makes it sound like a justice-type murder-suicide, similar to that perpetrated by George Zinkhan. But there is a key difference: Zinkhan planned his suicide; Pardo planned his escape (to Canada). But when Pardo set the fire, it also ignited his fuel-soaked suit, causing third-degree burns. He was forced to change plans, which, for Pardo, involved death by self-inflicted gunshot wound.

Because suicide was not primary in Pardo's planning, I view the incident as just outside the definitional border of true murder-suicide. It can be viewed as a closely adjacent phenomenon; the more suicide is involved in the initial planning of such incidents the more closely it approaches the category of genuine murder-suicide. Indeed, if the planning is such that suicide is primary and escape is considered but is dismissed or is otherwise clearly secondary, the diagnosis of true murder-suicide seems to be more apt.

The "Santa Claus" incident illustrates an important principle: although, as this book has argued, genuine murder-suicides can be classified within a taxonomy based on distorted virtue and most fit cleanly within one category, some events span categories; some incidents fall outside the framework entirely. Pardo's killing spree would not have included suicide at all if not for his failed escape plan and his invoking self-control in his decision to kill himself, and so it belongs in a category outside of the current framework, if only just. But there are clear elements as well having to do with Pardo's distorted sense of justice: he meted out revenge—his version of justice—on his ex-wife and her family.

In nature, it is important to reiterate that even true categories have fuzzy edges, and occasionally the edges of adjoining categories overlap. This illustrates an advantage of the taxonomy that this book has proposed: despite nature's fuzzy edges, virtually all murder-suicides fit neatly within the proposed categories, and some killings followed by suicide fit just outside the proposed categories.

Interestingly, murders perpetrated for revenge and murder-suicides in the name of perverted justice share the commonality of meting out revenge and justice in the form of killing. They also differ, in that, in murder *per se*, the perpetrator views himself as judge and jury; in murder-suicides, the perpetrator first and foremost views himself as condemned victim, and then secondarily, flowing from the role of condemned victim, as judge and jury.[2]

As emphasized throughout this book, suicide is primary in murder-suicide, which means that incidents like the one perpetrated by Pardo do not qualify, despite the fact that they involve murder followed by suicide. These incidents do, however, involve the perversion of what some have considered a virtue: self-control or controlling one's destiny ("taking things into one's own hands").

These crimes appear to include a line of reasoning as follows: "If it's not going to be like this (escape), then, secondarily, it's going to be like that (suicide). Everything else (e.g., prison) is unacceptable to me, would compromise my sense of control. There are no other options." Individuals like this fully endorse the quote above from *Proverbs*—"a city broken into and left without walls"—that is how they would experience being in prison. They prefer death to the loss of self-control (and they prefer escape to suicide, which is why their crimes, according to the current conceptualization, are not genuine murder-suicides).

Control in general and self-control in particular are more important to some personalities than to others. An intriguing aspect of killings related to perversions of self-control is that almost all—perhaps all—are committed by "Cleckley psychopaths." In his 1941 book *The Mask of Sanity*, Hervey Cleckley described individuals characterized by controlled, callous, sometimes charming con-men presentations, who also show marked emotional detachment (i.e., low anxiety, fake or shallow emotions, immunity to guilt and shame, and incapacity for love, intimacy, and loyalty).[3] The "Cleckley psychopath" can be very much in control, angles to be in control, and in the rare instance he finds himself out of control (e.g., will face a murder charge and life in prison or death on someone else's terms) may view it as intolerable.

Though extremely rare for the reasons just articulated, murder-suicides perpetrated by "Cleckley psychopaths" do occasionally occur. In June 2007 in the Miami area, a murder-suicide occurred that may have involved one such individual. Helder "Sonny" Peixoto, who had been in several legal and interpersonal disputes throughout a career involving security and police work (which work, interestingly enough, is associated with above-average psychopathy scores)—including a charge of vehicular homicide—was described by many as charming and always in the middle of fashionable parties in the Miami area. He had been dating a Miami model, who was beginning to ponder ending the relationship, which caused Peixoto to become even more possessive and controlling than he had been. It is not clear what escalated the situation to the point of violence, but, in what may have been a perverted-justice scenario, Peixoto killed his girlfriend with a hammer and left her in his apartment. He then engaged a real estate agent to show him a vacant 11th-story condominium, the balcony of which he jumped off to his death, "calmly" in the words of the real estate agent.[4]

These incidents are rare, largely because it rarely comes to such lengths for "Cleckley psychopaths." They usually work a con or otherwise manipulate others to escape instead. It is, in fact, quite possible that this entered into Peixoto's mind, and it is conceivable that, instead of being an instance of a murder-suicide involving perverted justice, Peixoto killed his girlfriend with plans of escape afterwards, and for reasons now lost to history, he found these plans ultimately unworkable. Suicide may have been his "Plan B," as it was for "Santa Claus" killer Bruce Pardo. Or, perhaps Peixoto was the very rare individual with psychopathy to choose suicide. I would expect that, assuming a psychopath does decide on suicide, the likelihood that he decides to first perpetrate a murder is many times the corresponding likelihood for the non-psychopathic, suicidal individual.

That the perversion of self-control is rarely if ever a motive in genuine murder-suicide mirrors the fact that self-control is rarely if ever a reason for suicide *per se*. This fact has been repeatedly misunderstood in the literature, I believe, because clinicians and others have confused two distinct phenomena. It is crucial to distinguish between, on the one hand, wanting an array of options including the last-resort option of suicide, and, on the other hand, deciding to die by suicide. In the former state of mind, there are multiple options, and this alone distinguishes it from the state of mind of the truly suicidal individual, for whom there is only one option (or perhaps more accurately, for whom the option of death is increasingly crowding out other options). The person who wants to keep suicide as a last-resort option is clearly implying that there are other "resorts" that can be tried out first. In saying they want control over the option to die, they are affirming that there are prior options involving living.

Dave Grossman's 1995 book *On Killing* is very illuminating and, in my judgment, gets virtually everything right. An exception is a reference to murder-suicide,[5] which the author viewed as a situation in which a person kills, feels elation, but then a new stage, revulsion/remorse kicks in, leading to suicide. This description seems to fit few actual cases, certainly not true murder-suicides, and not even situations like Peixoto's or the "Santa Claus" killer's.

The Perversion of Fate

"Hast thou considered my servant Job, that there is none like him in the earth, a perfect and an upright man, one that feareth God, and escheweth evil?" (God speaking to Satan about a soon-to-be afflicted Job; *Job* 1:8)

Job's tale of woe is long, and more, he was selected to suffer not because he deserved it, but precisely for the opposite reason: because he was virtuous and did *not* deserve it. Satan predicted, mostly wrongly, that even the virtuous Job would crack under the pressure of affliction and turn his back on God. The lack of contingency between Job's behavior and his fate conveys much of the Biblical tale's pathos. God and Satan conspired to pervert Job's fate.

What happened to Job is not just unfair, it is also mercifully uncommon. What can be said of Job also can be said of those involved in perversions of fate in which someone else's suicide inadvertently harms or (rarely) kills them.

These incidents resemble murder-suicides, in that a suicide is involved and in the process of it, another person is killed. But I think it is a mistake to lump together genuine murder-suicides with accidental perversions of fate, because the underlying processes are distinct. In accidental perversions of fate, the starting point is similar to true murder-suicides—the decision to die by suicide—but there the similarities end. Individuals in accidental perversions of fate are like all suicide decedents not involved in murder-suicides; they are very focused on their own deaths, and only their own deaths. This focus narrows their attentional capacity so that they cannot think of much else, certainly including other people's deaths. That their actions occasionally misfire and accidentally take someone else's life is a reflection of this narrowed focus and the poor thinking it can produce, and is not a reflection of malice toward others. This is the same state of mind that George Orwell referred to in *1984* when he wrote, "in the torture chamber...the issues that you are fighting for are always forgotten, because the body swells up until it fills the universe."[6]

An example of this phenomenon occurred in early 2009. A woman jumped from the fourth floor to her death inside a mall in New York City. Even at this point in the story, it is unusual—jumping from a height is a relatively rare suicide method. In the United States just over half of all deaths by suicides are by self-inflicted gunshot wound; 40% are by suffocation/hanging or by overdose/poisoning. The remaining methods, including jumping from a height, are infrequent. It is not that heights are infrequent—in many areas they are quite common (e.g., cities; mountainous regions)—and for many people, the experience of being on a high place is more familiar than, for example, handling a gun. The daunting nature of jumping from a height accounts, in part, for its overall rarity. It is noteworthy as well in the story of the woman in New York that she did not jump from a particularly high place, the fourth floor.[7] The act was daunting and proved fatal but is less fearsome than jumping from several times that height, which is more usual in deaths by suicide from a height.

This incident, already unusual in some of its features, was made much more so by the fact that the woman landed on a 17-year-old youth. Bizarrely, the young man was sitting in a massage chair with a sign that read "sit back and relax." The youth was knocked unconscious and had a cut on his head, but, mercifully, was in otherwise good condition. Tragically, the fall was fatal for the woman.[8]

The physics of these incidents can be unpredictable and complex, but a common outcome is that one person dies, and the other is injured but survives—another reason this type of occurrence is not really a murder-suicide *per se*. The main reason that this was not a murder-suicide was not only that the young man was not killed, but that the woman did not intend anyone's death but her own. She viewed the jump as an unpeopled landscape; that she was mistaken in this is not evidence of malice, but rather of poor foresight due to the unusually narrow and concrete mindset of the suicidal individual. The young man's involvement was wholly accidental and incidental, a perversion of fate.

Reports suggest that the person on the ground is just as likely to die as the person jumping. For example, also in 2009, a man in southeastern China knew his girlfriend was suicidal, spotted her from the ground on the seventh floor of a building, and pled with her, unsuccessfully, not to jump. He tried to catch her; the impact killed him, and, though she was seriously injured, the woman survived.[9] We will see this pattern again shortly; it involves the ironic fact that intently suicidal people can engage in actions like falling from a height or accelerating in their car, which they believe will result in their deaths but instead cause others' death due to the transfer of momentum. In this example, the woman intended her death and only her death; that she survived and her boyfriend did not is a tragic perversion of fate, not a genuine murder-suicide (or murder and suicide attempt).

As another example, consider an event that involved a suicide *qua* suicide but that might well have resulted in others' death as well. I described this June 2008 incident, and the media reporting of it, in the 2010 book *Myths About Suicide*, because it illustrates how widespread is the myth that people frequently die by suicide on impulse, in spur-of-the-moment fashion. A man in his late 20s went on a skydiving trip with a few other people. He explained to the pilot that he was a photography buff and simply wanted to take pictures; he did not intend to skydive, had no training in it, and had no parachute or other gear for it. At an altitude of 10,000 feet, the pilot turned on the auto-pilot and went to the back of the plane to assist the parachuters; the three people with parachutes jumped and, after a brief struggle with the plane's stunned pilot, so did the man, whose death caused damage to a house below.

Contrary to initial reports, the man's death was far from impulsive; he had been planning it for months if not longer. In the weeks before his death, for example, the man frequently queried puzzled co-workers with a question along the lines of "If you were going to fall to your death from a great height, which would you prefer, to jump off a tall building or to jump from a plane?" Notice, in this line of questioning and all it implies, that the man was focused on his death and only on his death; the risk to others was not prominent in his thinking.

And in the event, others were spared, but it is not hard to imagine how the man's actions could have resulted in the deaths of others. Not only might he have killed someone on the ground—in fact he landed on someone's residence but others were uninjured—but in the brief struggle that occurred between the man and the pilot, the latter, unparachuted, might have been pulled out of the plane. He too would have been killed and, furthermore, may have landed on someone; the crash of the pilotless plane might have killed others as well. Would it have constituted murder-suicide, had others died? I do not believe so; the intention, motives, and mindset of the individual in question are too distinct from those of the perpetrators of genuine murder-suicides, who, unlike the young man, become very preoccupied and focused on the deaths of others.

Admittedly, incidents in which people's suicides accidentally cause others' deaths can be very difficult to come to terms with in certain scenarios, because some can involve the deaths of others in ways that seem, on the surface, not only thoughtless but also deeply callous. For example, people die by suicide in their cars relatively frequently. The most common scenarios do not involve others' deaths; usually suicides in cars are from carbon monoxide poisoning from the car's exhaust, or from self-inflicted gunshot wound occurring in a parked vehicle. However, suicides in moving vehicles do occur. A common form of this, somewhat surprisingly, is for someone to self-inflict a lethal gunshot wound while driving. Of course there is a motor vehicle accident of some sort in the aftermath (a fact that can later confuse investigators, who may initially view the cause of death as the motor vehicle accident). However, to my knowledge, none of these motor vehicle accidents have ever resulted in the deaths of others, though it is easy enough to imagine how they might. Had such deaths occurred, they would be viewed according to this book's framework not as genuine murder-suicides, but as perversions of fate. The accidental nature of anyone else's death is relatively easy to discern in such scenarios; one would not view the suicidal individual's actions as necessarily callous, though one would view them as distinctly lacking in foresight. This concrete, here-and-now focus is a common signature of the suicidal mind.

There is another phenomenon, however, that definitely has taken the lives of others, and in which the accidental nature of the others' deaths is harder to see. These deaths seem very callous, but I will argue they mostly are not. Consider, for example, the suicide attempt of a teenage girl in the Atlanta area, who drove her car at an accelerating speed into oncoming traffic as a means to cause her own death. Her car struck a vehicle driven by a young woman; the woman's child was with her in the car. Both were killed instantly. The teenage girl survived the attempt, largely because she accelerated toward the other car as it slowed in anticipation of the accident, thus transferring most of the momentum to the other vehicle. The girl had assumed that increasing her speed would ensure her death, but the basic physics of the situation dictated otherwise.[10]

The girl's actions seem callous indeed, in that she carelessly took strangers' lives. A key point, however, is that the others' deaths were, in her mind, purely incidental to her own. Her thought processes were likely to be "I will cause my death by driving into something lethal" rather than "I will cause my death and I will do it in a way that is likely to kill others." To counter "but she should have known the consequences of her actions" is to misunderstand the state of mind of the intently suicidal—a state of mind characterized by narrow focus on death, with little processing capacity left over to ponder any further consequences of one's actions. Here, as in other suicides that accidentally take others' lives, the most accurate classification is not murder-suicide, but rather a perversion of fate.

It is noteworthy, of course, that the girl survived her suicide attempt. A similar incident occurred on a bridge in Virginia in which the suicidal person did not survive. A man in his 40s drove head on into a car driven by a man in his 70s. Both men died at the scene. How, one might ask, is it possible to know this was a suicide; isn't it possible that the man had a heart attack or stroke, lost consciousness, and unintentionally drove to his and the other man's deaths?

It is a very plausible possibility, because this very thing does occur. However, for two reasons, there is no doubt at all that the man in this particular case intended his own death. First, a very lengthy suicide note was later discovered in his home. Second, his wife was with him in the car and survived to report on what happened.[11]

The man informed his wife as they were driving that he intended murder-suicide by driving into oncoming traffic, by which he meant her and his own deaths not the deaths of others in oncoming traffic (though as we will see that was one result). She then unbuckled her seatbelt and climbed into the backseat, a move that ultimately saved her life. A man driving in the other direction, however, was not as fortunate.

In what was most likely a perversion of justice, the man had decided on his suicide—recall his suicide note—and reasoned that, as long as he were to die, so should his wife. His intent to kill really did not extend beyond himself and his wife; the fact that he did kill an oncoming driver was, as awful as it sounds, incidental to his primary intentions. Like the girl who drove her car into oncoming traffic, this man was likely not conceiving of oncoming traffic as containing people who could be hurt or killed. Rather, he was viewing it as a means to his and his wife's deaths, and did not consider the matter further. The death of the oncoming driver was not part of the murder-suicide plan; it was a perversion fate. To the suicidal people in such incidents, oncoming traffic is unpeopled, much as jumping to her death was for the woman who happened to land on the reclining teenage boy.

The cases of people driving into oncoming traffic, I am arguing, do not, in the minds of the suicidal individuals in question, involve other people as victims. That there most definitely are victims does not change the fact that they are outside of the suicidal individuals' awareness. Much as it can be hard to grasp murder-suicide as in any way involving virtue, it is hard to conceive of someone driving into oncoming traffic without awareness of the distinct possibility of the injury or death of others. But difficulty in understanding something does not necessarily bear on whether that thing is true or false. The state of mind of the murder-suicide perpetrator or of the suicidal person driving into oncoming traffic is difficult to understand but comprehensible nevertheless.

It is possible that some occasional and dim awareness of potential victims flashes into the consciousness of suicidal individuals driving into oncoming traffic; if so—and I somewhat doubt the fact—then the awareness is of an abstract other, not a human being with hopes, dreams, and loved ones. Suicidal individuals' whole focus is on their own death, so much so that they have no attention left over to focus on the deaths of others.

Unless, that is, they are among the approximately 2% of suicide decedents who plan and perpetrate a murder-suicide. For this latter subgroup, their preoccupation is also about death, but it has widened to include others' deaths besides their own. To plan and enact one's own death requires so much resolve that, to use Orwell's phrasing, it usually "fills up the universe." But for murder-suicide perpetrators, plans of their own death do not fully deplete their mental resources; they have resources left over to plan and enact the deaths of others. This perspective suggests a prediction to be tested in future research: murder-suicide perpetrators may have pondered and planned suicide for a longer amount of time even as compared to suicide decedents. This longer timeframe might allow murder-suicide perpetrators to more fully habituate to the idea of suicide,[12] which, in turn, will make it less fearsome and thus will leave over more mental resources to ponder others' deaths as well.

The phenomenon of "suicide by cop" is relevant to what I have labeled here "the perversion of fate." Recall that the term "suicide by cop" refers to a suicidal person whose intention is to provoke a police officer into killing the individual. Why, incidentally, would someone choose this method of suicide? Here again, a major part of the answer to that question involves how daunting and fearsome it is to enact one's own death. Those who are suicidal and want others to kill them want that because they feel too daunted to enact death on their own. The main intent is suicide; it is not to harm the police officer or anyone else. Often, the person's intent is seen through; the individual draws a weapon on an officer in a threatening manner, and the officer shoots the individual in self-defense. Occasionally, however, an officer is killed as well in these incidents, due to accidental fire from other officers or to the individual who initiated the incident accidentally discharging the brandished weapon. In this harrowing scenario, murder-suicide would not be the accurate classification; this scenario, like those involving the drivers who steer into oncoming traffic, is a suicide that incidentally and deeply tragically involved another's death.

Can someone intentionally kill someone else, with full knowledge of what he is doing and to whom he is doing it, all in the process leading up to suicide, and it *not* count as murder-suicide? Almost always the answer to this question is no; these parameters strongly indicate murder-suicide. And yet, I am aware of at least one case that might be an exception to the rule, a case alluded to earlier in the book.

As referred to earlier,[13] a Florida man serving a life sentence became suicidal in prison, but as many people do, blanched at the prospect of enacting his own death. He resolved therefore to kill his cellmate, plead guilty to first-degree murder, and waive all appeals, all as a means to cause his eventual death by execution, which is what occurred. He died not by "suicide by cop," but rather by "suicide by the State of Florida."

Regarding murder-suicide, the incarcerated man killed someone else in the course of enacting his own death, and thus the appalling deed seems to qualify as a genuine murder-suicide. However, unlike in true murder-suicide, the man killed his cellmate *in order to* kill himself. As horrific as it is to state, the man viewed his cellmate much as he might a gun, knife, or noose . . . or as suicidal individuals driving a car view oncoming traffic—as the means to the end of one's own death. The underlying process in the man's killing of the cellmate was fundamentally different than that in the true murder-suicides described throughout this book. In these latter instances, the killing of others is an end in itself, an end predicated on the fact of one's own suicide and justified by an appeal to perverted virtue. In the case of the felon and those of the suicidal drivers, the killing of others is not an end in itself; rather, it is part of the method for one's own suicide. Had someone else died in the incident, described earlier in the book, in which the young woman used chemicals to produce toxic fumes in her car, the same analysis would apply. Had the man who jumped to his death on the skydiving expedition landed on and thus killed someone, the same would apply. Neither person in these latter two instances was focused on others' death; the perpetrators of murder-suicide are defined in part by their preoccupation with others' death (in addition to their own).

Fate is not a virtue; the perversion of fate is not murder-suicide. The clearest instance of this I have ever learned of occurred in Wichita in 2010. A 70-year-old man and his wife were both found in their bed, dead from gunshot wounds. Investigators' initial take on this tragedy was that it was very likely a murder-suicide involving the man shooting his wife and then shooting himself. But in actual fact, he shot himself to death and then shot his wife to death. This sounds improbable, but, try as they might, investigators could only discover one bullet, which was located in the wife's body. That is because there really only was one bullet: the man shot himself in the head; the bullet passed through his head and then struck his wife, who was asleep next to him and who died as a result.[14]

In the reporting of this incident in the media, it was referred to as a "murder-suicide," presumably because it, like genuine murder-suicides, entailed one person killing both himself and another individual. But, on deeper reflection, this is a superficial consideration; murder requires premeditation. The man certainly premeditated his own death but not that of his wife, whose death was accidental.

This awful tragedy illustrates other important truths about suicide and murder-suicide. In suicides that do not involve murder, the person's attention is wholly captured by his or her own death; other considerations beyond that fact often do not enter into awareness. This is why suicide decedents rarely leave a note and why they sometimes die in ways that confront loved ones with horrific scenes—it is not that they intended horror, it is usually that they did not think it through past the fact of their own demise. It is highly likely that the man had not at all fathomed the possibility that the bullet meant for him may have injured, much less killed, his wife. Additionally, although this hardly needs pointing out, in genuine murder-suicides, the murderous act occurs first and then the suicide ensues. In this tragic happenstance, the man's suicide occurred an instant before his wife's death, a death that was not intended, further corroborating the point that this was not a genuine murder-suicide but rather a perversion of fate.

Section 3
Implications and Conclusions

Prevention, Clinical, and Other Real-World Applications

IF THE POINT OF DEPARTURE FOR MURDER-SUICIDE IS suicide, a clear and important applied implication of the current framework is that suicide prevention is also murder-suicide prevention. That is, there may be no need for a separate set of guidelines and clinical approaches to the two topics, because the prevention of the one entails the prevention of the other. Suicide subsumes murder-suicide, according to this book; therefore, suicide prevention subsumes murder-suicide prevention.

Additionally, anyone with elevated suicide risk should be assessed, at least briefly, for potential for violence to others as well. Of course, such assessment may be met with silence or other forms of uncooperativeness, which points to another thing that should be assessed in such individuals: preoccupation with distorted versions of the four virtues of mercy, justice, glory, and duty.

Indeed, it is not difficult to imagine a scenario in which a potential perpetrator of murder-suicide comes to clinical attention and is asked "are you thinking of hurting yourself or someone else?" Despite the fact that the individual is consumed with such thoughts, he responds, tersely and unemotionally, "no."[1] This answer of "no" should not stymie the clinician; there remain at least two avenues of potentially fruitful inquiry, one suggested by the framework established in this book, the other by the literature on suicide risk assessment.

Warning Signs for Suicide and Their Relevance to Murder-Suicide

Regarding the latter, it would be reassuring if imminent warning signs for suicide existed that need not rely on patient self-report. Clinicians do not have to pine for such factors, because many have been established, and still others, though less well established, deserve consideration. Of those that have been well established, the leading few are agitation, insomnia, nightmares, and social withdrawal.[2] Agitation—extreme subjective turmoil combined with physical restlessness (e.g., pacing) and nervousness—is very frequently directly observable by clinicians; patients will often describe it in terms like "I'm so stirred up inside I want to crawl out of my skin." Insomnia, nightmares, and marked social withdrawal are observable by those living with patients; moreover, many patients talk freely about these factors, because they are not very stigmatized. Further still, and relatedly, patients are generally unaware of these variables' link to suicide risk; thus, even if a patient is attempting to conceal risk, he or she may openly discuss these risk indicators. A clinician from whom imminent murder-suicide plans are concealed may nevertheless become concerned enough about agitation, insomnia, nightmares, and marked social withdrawal that intervention becomes indicated and an imminent murder-suicide may be averted thereby. In fact, more than one case example of murder-suicide preceded by agitation has been described in the preceding chapters.

The 1981 book by Eli Robins, *The Final Months*, elaborates on the nature of marked social withdrawal. One main purpose of the book was to catalog the signs and symptoms present, according to interviews with those left behind, in 134 suicide decedents. Consistent with the foregoing discussion, of the top three signs and symptoms, numbers two and three were agitation and insomnia. The number one sign, however, was noticeable weight loss in the days and weeks preceding death.

In my opinion, this is understandable in light of a more general tendency in suicidal behavior of withdrawal from social discourse: people stop communicating (some of the decedents in Robins' study had become nearly mute in the days before their deaths, and relatively few people leave suicide notes, a form of communication); they lose interest in sex; many habitual drinkers, interestingly and surprisingly, lose interest in drinking alcohol (often a facilitator of social interaction); and, relevant to noticeable weight loss, many lose interest in the socially relevant activity of mealtime. This latter sign was evinced by the perpetrator of a murder-suicide in Mahopac, New York, in November of 2011. An officer said of the perpetrator, "I had seen him a couple of weeks earlier and he had lost a lot of weight, so I asked him if everything was all right." Notably, the officer did not wonder whether the eventual perpetrator had been exercising more or dieting; the kind of weight loss involved tends not to occasion such questions. Rather, as in this case, people have the thought that something is wrong with the person, and that the weight loss looks unhealthy.[3]

Beyond these well-established, observable risk indicators, I suggest two more that, though not as well researched, have anecdotal support and also make intuitive sense. I alluded earlier in the book to the phenomenon of the "thousand-yard" stare—a look in the eyes that conveys the impression of a distant, faraway gaze, combined with internal preoccupation with a thought or a problem. It is my distinct clinical impression that people who are very seriously contemplating their imminent death by suicide frequently show this sign; the processes leading up to suicide involve marked withdrawal, taking them "far away," and the daunting prospect of death is their internal preoccupation. One can observe a similar phenomenon, by the way, in boxers in the moments before a bout, who are preoccupied by the task at hand, a rather grueling one; interestingly enough, boxers also show another feature in the moments before a fight, namely agitation. Very daunting prospects of any sort, including one's imminent death, are agitating and preoccupying.

Relatedly, it can be of clinical interest when someone blinks very infrequently. The usual blink rate is about once every three seconds, or about 20 times per minute.[4] If someone blinks, say, twice per minute, it suggests that the individual is either intensely concentrating on something,[5] is feeling a sense of danger, or both. A memorable example of this phenomenon is Tiger Woods in his prime, before his recent troubles. Golf fans will have little trouble picturing Woods sizing up a putt, concentrating very intensely, and hardly blinking.[6] In mental health settings, if a person's blink rate is low and he or she is not communicative, the clinician should attempt to infer the individual's preoccupation or fear. A usual inference is that the person is preoccupied with and concentrating on death, and, because death is fearsome, is attempting to "stare it down." This can be a particularly useful sign, because it may differentiate depressed, uncommunicative patients not at risk for suicide (whose blink rate is usually *increased*, and whose rate normalizes with successful treatment)[7] from those who are at high risk (whose blink rate tends to be reduced).

This discussion is not merely hypothetically relevant to murder-suicide. On December 13, 2005, a young man was evaluated in a mental health facility in the vicinity of Blacksburg, Virginia. The evaluation was occasioned by some vague threats of suicide made by the young man to roommates. The evaluation reads, "The patient denies suicidal ideation…Patient very nonverbal, very quiet, sits in the chair looking down at the floor…Patient does not blink."[8] The young man was deemed not to be a danger and was released. Sixteen months later—April 16, 2007, a spring date, which, as alluded to already, is probably not coincidental—Seung-Hui Cho perpetrated a horrific murder-suicide at Virginia Tech.

Were agitation, insomnia, nightmares, and marked social withdrawal assessed in Cho? In the available medical records, there is a checklist in which sleep problems are referred to; the item was checked by the clinician in a fashion indicating that insomnia was absent. To my knowledge, there is no mention of nightmares, one way or another, in Cho's records. The records do refer to Cho's social isolation; they indirectly refer to absence of agitation, in that Cho is described as quiet (it is possible, however, to be both agitated and quiet; most people express agitation through physical restlessness but not all—the quiet agitated person, if my experience is any guide, has a distinctly preoccupied air and does not blink much; see Footnote 9 regarding sourcing for Virginia Tech tragedy). Although very speculative, one wonders about ultimate outcomes if these factors had been more extensively evaluated; might Cho have gotten hospitalized for more than just a few hours, and then received systematic and comprehensive treatment? If so, might this have averted disaster?[9]

Discussions of Virtue in Clinical Settings

There is another line of questioning that might have alerted clinicians to Cho's potential dangerousness, and that is generally useful in situations in which a person seems at risk for suicide and/or violence but is uncommunicative to usual questioning. And that line of questioning involves virtue.

For anyone harboring a plot to enact what they view as a just or glorious thing (to take two of the four virtues emphasized here as examples), they are unlikely to talk about the plot itself but may be less reticent—and in some cases even effusive—about the virtue in question. Consider the examples of Timothy McVeigh, Nidal Malik Hasan, and the pair who perpetrated the Columbine killings. In the months leading up to the atrocity in Oklahoma City, it would not have been difficult to induce Timothy McVeigh to talk about issues of justice; indeed, the record indicates he talked of little else (and, as mentioned already, it is plausible to view McVeigh's actions as a murder-suicide, as he must have understood that his own death would ensue as a result, sooner or later, as it in fact did).[10] In the hours before he went on a rampage at Ft. Hood—an incident that has similarities to Oklahoma City in that the perpetrator likely viewed his own death as probable—it likely would not have been hard to elicit Nidal Malik Hasan's thoughts on the topic of justice. He was consumed with such thoughts, and reportedly mentioned to a neighbor that he was off to do God's work[11] as he left to perpetrate the incident that took 13 lives (14 if the unborn child of one of the victims is included) and injured 29 others. Hasan was nearly killed in the chaos but survived, paralyzed from the chest down; the possibility remains that he, like McVeigh, will be executed for his crimes. In the timeframe before the Columbine incident, the perpetrators talked frequently to friends and recorded themselves talking about the glory that they anticipated.

Regarding the Virginia Tech tragedy, what might have occurred had a clinician, after asking Cho about his social functioning and his sense of deep isolation from others, enquired about Cho's views on justice? One speculates that this might have been the one topic about which he might have opened up. It is conceivable that much could have been learned as a consequence.

Should those voicing homicidal ideation, by the same logic, be assessed for suicide risk? Yes, because past research has shown that ideation about violence of any sort constitutes a risk for suicidal ideation and behavior.[12] Additionally, suicide is primary in murder-suicide in the sense that it initiates the process. But by the time a clinician is interviewing someone as this process is unfolding, the individual's attention may have turned to the murder element of murder-suicide.

To summarize, based on this book's conceptualization, in clinical situations in which a person is relatively uncommunicative and in which the clinician has the feeling that some form of dangerousness is possible, several signs and symptoms should be assessed. These include, either by direct observation, interviews with collateral informants like family and roommates, or (less likely successful) asking the patient himself or herself, agitation, insomnia, nightmares, and marked social withdrawal, all of which are highly relevant to suicide risk, whether the suicidal individual harbors plans for murder or not. It is not coincidental that authors focusing on murder-suicide recommend these same, longstanding suicide prevention approaches,[13] corroborative of the view that murder-suicide prevention is accomplished by suicide prevention.

Observations of the "thousand-yard" stare and blinking rate also should be made; these too can be relevant to suicide and to murder-suicide. And, most central to the concerns of this book, the patient should be invited to express opinions and views on the topics of justice, mercy, duty, and glory.

This approach is by no means failsafe, for a few reasons. With regard to the suicide risk indicators of agitation, insomnia, nightmares, and marked social withdrawal, as well as with regard to the "thousand-yard" stare and blink rate, there are problems related to both false-positive and false-negative scenarios. That is, patients who are positive for these signs may not in fact attempt or die by suicide; and those who are negative for these signs—or, perhaps, more accurately, are able to appear negative for these signs—may attempt or die. These signs are probative enough that, in my opinion, it is clinically irresponsible not to assess for them (at least in mental health settings, perhaps in all health settings), but they are nevertheless imperfect.

Asking patients about virtue presents challenges too. First, it is understandably not immediately evident to many clinicians how to broach the question. I would like to suggest something along the following lines: "It appears to me that something is on your mind, but I see that you don't want to talk about problems. Let's shift gears then and change the topic altogether. What if we talked for a while about the positive? In particular, I would be interested to know your views on positive qualities like honor, justice, mercy, duty, and heroism."

The wording emphasizes "honor"—not because it is one of the specific virtues perverted in murder-suicide, but because it is applicable to the four that are, and also because it is mildly provocative, putting the issue of one's honor on the table if not at stake. For an individual preoccupied by something as momentous as causing others' death as well as suicide, all for the sake of a virtue (even if perverted), silence in reply to a question about honor is improbable.

It is certainly possible that, in reply to this question, the patient does not answer but instead asks a question in turn, along the lines of "Why do you want to know that?" My suggested answer is "Because I am interested in them as essential aspects of human nature. I am curious about and interested in other people's opinions on these fundamental things, including your opinion." Clinicians should of course feel free to amend this phrasing so that it suits the context.

It is also quite possible that a question on virtue may puzzle patients. I would suggest, however, that this is valuable information in itself. More specifically, someone preoccupied by virtue, including those in the process of planning to pervert it in a murder-suicide incident, may answer it readily, may express suspicion at the question, or may refuse to react to it, but they will not find the question perplexing. They are so focused on the question, have given it so much thought, and feel the question to be so deeply resonant, that puzzlement is unlikely, and even the feigning of puzzlement, in the unlikely event that it occurred to the person to attempt, would prove exceedingly difficult. An analogy to someone lacking oxygen may be instructive. To the random person, the question "Do you have enough oxygen?" seems very peculiar; but to the person in need of oxygen—preoccupied by it—the question has a different impact. Anyone who is genuinely puzzled by the question about oxygen is unlikely to be lacking it, just as anyone who is perplexed by the question on virtue is not in the midst of planning a murder-suicide.

Another useful applied aspect of the conceptualization developed in this book is that it can inform early conjectures regarding motives in particular murder-suicide scenarios. From a relatively spare fact pattern (and by ignoring media speculations that ring false), it is possible to arrive at early and correct conclusions. Examples include the Zinkhan case, in which the perpetrator was found dead by suicide in a camouflaged pit in the woods (not in Europe, as some in the media guessed), and the case in which a mother killed her children before setting her house on fire, causing her own death in the process (not in which her adolescent son was the perpetrator, as some in the media speculated).

A murder-suicide occurred in Florida in late May 2011, for which the current framework makes a plausible motive reasonably clear. A transplant surgeon in his mid-40s was killed by an older man, who then killed himself. The latter was a patient of the former.[14] A plausible conjecture, consistent with this book's approach, is that the perpetrator felt medically wronged by the doctor and decided that it was unjust for the doctor to live on if the man himself would not. A further speculation is that the man was motivated not only by perverted justice, but also by a perverted sense of duty to protect other patients of the doctor's.

Another potential applied application involves the finding, described in an earlier chapter, that disabling the right temporo-parietal region reduces harshness of moral judgments. This could equate to inducing the leavening effects of empathy in patients at high risk for violence. A similar technique, transcranial magnetic stimulation, has been successfully used in the treatment of depression.[15] Might it do so partly by reducing recriminations, including self-recriminations?

Psychotherapy with people harboring a mix of suicidal and homicidal ideas should focus on empirically supported approaches like cognitive-behavioral therapy and should apply these approaches to psychological themes related to mercy, justice, glory, and duty. Indeed, a main point of this book is that these virtues are distorted in murder-suicide, and a main point of cognitive-behavioral therapy is to address such distortions. Of course, such treatment should not ignore the basics, including aggressive treatment of underlying mental illnesses, and practical matters such as safety planning and means restriction (e.g., firearm safety and removal).

An August 10, 2009, article in the *Columbus Dispatch* points to other things that can be done to potentially head off unfolding murder-suicides. Referring to murder-suicide expert Donna Cohen, the article stated, "She said family members, friends and co-workers of victims often are aware of problems that precede murder-suicide. But, she said, they don't intervene." The article quoted Dr. Cohen directly; justice-type events were evidently on her mind: "There are a lot of things that can be done to increase awareness. People shouldn't be afraid to recommend resources, to know where a shelter is or how to contact a domestic-violence program."[16]

The framework developed and defended in this book suggests still other real-world applications. For example, in a standoff involving a distressed, armed individual and a hostage, authorities may be aided in averting a murder-suicide if they know the individual's motive (i.e., which virtue is being distorted), which could help in the process of negotiation and de-escalation. A crisis negotiator who understands that an incident is about, for example, perverted mercy might shape his or her interactions differently than if the incident is about perverted justice. As another example, murder-suicides are routinely reported in the newspaper and other media, far more so than are suicides and more so even than are murders. As has been shown regarding suicide, the way that these reports are phrased can encourage or discourage those who are considering similar actions. A fuller understanding of the phenomenon of murder-suicide—the goal of this book—may inform and refine reporting guidelines.

Conclusion: Human Nature and the Perversion of Virtue

"[The writer] must teach himself that the basest of all things is to be afraid; and, teaching himself that, forget it forever, leaving no room in his workshop for anything but the old verities and truths of the heart, the old universal truths lacking which any story is ephemeral and doomed—love and honor and pity and pride and compassion and sacrifice...It is easy enough to say that man is immortal simply because he will endure: that when the last dingdong of doom has clanged and faded from the last worthless rock hanging tideless in the last red and dying evening, that even then there will still be one more sound: that of his puny inexhaustible voice, still talking. I refuse to accept this. I believe that man will not merely endure: he will prevail. He is immortal, not because he alone among creatures has an inexhaustible voice, but because he has a soul, a spirit capable of compassion and sacrifice and endurance. The poet's, the writer's, duty is to write about these things. It is his privilege to help man endure by lifting his heart, by reminding him of the courage and honor and hope and pride and compassion and pity and sacrifice which have been the glory of his past."—William Faulkner's Nobel Prize acceptance speech, given in Stockholm on December 10, 1950

FAULKNER'S VISION OF THE HUMAN CONDITION WAS NOT only incisive, but sweeping. An Achilles' heel of such an approach, of course, is overgeneralization. The current book claims a framework that applies to all genuine instances of murder-suicide, and in this it is subject to Hamlet's reproach to Guildenstern, "You would pluck out the heart of my mystery." In his book 2011 *Anything Goes*, Theodore Dalrymple concurred that "there is always something incalculable about human conduct." Consider, however, his very next line, "Nevertheless, there are certain regularities...."[1]

One goal of this chapter is to ponder both the incalculability and the regularity in the perpetration of murder-suicide. I eagerly await challenges to the universality of the conceptualization proposed in this book, and relish such challenges because only two outcomes are possible in their wake, and both outcomes mean an advance in our understanding: either the framework survives all challenges, and thus is corroborated in the Popperian sense of that word, or the framework's limitations will emerge, which is likely to prove as illuminating as corroboration, or even more so. Seminal philosophers of science, from Popper to his student Lakatos to Kuhn, though they disagree with each other on many things, agree with the premise that science proceeds well under conditions of sweeping theoretical claims open to empirical correction.

The case of Charles Whitman provides an interesting potential challenge to the framework developed in this book. Whitman, having already killed his wife and his mother, took the elevator up to the top floor of the central tower of the University of Texas at Austin (which one can now do only with some difficulty, in part as a result of the horror Whitman perpetrated), bludgeoned a receptionist to death, shot at two families who had scaled the stairs in the meantime, and then began shooting at people on the campus grounds below, eventually killing a total of 13 people and injuring 32 others.[2] The incident occurred on August 1, 1966, consistent with an observation that has been made throughout this book—murder-suicide peaks in the spring-summer timeframe (as do suicide and murder). Also illustrative of an issue discussed earlier—namely, that many people who die by suicide tell others of their intentions in the days and weeks leading up to the event—Whitman discussed his violent ideas with a psychiatrist about four months before the killings. Hauntingly, the psychiatrist's progress note stated that Whitman was "thinking of going up on the tower with a deer rifle and start [sic] shooting people."

Whitman fully expected his own death in the midst of this incident, as a suicide note he left amply shows. Indeed, police shot him dead at the site.

What the note also shows is that Whitman believed something was wrong with his brain—not just his mind, but his brain specifically—and he requested in the note that an autopsy be performed to test his suspicions. In this, he was mindful not only of his increasingly violent impulses but also of severe headaches. He wrote, "I don't really understand myself these days. I am supposed to be an average reasonable and intelligent young man. However, lately...I have been the victim of many unusual and irrational thoughts." Elsewhere in the same note, he wrote, "I talked with a Doctor once for about two hours and tried to convey to him my fears that I felt...overwhelming violent impulses...I never saw the Doctor again, and since then I have been fighting my mental turmoil alone, and seemingly to no avail." It is worth noting that, in this note, Whitman refers not only to the risk factor of loneliness, but also that of agitation (which is what I believe he meant, at least in part, when he referred to "mental turmoil"). These are risk factors for violence, including suicide as well as violence directed toward others.

Whitman's autopsy confirmed his suspicions—there was a nickel-sized tumor, a glioblastoma, which impinged on several brain regions, including the amygdala. As noted earlier in the book, this brain area is centrally involved in fear processing; when it is impaired, people tend to do things that fear would usually have kept in check. These can include, as in Whitman's case, aggression toward others.

It would be plausible to simply attribute Whitman's violence to his brain tumor and view it as having nothing to do with the framework outlined in the previous chapters. For two reasons, however, I am reluctant to do that. The first reason is that many people have had tumors similar to Whitman's, and yet none of them, to my knowledge, has perpetrated a similar atrocity. In a previous chapter, I discussed a woman whose amygdala was completely impaired by a rare genetic illness; she experienced many close calls because of her lack of fear but, quite unlike Whitman, was not preoccupied by violence, much less did she perpetrate it.

Second, there are allusions to perverted virtue in the writings Whitman left behind. In the same suicide note quoted above, he stated, "It was after much thought that I decided to kill my wife,

Kathy, tonight...I love her dearly, and she has been as fine a wife to me as any man could ever hope to have. I cannot rationally pinpoint any specific reason for doing this."[3] If it is difficult for Whitman to explain his own motives, it follows that it will be difficult as well for everyone else. A possibility, however, is that, earlier in the progression of his brain disease and his mental disorder, Whitman had first fantasized and then decided on a murder-suicide perverting the virtue of glory. Having decided this, he then reasoned that leaving behind his wife (and mother) to deal with the aftermath was worse than their deaths, so he decided to kill them as well—a perversion of mercy. By the time Whitman wrote his note, his illnesses may have been too advanced for him to articulate and write out this train of thought (though he did make some vague references in the note to relieving his wife and mother of suffering).

Whitman's case thus may fit within the perverted-virtue conceptualization of murder-suicide developed in this book. By the same token, it could be construed as a counterexample. Only more information about Whitman's inner thoughts in the time leading up to the incident would resolve this issue. It could be argued that it is Procrustean to fit Whitman's case to the present framework. Perhaps, but none of the facts of the case disconfirms the narrative of Whitman's actions inspired by this book: that, having first decided on suicide, he then decided to give in to his impulses to go out in what he construed as a blaze of glory; and having decided that, he in turn perverted the virtue of mercy and reasoned that his wife and mother should be spared the suffering that his actions would entail.

The shootings perpetrated by Jiverly Wong in Binghamton, New York, on April 3, 2009, can, like those carried out by Whitman, be viewed as either challenge to or corroboration for the current conceptualization. The incident bore some similarities to the Virginia Tech tragedy. Wong first barricaded the rear door to the Binghamton American Civic Association, an immigration center, and then entered the front door, wearing a bulletproof vest. He fired at everyone he encountered, killing 13 people and wounding 4 others. When Wong heard police sirens approaching, he killed himself.[4]

Like Cho at Virginia Tech, Wong had mailed materials to a news station in advance of the shootings. The letter received by News 10 Now, a local station, was postmarked on the day of the killings, but it was dated 16 days earlier. The letter, mostly in capitals and with many grammatical errors, opened ominously: "I AM JiVERLY WONG SHOOTING THE PEOPLE." The letter also suggests that Wong harbored paranoid delusions about police activities regarding him: "COP USED 24 HOURS THE TECHNiQUE OF ULTRAMODERN AND CAMERA FOR BURN THE CHEMICAL IN MY HOUSE. FOR SWITCH THE CHANNEL Ti.Vi. FOR ADJUST THE FAN. FOR MADE ME UNBREATHABLE. FOR MADE ME VOMIT. FOR CONNECT THE MUSiC INTO MY EAR."

Given the delusional character of these and others of Wong's statements, perhaps his actions should simply be attributed to psychosis and not to anything having to do with the perversion of virtue. Although it should not be disputed that mental disorder played a clear and substantial contributory role in the tragedy, it does not in my opinion represent a full explanation, in part because the vast majority of psychotic people do not perpetrate violence, and because most murder-suicide perpetrators are not psychotic.

Can the framework presented in this book shed further light on Wong's actions? His letter concludes, "I CAN NOT ACCEPTED MY POOR LiFE. BEFORE I CUT MY POOR LiFE I MUST ONESELF GET A JUDGE JOB FOR MAKE AN IMPARTiAL WiTH UNDERCOVER COP BY AT LEAST TWO PEOPLE WiTH ME GO TO RETURN TO THE DUST OF EARTH." Wong's premeditation is clear: he apparently wrote the letter over two weeks in advance; he mailed it on the morning of the shootings; he barricaded the back entrance of the center; and he was heavily armed, wearing a bulletproof vest. The letter's content corroborates the planful nature of this incident. Furthermore, Wong's words "before I cut my poor life" and his reference to impartial judgment as well as to killing a minimum of two people before he kills himself suggest a murder-suicide involving the perversion of justice. To be sure, the logic is indirect and difficult to follow, due largely to Wong's probable psychosis and his language difficulties. Nevertheless, suicide seems a foundation from which Wong reasons; his words imply that he had decided on suicide, but he felt he must kill others first as a way to attribute blame and responsibility to police, which, in turn, Wong believed would accomplish justice. The second-to-last line of his letter supports this perspective: "COP BRiNG ABOUT THiS SHOOTiNG COP MUST RESPONSiBLE."[5]

Given Wong's views that he had been regularly persecuted by the police, so much so that he was driven to murder and suicide, it is perhaps peculiar that Wong did not directly target police. Indeed, when he heard the sirens approaching the immigration center, he turned his weapon on himself. Given his mental state, it is not too surprising that Wong's decision-making process was peculiar; furthermore, perhaps he was too afraid of police officers to target them directly or calculated that he might not be successful in killing at least two people if he targeted police officers.

The peculiarity of some of Wong's decisions affected the process and outcome of the tragedy—police officers were not targeted; people at the immigration center were—but, I suggest, Wong's mental state did not fundamentally alter the fact that this was very likely a murder-suicide perverting justice.

This same process of psychosis affecting but not fundamentally changing the essential underlying motivation occurs in suicide *qua* suicide as well. In his classic *Dementia Praecox*, Bleuler[6] described the self-concept of schizophrenic patients as often including delusions of inferiority, poverty, and sinfulness. He stated, "The delusions then have the same content as other melancholias, except that schizophrenia often tinges them with its own peculiar coloring of contradiction, incompleteness and senselessness." Bleuler cited an example of a schizophrenic patient at high suicide risk who believes that God has withdrawn from him through his belly; a second schizophrenic patient, in explaining a suicide attempt, stated, "All the world's murderers wait for me; they cannot die without me."[7] In both these instances, a fundamental aspect of the suicidal mind can be discerned—namely, perceived burdensomeness. Psychosis does not change this fundamental aspect, but rather, to use Bleuler's phrasing, lends it a "peculiar coloring."

Still another kind of incident that may challenge this book's approach is that in which a conflict occurs between two parents, and one parent kills the couple's child and then dies by suicide, seemingly as a way to vent anger toward the surviving parent and to others associated with the surviving parent. For example, in early 2010, Stephen Garcia killed his infant son and then himself, in the context of a very tempestuous separation from the child's mother. The perpetrator in this case certainly did intimate that his motive was spite; for example, he wrote to his ex and her family and friends, "I will see you in fucking hell. I held the gun, you pulled the trigger...the blood is on your hands." In this, he sounded somewhat like Wong, and also like some of those, alluded to in an earlier chapter, in the moments before their execution by the state, spitting vengeance.[8]

However, Garcia also wrote, "Find it in your heart to forgive me. It's my job to protect him. I know God will welcome our son with open arms." Garcia was a very confused and troubled person, and thus it is unsurprising that he voiced many different motives for his appalling actions. But, at bottom, he seemed to believe that death was a protection to his son; his motive might well have been mercy, albeit a profoundly distorted version of it.

What constitutes the full set of human virtues? Peterson and Seligman's[9] handbook devotes over 500 pages to this question. Many more pages than that have been written by theologians and philosophers over the centuries on the question. The question has been answered in the negative, too (e.g., the Ten Commandments, the Seven Deadly Sins). It is not the main goal of this book to fully elucidate the nature of virtue, but the conceptualization articulated here points to an intriguing possibility: murder-suicide involves ultimate, life-or-death decisions not just for oneself but for others as well; might the virtues it perverts therefore constitute the collection of human virtues that best balances parsimony and comprehensiveness?

As a reminder of this book's approach to the virtues perverted in murder-suicide, Figure 11.1 depicts the four essential virtues, with a close (indeed overlapping) connection between glory and justice and between mercy and duty, and with fate and self-control as neighboring but non-overlapping phenomena. One possible reaction is that an even more parsimonious categorization is workable. In fact, in an earlier chapter, I noted that the four virtues of mercy, duty, justice, and glory can be organized into two categories: one, combining mercy and duty, in which feelings of care and empathy for others are high (if distorting), and another, combining justice and glory, in which callousness and carelessness toward others predominate. In creatures as gregarious as we, and, at the same time, as warring, it is no surprise that duty and mercy (because our sociality binds us to one another) and glory and justice (because we need heroes and stalwarts, and not just in wars) are primary virtues. Though there is utility to this categorization scheme, specific instances of murder-suicide show why it violates the dictum, often attributed to Einstein, that a concept should be as simple as possible but no simpler. A murder-suicide

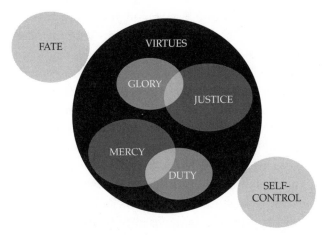

FIGURE 11.1 The four essential virtues, with fate and self-control as neighboring but non-overlapping phenomena.

perverting justice, like that perpetrated by the University of Georgia business professor George Zinkhan III, is fundamentally different than the Columbine killings, which were motivated by perverted glory. To view them as fundamentally similar would be misleading. The differences are several, but a primary one has to with motive— Zinkhan was preoccupied by justice, the Columbine killers by glory. Even limiting the examples to school shootings, it would not do to view them all as in the same category, as some involved the perversion of justice (e.g., Virginia Tech), whereas others involved the perversion of heroic glory (e.g., Columbine).

The differences between the incidents at Columbine and Virginia Tech show the shortcomings of too parsimonious a framework—two virtues are too few—but a related and quite reasonable question is why stop at the four virtues of mercy, justice, duty, and glory? Why not include five, six, or more?

Regarding virtue as a general matter, as distinct from its perversion in murder-suicide, it is again not the main aim of this book to fully elucidate it (which would be ambitious indeed, given that this has been a preoccupation of philosophical and religious scholarship for millennia), but nonetheless, it is at least plausible to view the four virtues highlighted in this book as fundamental, irreducible, and comprehensive (others have provided a compatible account).[10] Consider, for example, the ones highlighted by Faulkner in his Nobel speech, quoted in this chapter's epigraph. He lists "courage and honor and hope and pride and compassion and pity and sacrifice." It is not particularly mentally taxing to imagine how each of these could be viewed as derivative of mercy, justice, duty, and glory.

In an earlier chapter, I pointed out that these four virtues are interpersonal in essence. It is therefore of interest to wonder whether even non-interpersonal virtues might be subsumed by these four interpersonal virtues. Non-interpersonal virtues are somewhat difficult to think of, a fact that is not without meaning. Honesty? At first blush it seems relatively unpeopled, but on further reflection, it clearly has a social dimension—honesty exists within and characterizes relationships, as words like "confess" show. It is true that one can be honest to principle as opposed to people, but that begs the question of what those principles are; I contend that they are the virtues of mercy, justice, duty, and glory. Much the same analysis would apply to the virtue of patience.

The virtue of autonomy or freedom may not fit well within the four virtues highlighted here. Nevertheless, it is of interest to note that the murder-suicide perpetrator takes freedom too far; he abandons the individual restraint that is the bedrock of a free and just society. Freedom rings in the heart, mind, and ears of the murder-suicide perpetrator, but it is an ersatz version of freedom, a perversion of virtue. In a free society, everyone has a duty to restrain individual feeling and impulse at least to a degree—Rousseauian claims notwithstanding, the absence of individual restraint leads not to an Eden of freedom but to a Hades of chaos. Murder-suicide perpetrators, in abandoning restraint, abjure duty, bringing even the virtue of freedom back around to one of the four interpersonal virtues emphasized in the current framework.

I acknowledge that the nature of my overall conjecture is both sweeping and speculative, a combination that cries out for systematic scientific research. One potential avenue for future research involves the application of psychological autopsy methodology to large numbers of murder-suicide perpetrators. Such studies might strive not only for rich description,[11] but also for specific empirical tests of predictions stemming from this and other frameworks on murder-suicide. Analog experimental tests are also conceivable, for example using variants of the "trolley problem."[12] In the classic version of this dilemma, most people consider it morally just to direct a trolley about to collide with and kill five people onto a different track on which only one person would die, but they find pushing a person in front of a trolley to prevent it from killing five people down-track much less acceptable. Versions of this problem in which the respondent and others die (cf. murder-suicide) could be used under experimentally manipulated conditions in which different virtues are more or less salient.

One might protest that such experiments are not feasible or relevant enough. Having done my fair share of scientific work on a hard-to-study phenomenon in suicidal behavior, I have some sympathy for the plea that scientific work, at least that with any sort of controlled design feature, is too difficult. I sympathize but do not agree. A fully experimental test of a theory of suicidal behavior in the laboratory is not merely possible but has been done.[13] We cannot give up easily regarding a phenomenon that kills many innocents, like, for example, the children of the Beadle and Lupoe families.

Faulkner's Nobel acceptance speech emphasizes that anything other than verities and virtues like honor, love, compassion, and pity is not worth the artist's attention. These virtues and verities define us, and this book has shown that they are at play even in great evil and tragedy. Murder-suicide shows that people can prevail even over the ancient and powerful proscription, written in our cells and souls, against killing. That this is so is horrible. If there is a hopeful flipside to this horror, it is that there are future avenues for prevention, clinical, and scientific research, to eventually prevail over a misery this extensive.

Notes

Preface

1. Liem and Nieuwbeerta (2010), pp. 133–134.

Chapter 1

1. Alden (1814).
2. The quote is from Terence's comedy, *The Self-Tormentor* (i.77).
3. Sullivan (1953), p. 7.
4. Hardy (1940).
5. Huxley & Huxley (1916), p. 183; in fact, many did think of evolutionary principles even before Darwin; for example, early work in linguistics on the relation of earlier to later languages invoked explanations that are Darwinian in character (e.g., Wilhelm van Humboldt).
6. Joiner (2005).
7. Joiner (2010).
8. Compare to Bandura (1999).
9. See Ball (2012) for a recent treatment of physician-assisted suicide.

10. Hendin (1997).
11. Media coverage of this incident is available from several news outlets (e.g., a January 27, 2009, *New York Times* article by Rebecca Cathcart and Randal Archibold).
12. For example, Guileyardo et al. (1999); Marzuk et al. (1992).
13. Compare to Liem & Nieuwbeerta (2010), pp. 133–134.
14. Throughout I use gendered pronouns as I think—and as the data indicate—is appropriate to the phenomenon. For example, the vast majority of "justice"-type murder-suicides is perpetrated by men, so when discussing them, I often use pronouns like "he."
15. As will be drawn out in some detail in a later section, murder-suicides involving the perversion of duty and mercy share some similarities but remain discernible from one another nevertheless.
16. Cullen (2009).
17. A quite useful Secret Service report on school shootings makes this same point; the report is available at http://www.secretservice.gov/ntac/ssi_final_report.pdf
18. Cohen, Llorente, & Eisdorfer (1998); Eliason (2009).
19. Media coverage of this incident is available from several news outlets (e.g., a December 30, 2008, *New York Times* article by Solomon Moore). This incident is distinct from that which occurred in December 2011 in Grapeville, Texas, in which a man dressed as Santa Claus killed six relatives before killing himself. This 2011 incident was a genuine murder-suicide.
20. Roth (2009).
21. Darwin, from the *Origin of Species*, Chapter IX: "It can be shown that plants most widely different in habit and general appearance, and having strongly marked differences in every part of the flower,…plants inhabiting different stations and fitted for extremely different climates, can often be crossed with ease."
22. Of course extensive media coverage of this incident is available via several news outlets (e.g., an April 17, 2007, article in the *New York Times* by Brian Knowlton).
23. This statement appears in Appendix N (on p. N-5) of the Governor of Virginia's Virginia Tech Review panel report, which appeared in August 2007.
24. The president's remarks received considerable media attention (e.g., a November 10, 2009, *New York Times* article by Peter Baker and Clifford Krauss). In his *The Gulag Archipelago* (1973),

Aleksandr Solzhenitsyn wrote, "To do evil a human being must first of all believe what he is doing is good"—a similar view, in a quite different context, as those articulated by the Virginia Tech panel and President Obama. As true as this often is, there are exceptions to the rule, as we will see in the chapter on murder per se (e.g., serial killers often clearly understand and enjoy that they are perpetrating evil).

25. Cleckley (1941).
26. The quote is attributed to Archimedes by Pappus of Alexandria and appears in the latter's *Synagoge*, Book VIII.
27. For example, Meloy (2006).
28. See also Hempel et al. (1999); Meloy (1999).
29. See, for example, Bushman & Anderson (2001); Cornell et al. (1996); Crick & Dogde (1996).
30. Linde (2010).
31. Jamison (1995).
32. Ibid., p. 115.
33. Wilson (2010).
34. Ibid., p. 56.
35. A team led by Mike Anestis has recently conducted an in-depth scholarly review of the literature on impulsivity and suicidal behavior; the review, currently under peer review, rejects the notion that suicide occurs on a whim.
36. A September 27, 2010, article posted to boston.com by David Abel described this incident.
37. The 2006 documentary film *The Bridge*, directed by Eric Steel, demonstrates this vividly in its interview of Kevin Hines, who described surviving a jump from the bridge.
38. The program is the Henry Ford Health System's Depression Care Program.
39. See *The Works of Francis Bacon*, edited by J. Spedding, R. L. Ellis, and D. D. Heath (1869, p. 210).
40. Cleckley (1941), p. 399.
41. As will be noted again later in the book, evolution has derived self-caused, self-initiated death under very specific circumstances as a means of inclusive fitness in many species, but this is quite a distinct matter from the idea of a generalized death wish.
42. Isbell (2010), p. 94; I would suggest a similar mechanism is at play in the following quote from an article in the March 2012

issue of *Esquire*, describing a Zanesville, Ohio, resident who chanced upon an area in which a neighbor had released numerous exotic animals: "[he] suddenly felt a shiver go over him. 'I can't really explain it,' he says today, 'except to say that I felt like I was being watched...' Then [he] saw the lion."

43. See, for example, Kahneman (2011).
44. Bowker (2003), p. 36.
45. Hames and colleagues (2011).
46. Herbert (2010).
47. Ibid., pp. 31–32.
48. Covington (1995).
49. It made Julian Jaynes wonder, and a similar view is at the heart of his intriguing life's work *The Origin of Consciousness in the Breakdown of the Bicameral Mind*—a book that was (and remains) underappreciated.
50. Darwin (1872), p. 38.
51. Feinstein et al. (2010).
52. Sullivan (1953), p. 7.
53. Ibid., p. 26.
54. In this, I believe Soame Jenyns, writing (at first anonymously) in 1756, would agree. He asked, "what numberless lives would be lost...was the piercing of a sword no more painful than the tickling of a feather?"
55. An article describing this incident was posted to the following news site on May 11, 2011: http://www.wftv.com/news/news/cops-man-bonded-out-of-jail-killed-wife-self/nJ2R5/
56. This is consistent with the study by Malphurs and D. Cohen (2005); these researchers reported that a main differentiating variable between older male suicide decedents and older male perpetrators of murder-suicide was that the latter were much more likely to have history of domestic violence (see also D. Cohen, Llorente, & Eisdorfer, 1998).
57. West (1966) used this term as well.
58. This very term has been suggested in the literature (for example, van Wormer & Odiah, 1999).
59. Although I am aware of one exception to this rule, a bizarre shooting incident discussed later in the book.
60. For example, Zimring (2011).
61. For example, West (1966); Anderson & Anderson (1984).

62. For example, Joiner (2010).
63. For example, West (1966).
64. Masters (2006).
65. Ibid., p. 194.
66. Marzuk et al. (1992), p. 3179.
67. This incident is described in a November 18, 2011, report by Mead Gruber; it is available at http://www.huffingtonpost.com/2011/11/18/wyoming-car-crash_n_1101281.html. We will see a similar case involving driving into traffic in Chapter 9; that chapter makes the argument that these incidents pervert fate, but that fate is not a virtue and thus these incidents are distinct from those that clearly do pervert virtue. In suicides in which an individual drives into oncoming traffic, the suicidal person's car is usually traveling at a far higher rate of speed than the other car involved in the tragedy, and those in the other car usually die instantly, whereas the suicidal individual either survives (as in the example discussed in Chapter 9) or dies in the hospital. In the Wyoming case, the difference in speed was 100 mph versus 50 mph; the four in the other car died at the scene and the suicidal individual died later in the hospital.
68. Camus (1957).
69. Ibid., p. 25.
70. Eliason (2009), p. 374.
71. Malphurs & D. Cohen (2005).
72. This is because decedents were, in many cases, being treated for serious mental illnesses, which in the end proved fatal, not because the medicines caused suicide (see Simon & Savarino, 2007, for a sophisticated and persuasive treatment of the relevant issues).
73. 2010.
74. Liem & Roberts (2009).
75. Joiner (2010).
76. Felthous & Hempel (1995).
77. Abraham understood the $N + 1$ problem and used a version of it to try to persuade God to spare Sodom and Gomorrah, as described in *Genesis* 18. God agrees to relent if there are 50 holy people there; Abraham respectfully asks if it is fair to destroy the area if there are 45 but not 50. They keep at this until the number 10 is agreed upon. Unfortunately for the inhabitants of the area, according to *Genesis*, it turned out that there were fewer than 10 holy people in Sodom and Gomorrah.

78. A September 18, 2009, article by Tiffany Gibson and Mary Manning in the *Las Vegas Sun* described this incident.

79. Grossman (1995); but see Buss (2005).

80. Hendin (1997), p. 160.

81. These events are described in detail in a series of articles in the *New York Times* by Michael Arkush and Mike Wise in September and October 2002.

82. Extensive media coverage of these events is widely available (e.g., a January 6, 2009, article by Denise Lavoie posted to the Huffington Post at http://www.huffingtonpost.com/2009/01/06/richard-sharpe-crossdress_n_155723.html).

83. The details of Bishop's case are described in various news outlets (e.g., a June 19, 2010, article by Shelley Murphy and Donovan Slack in the *Boston Globe*).

84. Joiner (2005).

85. Roth (2009).

86. Eliason (2009); West (1966).

87. See also Atran (2003).

88. Pape (2003), p. 343.

89. Ibid., p. 344.

90. West (1966).

91. van Wormer & Roberts (2009).

92. For example, Marzuk et al. (1992).

93. Large et al. (2009).

94. The 2010 toll was 38,364 (see the Statistics section of the website of the American Association of Suicidology, which is at www.suicidology.org).

95. The report is available at http://www.vpc.org/studies/amroul2012.pdf.

96. Robins (1981).

97. Large et al. (2009).

98. Roth (2009).

99. Large et al. (2009).

100. For example, Zimring (2011).

101. Milroy (1995).

102. West (1966) made a similar point.

103. Barber et al. (2008).

104. Compare to Logan et al. (2008).

105. Large et al. (2009).

106. See also Liem & Nieuwbeerta (2010) for an account compatible with Large et al.
107. All quotes are from Robins (1981), p. 427.
108. Compare to Stack (1997).
109. Roth (2009); Joiner (2005).
110. Cohen et al. (1998).
111. Compare to Liem & Nieuwbeerta (2010).
112. This incident was described in a March 16, 2011, *New York Daily News* article by Kerry Burke and Bob Kappstatter.
113. This incident was described in a June 22, 2011, article available at http://abclocal.go.com/wpvi/story?section=news/crime&id= 8198278. No one on the train was hurt, but as we have seen and will see again, there certainly are incidents in which other people are hurt or killed accidentally in the course of a suicide.
114. Quotes are from a June 22, 2011, article available at http:// www.phillyburbs.com/news/crime/double-murder- suicide-in-warrington-hatboro/article_49d10987-9c83-518b-a 4ad-99f09186805b.html.
115. Santayana (1905).

Chapter 2

1. An illuminating account of West's crimes appears in Dalrymple (2005, pp. 260 ff.).
2. Grossman (1995).
3. Ibid.
4. Vaillant (2010), p. 140.
5. Vaillant (2010).
6. p. 29; Anthony Daniels (2011), who usually writes under the pen name Theodore Dalrymple and whose observations and con- clusions are often uncannily similar to Cleckley's, described an incident with some similarities, but involving the threat of sui- cide: "when we reached the roof the psychopath warned us not to come any closer, or he would jump. I disbelieved him, and we ran forward to grab him. Whether by intention or accident I do not know, he slipped off the ledge. By luck each of us caught one of his wrists...and we held him dangling from the roof, seventy feet above his death. We held him through the railings but we were not strong enough to haul him up. 'Let me go you bastards!'

he shouted, and then, 'Help, I'm falling!'" (pp. 225 ff). The individual in question was hauled up, after all.

7. Dewey (2004), p. 31.

8. War propaganda often uses such imagery, dehumanizing the enemy through comparisons to insects for example (see Harris & Fiske, 2011, for a laboratory demonstration of this phenomenon).

9. Wayne, "The Shootist," 1976. Directed by Don Siegel.

10. Dewey (2004), p. 15.

11. Grossman (1995), p. 110.

12. Dewey (2004).

13. Bohrer et al. (2008).

14. Ibid.

15. According to a 2012 report from the National Law Enforcement Officers Memorial Fund, 173 federal, state, and local law enforcement officers were killed in the line of duty in 2011, up from 153 in 2010 and 122 in 2009. Of the 173 officers killed in 2011, 68 died from gunshot wounds.

16. Dewey (2004).

17. Ibid., p. 19.

18. Krakauer (2003), pp. 188–189.

19. Dalrymple (2008), p. 5.

20. Solomon (1980).

21. The quote is from a 1764 pamphlet entitled *Crimes and Their Punishments*.

22. Camus (1957).

23. Ibid., p. 23.

24. Or whoever authored it—there is some controversy on the question. The passage appears in Chapter 1, Verse 8 and Chapter 5, Verse 10.

25. The quote is from a taped lecture Faulkner gave on May 7, 1958; the lecture is available through a University of Virginia archive at http://faulkner.lib.virginia.edu/display/wfaudio28_1#wfaudio28_1.7.

26. Dalrymple (2005).

27. Ibid, p. 249.

28. These are the last lines in the poem "The Voyage," which appeared in Baudelaire's collection "Fleurs de mal," a definitive edition of which was published in 1868, one year after the poet's death.

29. Fischer et al. (2008).

30. This latter claim is documented in the March 2010 *Atlantic Monthly* article by Bruce Falconer.
31. Compare to Hendin (1997).
32. p. 111.
33. I have a similar reaction to a Dutch physician who, according to Herbert Hendin's (1997) *Seduced by Death*, described euthanasia as "dignified, beautiful, and peaceful, almost festive" (p. 126).
34. Camus (1957).
35. Ibid., p. 25.
36. For example, L. Dahmer (1995).
37. Dahmer describes his reactions in, among other places, the 1994 interviews conducted by Stone Phillips and shown in the documentary film *Jeffrey Dahmer: Confessions of a Serial Killer*.
38. Act IV, Scene 1.
39. Wortman (2006), p. 221.
40. Sullivan (1953), p. 7.
41. Freud (1920) wrote about a death instinct in, among other places, *Beyond the Pleasure Principle*.
42. Menninger (1938), p. 24.
43. Mitani et al. (2010).
44. Cullen (2009).
45. Ibid.
46. Compare to Skeem et al. (2011).
47. Dalrymple (2005).
48. For example, Skeem et al. (2011).
49. Dewey (2004), p. 110.
50. Ibid., pp. 82–83.
51. Wortman (2006), p. 192.
52. Grossman (1995), p. 234.
53. Ibid.
54. *The New Yorker*, May 4, 2009, p. 40.
55. Hatzfield (2005), pp. 213–214.
56. Camus (1957), p. 23.
57. Described in the July 27, 2009, *New Yorker*, pp. 33–35.
58. As to why it follows that, given that one has nothing to lose, one therefore should kill others, as opposed to devoting oneself to charity, for example, Johnson offers little insight, unsurprisingly.
59. Some object to the use of the term "suicide by cop," in part because it is too colloquial for such a grave matter—a point of

view with which I am in sympathy. However, I am aware of no other apt terms; the terms "suicide by police," "police-assisted suicide," and "victim-precipitated homicide" all have short-comings that, in my judgment, exceed those of "suicide by cop."

60. Joiner, Petty, Perez, Sachs-Ericsson, & Rudd (2008).
61. For example, Baumeister, Smart, & Boden (1996).

Chapter 3

1. The filmmakers also alerted police about anyone whom they thought was in danger.
2. Compare to Rosen (1975).
3. See Holm-Denoma et al. (2008).
4. There could be, however, in the case of someone who both desired to travel to India and was intimidated or otherwise afraid of some aspect of the trip.
5. Robins (1981).
6. Ronald Maris' (1981) *Pathways to Suicide* provides a compatible account.
7. Joiner (2010).
8. A summary of the case can be found in an Associated Press article posted on January 15, 2010, by Roger Alford.
9. The resolve required to enact this is considerable, another illustration that serious suicidal behavior is characterized by factors like intent, planfulness, and resolve.
10. Regarding life insurance, it is worth emphasizing that the usual policy is structured so that benefits are paid in the event of suicide, as long as the death occurs more than two years after the policy is issued—a reasonable approach in my opinion, in that life insurance companies have chosen to pay benefits for suicides as for other deaths—just as they should—but are protected from people who have decided on suicide from taking out a policy one day and dying by suicide the next. The Census worker's policies—for accidental/homicidal death only—represent a relatively unusual form of life insurance.
11. Joiner (2005).
12. The incident is described in a June 1, 2009, *New York Post* article by Clemente Lisi.

13. Quote is from an interview aired on *This American Life* on March 29, 2002.

14. Sheehan-Miles (2008), p. 81.

15. Minois (1999).

16. The case is described in an article available in the *New York Times* archive, dated May 27, 2004, at http://www.nytimes. com/2004/05/27/us/execution-for-man-who-sought-death.html.

17. West (1966) described some similar cases.

18. It should be remembered, however, that death by suicide is more common than death by homicide. A related question, which is very hard to answer given current surveillance practices and data, is whether serious violence to others in general (e.g., assault, rape) is more common than serious violence to self (e.g., non-lethal suicide attempt). On the logic elucidated in this passage, I would predict that serious other-directed violence is more common than serious self-directed violence.

19. p. 54; Koestler had his own credibility problems, it should be acknowledged, and furthermore was likely misled by the psychoanalytic view that suicide is merely "aggression turned inward."

20. Joiner (2005); Van Orden et al. (2010).

21. Pascal (1670); the quote is from the 148th *pensée*.

22. Compare to Van Orden et al. (2010).

23. For example, Beck et al. (1985).

24. For example, Shneidman (1996).

25. For example, Kessler et al. (2003).

26. For example, Joiner et al. (2002).

27. Quote is from an interview aired on *This American Life* on March 29, 2002.

28. For example, Joiner et al. (2002).

29. Nearing (1992), p. 183.

30. Cleckley (1941), p. 306.

31. Hamilton (1964).

32. This has been viewed as the third most important contribution to evolutionary thought, behind those of Darwin and Mendel, but, in a decision that should give Ph.D. students both pause and hope, the originator's dissertation committee did not appreciate the contribution and deemed it "insufficient" as a dissertation. Richard Dawkins' (1976) *The Selfish Gene* popularized a compatible account. Eminent evolutionary biologist E. O. Wilson has

recently dissented from this viewpoint, a change of heart that has produced considerable controversy and debate (see Nowak et al., 2010).

33. See, for example, McAllister et al. (1990).

34. See Shorter & Rueppell (2012).

35. McAllister et al. (1990).

36. It should be acknowledged, however (and will be more fully in Chapter 8 on the perversion of glory), that some have argued that suicide terrorism *is* motivated by personal feelings of hopelessness and emotional pain.

37. DeAngelo et al. (1990).

38. Ibid.

39. That self-injury can be calming may seem quite paradoxical but it is nevertheless quite true, and is the major reason that people engage in this type of behavior. The calming effects represent the opponent process; through repetition, people habituate to the negative effects of the behavior, such as pain and fear.

40. See Favazza (1996).

41. Minois (1999).

42. James (1910), p. 1.

43. p. 56.

44. The video can be found in a story about the work of Princeton biologist John Bonner at http://www.princeton.edu/main/news/archive/S26/40/89S11/index.xml?section=featured.

45. Heinze & Walter (2010), p. 249.

46. The researchers showed, by the way, that this is unlikely the result of the fungus deranging the ants' nervous system, because the same behavior occurred in ants exposed to 95% carbon dioxide in laboratory settings, and was observed time and again in the wild. In the researchers' words, all ants under clear mortality threat "exhibited the same suite of behavior of isolating themselves from their nestmates days or hours before death. Actively leaving the nest and breaking off all social interactions thus occurred regardless of whether individuals were infected or not."

47. For example, Rudd et al. (2006).

48. The passage is on p. 26 of the 1977 Signet Classics edition of the novel.

Chapter 4

1. Bartram (1791), pp. 45–46.
2. Peterson & Seligman (2004).
3. Ibid., p. 13.
4. Elder (2010), p. 258.
5. Ibid., p. 206.
6. Ibid., p. 183.
7. Darwin (1871), p. 101.
8. Vaillant (2010), p. 136.
9. Brosnan & de Waal (2003).
10. A sense of justice is present in eight-month-old human infants. To demonstrate this, researchers showed babies different puppet shows. In some shows, the puppets behaved prosocially; in others, antisocially; and in still others, puppets were shown either rewarding or punishing the prosocially or antisocially behaving puppets. Which were the babies' favorite puppets (as indexed by which puppets they reached for the most)? The puppets who punished antisocial acts (Hamlin et al., 2011).
11. Bartel et al. (2011).
12. These four virtues also can be viewed as summarizing the entirety of the interpersonal virtues. For example, in his Nobel acceptance speech (quoted at length later in the book), William Faulkner refers to the following: "love and honor and pity and pride and compassion and sacrifice." Faulkner's and other similar lists are covered well by the four virtues emphasized by the present framework.
13. Dalrymple (2008), p. 68.
14. For example, Raskin & Shaw (1988).
15. Cukrowicz & Joiner (2005).
16. Hardy (1940), p. 77.
17. Ferguson (1792), p. 258.
18. This appears on p. 125 of the 1977 Signet Classics edition of the novel. The slogan "War is peace, freedom is slavery, ignorance is strength" appears on p. 4 and throughout the rest of the novel.
19. In this, the justice–glory murder-suicide perpetrator resembles, to a degree, the suicide decedent who incidentally kills others in the process of suicide (e.g., the driving incident in Wyoming already noted).

20. Thomas Aquinas made this and related points throughout his *Summa Theologicae*.
21. Pyszczynski, Greenberg, & Solomon (1999).
22. Becker (1973), p. 99.
23. Quoted by Cleckley (1941), p. 415.
24. The apostrophe in DONT is not included on the flag.
25. For example, Haidt & Joseph (2008).
26. Haidt & Joseph (2008), p. 385.
27. For example, Ryan & Deci (2000); as with Terror Management Theory, the proponents of Self-Determination Theory have done an impressive job in putting the theory to challenging empirical tests. The theory has fared well in these tests and thus stands as corroborated (to use a favorite term of Sir Karl Popper's).
28. Hayek (1944), p. 232.
29. For example, Mischel, Ebbesen, & Zeiss (1972).
30. Work by Moffitt and colleagues is persuasively corroborative of the thesis that self-control as measured early in life predicts functioning later in life (e.g., Moffitt et al., 2011).
31. 2004.

Chapter 5

1. The quote can be found in the 1977 *Portable Nietzsche*, p. 127.
2. Marzuk et al. (1992).
3. Guileyardo et al. (1999).
4. Stack (1997).
5. Thomas Aquinas in *Summa Theologicae*, II-8, Q. 62, arts. 3-4.
6. Compare to Stack (1997).
7. Selzer (2002), pp. 134–135.
8. The article appeared on August 9, 2010.
9. Koestler (1957), p. 166.
10. This incident is described in a May 25, 2011, article by Richard Marosi and Don Bartletti in the *Los Angeles Times*.
11. This observation regarding alcohol is consistent with the fact that far more than half of suicide decedents have a blood alcohol level of 0.00%—a fact, as noted above, that is underappreciated.
12. If her testimony is to be believed, she fully intended her own death; some do not believe her, and a trial is pending as of 2012.

This incident is described in a March 12, 2010, Associated Press article by Jennifer Peltz.

13. Devji (2005), pp. 37–38.
14. In the study by Stack (1997), mentioned earlier, approximately 12% of the murder-suicides involved parents and children.
15. The incident is described in a July 17, 201,0 article by Brandon Formby in the *Dallas Morning News*.
16. Not a terribly rare occurrence in that about 1 in 10 self-inflicted gunshot wounds are non-lethal (e.g., Selden et al., 1988).
17. The incident is described in a July 29, 2010, article by Karen Zraick in the *New York Times*.
18. The incident is described in an April 14, 2011, article by Daniel Bates and Mark Duell in the *Daily Mail*.
19. See Koren & Negev (2006).
20. Ibid., p. 213.
21. See Sheybani (1987).
22. Why not simply let the cows go free? The man may have been concerned that this would be an abrogation of duty. As described in the March 2012 issue of *Esquire*, a man in Zanesville, Ohio, did in fact let his animals free before his death by suicide, which decision created an enormous burden on local law enforcement. A major aspect of this burden was that the animals included several each of tigers, lions, and bears.
23. The sad tale of the dairy farmer ended with the burial of the cows on his farm, the difficult work for which his community pulled together to accomplish. This fact led some to question why the meat could not have been used instead, for example, in animal feed. The answer is that the cows were not killed according to regulations, and so could not be used in that manner; moreover, the community understood that there was a disturbing scene to handle as quickly as possible, so they took action to do so, to their credit. The incident is described in a January 24, 2010, article in the *Register Star* newspaper by Jamie Larson.
24. Dewey (2004), p. 205.

Chapter 6

1. See Judt (2005), p. 106.
2. Gilligan (1997), p. 11.

3. The choice of the codename "Geronimo" was offensive to many in that it equated bin Laden and a Native American hero. This was one of very few poor choices made in the entire operation.

4. The statement appears in Book XXII.

5. See Simms (1811), p. 337.

6. The quote is from the *Controversiae*, Book I.

7. *Protagoras* 324.

8. Roth (2009), pp. 450–451.

9. The incident is described in an August 5, 2010, Associated Press article by Stephen Singer.

10. The letter is dated February 22, 1787; a scanned version of the original letter is available through the Library of Congress website at http://memory.loc.gov/cgi-bin/ampage?collId=mtj1&fileName=mtj1page006.db&recNum=1250.

11. Letter to William Smith, November 13, 1787, available at Library of Congress website.

12. A similar view was put forth by Lord Acton, cited by F. A. Hayek in the often-misunderstood (because often unread) *The Road to Serfdom*: "at all times sincere friends of freedom have been rare, and its triumphs have been due to minorities, that have prevailed by associating themselves with auxiliaries whose objects often differed from their own; and this association, which is always dangerous, has sometimes been disastrous" (p. 42 of Caldwell edition of *The Road to Serfdom*).

13. A definitive treatment of McVeigh and his crime was provided by Michel and Herbeck (2001); see also Meloy (2004).

14. Lincoln had likely encountered these words, from Madison: "If men were angels, no government would be necessary" (see Brookhiser, 2011).

15. Camus (1957), pp. 18–19.

16. I have mentioned this very useful book a few times and will have occasion to mention it again. In the Internet age, books are remarkably easy to purchase, some more than others. Rather inane books are a click or two away, often costing a few cents (plus shipping and handling). Not so with *The Final Months* (or with Hervey Cleckley's equally accomplished *The Mask of Sanity*), leading me to suggest the possibility of a small negative correlation between quality of books and ease of access.

17. This incident is described in a June 7, 2007, Associated Press report by Lindsey Baguio.

18. The incidents in Japan and Massachusetts are described in the same *New York Times* piece mentioned in text, which appeared on June 18, 2011, and was authored by Erica Goode.

19. Robins (1981).

20. Ibid., p. 236.

21. Ibid.

22. Ibid., p. 235.

23. Joiner (2005).

24. For example, Vandello, Bosson, Cohen, Burnaford, & Weaver (2008).

25. On the point of "losable resource," notice the title of the paper in question: "Precarious manhood." The paper, by Vandello and colleagues, appeared in a 2008 issue of the *Journal of Personality & Social Psychology*.

26. This appears on p. 86 of the 1862 edition published by Sheldon & Co.

27. Brosnan & de Waal (2003).

28. Peterson & Seligman (2004).

29. Dewey (2004).

30. Ibid., p. 88.

31. Dalrymple (2001), pp. 42–43.

32. This incident is described in a May 9, 2009, Associated Press report by Kate Brumback.

33. This incident is described in an April 3, 2009, article in the *Daily Mail* by Sarah Knapton.

34. The incident is described in a February 9, 2010, article in the *Orlando Sentinel* by Henry Pierson Curtis and Willoughby Mariano.

35. The incident was described in a December 20, 2010, in an unattributed article by the Associated Press.

36. The panel took place at the annual meeting of the American Association of Suicidology in 2010.

37. This incident was described in an unattributed August 5, 2009, article in the *Pittsburgh Post-Gazette*.

38. My only quibble with Orwell on this point—and I for one do not take quibbling with Orwell lightly—is that fearlessness would be required even if very lethal means *were* easily available. The

quote appears on p. 102 of the 1977 Signet Classics edition of the novel.

39. A March 26, 2010, report on the incident is available at http://www.news10.net/news/local/story.aspx?storyid=78210.
40. *Columbus Dispatch*, August 10, 2009.
41. This incident is described in a July 8, 2009, article in the *Nashville City Paper* by Nate Rau.
42. This incident is described in a May 31, 2011, Associated Press report.
43. Güroğlu et al. (2010).
44. Young et al. (2010).
45. Adding precision and correction to an assertion in the July 2011 *Harper's Magazine* "Findings" section that "The sense of justice resides in the amygdala."
46. Of course extensive media coverage of this incident is available via several news outlets (e.g., an April 17, 2007, article in the *New York Times* by Brian Knowlton).
47. This incident is described in a January 15, 2005, *New York Times* article by Laurie Goodstein.

Chapter 7

1. As described in the opening pages of Richard Miles' 2011 history of Carthage, *Carthage Must Be Destroyed*.
2. Dalrymple (2001), p. 125.
3. The details of the burial were widely reported, including in a May 2, 2011, *New York Times* article by John Leland and Elisabeth Bumiller.
4. Not to imply, alas, that American service members are exempt from this kind of behavior; they are not (e.g., a video surfaced in January 2012 showing American Marines urinating on enemy dead in Afghanistan; the details of this latter incident are described in a January 12, 2012, article in the *New York Times* by Graham Bowley and Matthew Rosenberg).
5. Robins (1981), p. 139.
6. Ibid.
7. Ibid.
8. A description of this May 2010 incident is available at http://www.kdlt.com/index.php?option=com_content&task=view&id=2694&Itemid=57.

9. Daly & Wilson (1994).
10. See Joiner (2010), p. 165.

Chapter 8

1. Cullen (2009).
2. In addition to the Secret Service report footnoted earlier, a useful report on the Columbine tragedy is available at http://www.state.co.us/columbine/Columbine_20Report_WEB.pdf. Cullen's book, however, is the definitive source on the perpetrators' state of mind.
3. An important fact, because the perpetrators of bullying are as vulnerable to mental health problems as the victims of bullying (Klomek et al., 2007).
4. William Bartram, writing in the late 1700s of the Native people he encountered: "[they] make war against, kill, and destroy their own species, and their motives spring from the same erroneous source as they do in all other nations of mankind; that is, the ambition of exhibiting to their fellows a superior character of personal and national valour, and thereby immortalizing themselves..." (p. 183).
5. Roosevelt gave his "Strenuous Life" speech in Chicago on April 10, 1889, and the speech was later published along with other of Roosevelt's writings and speeches as a 1900 book entitled *The Strenuous Life*.
6. James (1903), p. 267.
7. The young man who shot Congresswoman Gabrielle Giffords and many others in January 2011 harbored similar fantasies (*Harper's Magazine*, March 2011). For what it is worth, I personally have never observed such fantasies in a non-psychopathic person.
8. Cullen (2009).
9. Compare to Large et al. (2010).
10. Merari et al. (2009).
11. See also Merari (2010).
12. The quote is from a February 24, 2010, article by Tom Jacobs in *Miller-McCune*, which has recently changed its name to *Pacific Standard*. Regarding Kruglanski's scholarship on this topic see also, for example, Kruglanski et al. (2009).

Chapter 9

1. Media coverage of this incident is available from several news outlets (e.g., a December 30, 2008, *New York Times* article by Solomon Moore). This incident is distinct from that which occurred in December 2011 in Grapeville, Texas, in which a man dressed as Santa Claus killed six relatives before killing himself. This 2011 incident was a genuine murder-suicide.

2. Eduard Shevardnadze, former foreign minister of the USSR and subsequently President of Georgia, wrote in 1991 (concerning a different topic): "The executioner has always been preceded by the inquisitor, the axe and block foreshadowed by the dogmas of faith" (p. 21).

3. Recent theorizing and empirical work point to the confluence of three traits in psychopathy: disinhibition, boldness, and meanness (Skeem et al., 2011).

4. Coverage of the incident is available in a June 3, 2007, *Boston Globe* article by Megan Woolhouse and Mac Daniel. Peixoto's brother died by suicide about a year later, also after having killed someone else (as described in an unattributed Associated Press article dated April 24, 2008).

5. Grossman (1995), p. 241.

6. This appears on p. 102 of the 1977 Signet Classics edition of the novel.

7. A fall from two stories can prove fatal; in a study by Türk & Tsokos (2004), no deaths by suicide by falls occurred from below two stories.

8. The incident is described in an April 8, 2009, article by Sewell Chan and Mick Meenan in the *New York Times*.

9. March 25, 2009, *Straits Capital News (Haixia Dushi Bao)*.

10. See Joiner (2010).

11. The incident is described in an April 28, 2010, article in the *Virginian-Pilot* by Kristin Davis.

12. The idea that one can get fully or near-fully used to the idea of causing one's own death is, I suggest, both peculiar and true (thus the need for book-length explanations of such phenomena as in my previous books *Why People Die By Suicide* [2005] and *Myths About Suicide* [2010]). Dostoevsky wrote, "Man is a creature who can get used to anything, and I believe that is the

very best way of defining him" (*Memoirs from the House of the Dead*, p. 9).

13. The case is described in an article available in the *New York Times* archive, dated May 27, 2004, at http://www.nytimes.com/2004/05/27/us/execution-for-man-who-sought-death.html.

14. This incident is described in a May 11, 2010, article by Stan Finger in the *Wichita Eagle*.

Chapter 10

1. It is not that the question is a bad one—quite the contrary, it most definitely should be asked. The problem is that it will not always be answered honestly, especially by people harboring plans involving murder.

2. Compare to Rudd et al. (2006); West (1966).

3. In his *Travels*, written in the 1700s, William Bartram describes a man who has threatened to shoot his wife "and afterwards put an end to his own life." In the same sentence, Bartram describes the man as "emaciated" (p. 110). The incident in Mahopac is described in a November 19, 2011, article in the *Lower Hudson* by Terrence Corcoran and Brian Howard.

4. For example, Mackintosh, Kumar, & Kitamura (1983).

5. For example, Karson et al. (1981).

6. I would venture to guess that Woods' total number of blinks per round of golf has increased in the wake of his personal problems and decreased golf performance, and that, should he return to his previous level of golf performance, his blink rate will decrease.

7. Mackintosh et al. (1983).

8. Psychiatrists who evaluated Anders Behring Breivik, the murderer in 2011 of 77 of his fellow Norwegians, described his blink rate similarly.

9. Appendix N (on p. N-5) of the Governor of Virginia's Virginia Tech Review panel report, which appeared in August 2007.

10. Michel & Herbeck (2001).

11. The neighbor believed Hasan was referring to an upcoming deployment. A definitive and comprehensive report on the Ft. Hood incident is available at http://www.defense.gov/pubs/pdfs/DOD-ProtectingTheForce-Web_Security_HR_13jan10.pdf.

12. For example, Conner et al. (2001).

13. Cohen & Eisdorfer (2011), p. 221.

14. This incident was described in a May 27, 2011, report for the *Orlando Sentinel* by David Breen and Jeff Weiner.

15. For example, Fitzgerald et al. (2003).

16. This statement could be broadened to include other kinds of programs, such as the National Suicide Prevention Lifeline (1-800-273-TALK [8255]), the website of which is at http://www.suicidepreventionlifeline.org/. Among many other positive contributions, this organization has partnered with Facebook so that users can anonymously report a Facebook friend's expression of suicidal intentions. The person making the suicidal comment then receives an immediate email from Facebook encouraging him or her to call 1-800-273-TALK (8255) or to click on a link that will initiate a confidential chat session with a crisis worker.

Chapter 11

1. Dalrymple (2011), p. 182.

2. There are numerous available sources on this incident; one that I found instructive appeared in the July/August 2011 issue of *Atlantic Monthly*.

3. Whitman quotes are from the July/August 2011 issue of *Atlantic Monthly*, p. 112, 114.

4. This incident is described in an April 11, 2009, *New York Times* article by Manny Fernandez and Nate Schweber.

5. The letter's last line reads, "AND YOU HAVE A NiCE DAY."

6. Bleuler (1911/1987).

7. Ibid., p. 122.

8. The incident is described in an unattributed April 4, 2010, Associated Press report.

9. Peterson & Seligman (2004).

10. For example, Haidt & Joseph (2008).

11. Compare to Robins (1981).

12. Thomson (1985).

13. In our laboratory at FSU, for example, we manipulated social exclusion and showed that the manipulation predicted a lab-based proxy for self-injury involving self-administered shock, particularly for people who were fearless of bodily ordeal.

References

Alden, T. (1814). *A collection of American epitaphs and inscriptions, with occasional notes.* New York: S. Marks.

Anderson, C., & Anderson, D. (1984). Ambient temperature and violent crime: Test of the linear and curvilinear hypotheses. *Journal of Personality & Social Psychology, 46,* 91–97.

Atran, S. (2003). The genesis of suicide terrorism. *Science, 299,* 1534–1539.

Ball, H. (2012). *At liberty to die.* New York: NYU Press.

Bandura, A. (1999). Moral disengagement in the perpetuation of inhumanities. *Personality & Social Psychology Review, 3,* 193–209.

Barber, C., Azrael, D., Hemenway, D., Olson, L., Nie, C., Schaechter, J., & Walsh, S. (2008). Suicides and suicide attempts following homicide: Victim-suspect relationship, weapon type, and presence of antidepressants. *Homicide Studies, 12,* 285–297.

Bartel, I., Decety, J., & Mason, P. (2011). Empathy and pro-social behavior in rats. *Science, 334,* 1427–1430.

Bartram, W. (1791/1928). *The travels of William Bartram.* New York: Dover.

Baudelaire, C. (1868). *Fleurs de mal.* Paris: Poulet-Malassis et De Broise.

Baumeister, R. F. (1996). *Evil.* New York: W. H. Freeman.

Baumeister, R. F., Smart, L., & Boden, J. M. (1996). Relation of threat-ened egotism to violence and aggression: the dark side of high self-esteem. *Psychological Review, 103,* 5–33.

Becker, E. (1973). *The denial of death.* New York: Free Press.

Bleuler, E. (1911/1987). *Dementia praecox.* Madison, CT: International Universities Press.

Bohrer, S., Kern, H., & Davis, E. (2008, March). The deadly dilemma: Shoot or don't shoot? *The FBI Law Enforcement Bulletin, 77,* 7–12.

Bowker, G. (2003). *George Orwell.* New York: Little, Brown.

Brookhiser, R. (2011). *James Madison.* New York: Basic Books.

Brosnan, S. F., & de Waal, F. B. M. (2003). Monkeys reject unequal pay. *Nature, 425,* 297–299.

Bushman, B., & Anderson, C. A. (2001). Is it time to pull the plug on the hostile versus instrumental aggression dichotomy? *Psychological Review, 108,* 273–279.

Buss, D. (2005). *The murderer next door.* New York: Penguin.

Camus, A. (1957). *Reflections on the guillotine.* Michigan City, IN: Fridtjof-Karla Publications.

Cleckley, H. (1941). *The mask of sanity.* St. Louis, MO: Mosby Co.

Cohen, D., & Eisdorfer, C. (2011). *Integrated textbook of geriatric mental health.* Baltimore, MD: Johns Hopkins University Press.

Cohen, D., Llorente, M., & Eisdorfer, C. (1998). Homicide-suicide in older persons. *American Journal of Psychiatry, 155,* 390–396.

Coid, J. (1983). The epidemiology of abnormal homicide and murder followed by suicide. *Psychological Medicine, 13,* 855–860.

Conner, K. R., Cox, C., Duberstein, P. R., Tian, L., Nisbet, P. A., & Conwell, Y. (2001). Violence, alcohol and completed sui-cide: a case-control study. *American Journal of Psychiatry, 158,* 1701–1705.

Cornell, D., Warren, J., Hawk, G., Stafford, E., Oram, G., & Pine, D. (1996). Psychopathy in instrumental and reactive violent offend-ers. *Journal of Consulting & Clinical Psychology, 64,* 783–790.

Covington, D. (1995). *Salvation on Sand Mountain.* New York: Penguin.

Crick, N., & Dodge, K. (1996). Social information-processing mecha-nisms in reactive and proactive aggression. *Child Development, 67,* 993–1002.

Cukrowicz, K., & Joiner, T. (2005). Treating the "mischances of character," simply and effectively. *Journal of Contemporary Psychotherapy, 35,* 157–168.

Cullen, D. (2009). *Columbine.* New York: 12 Books.

Dahmer, L. (1995). *A father's story: One man's anguish at confronting the evil in his son.* New York: Little, Brown.

Dalrymple, T. (2001). *Life at the bottom.* Chicago: Ivan R. Dee.

Dalrymple, T. (2005). *Our culture: What's left of it.* Chicago: Ivan R. Dee.

Dalrymple, T. (2008). *Not with a bang but a whimper.* Chicago: Ivan R. Dee.

Dalrymple, T. (2011). *Anything goes.* Leicstershire: Monday Books.

Daly, M., & Wilson, M. (1994). Differential attributes of lethal assaults on small children by stepfathers versus genetic fathers. *Ethology & Sociobiology, 15,* 207–217.

Daniels, A. (2011-03-31). *Fool or physician: The memoirs of a sceptical doctor (Kindle Locations 2520–2526).* Monday Books. Kindle Edition.

Darwin, C. (1871). *The descent of man.* London: John Murray.

Dawkins, R. (1976). *The selfish gene.* Oxford: Oxford University Press.

DeAngelo, M., Kish, V., & Kolmes, S. (1990). Altruism, selfishness, and heterocytosis in cellular slime molds. *Ethology, Ecology, & Evolution, 2,* 439–443.

Devji, F. (2005). *Landscapes of the Jihad.* Ithaca, NY: Cornell University Press.

Devji, F. (2008). *The terrorist in search of humanity.* New York: Columbia University Press.

Dewey, L., (2004). *War and redemption.* Burlington, VT: Ashgate.

Dickens, C. (1862). *Great expectations.* New York: Sheldon & Co.

Dostoevsky, F. (1862/2001). *Memoirs from the house of the dead.* Oxford: Oxford University Press.

Eliason, S. (2009). Murder-suicide: A review of the recent literature. *Journal of the American Academy of Psychiatry & Law, 37,* 371–376.

Favazza, A. (1996). *Bodies under siege.* Baltimore: Johns Hopkins University Press.

Feinstein, J. S., Adolphs, D., Damasio, A., & Tranel, D. (2010). The human amygdala and the induction and experience of fear, *Current Biology, 21,* 34–38.

Felthous, A., & Hempel, A. (1995). Combined homicide-suicides: A review. *Journal of Forensic Science, 40,* 846–857.

Ferguson, A. (1792). *Principles of moral and political science,* Volume II. Edinburgh: W. Greech.

Fischer, S., Huber, C., Imhof, L., Imhof, R., Furter, M., Zeigler, S., & Bosshard, G. (2008). Suicide assisted by two Swiss right-to-die organisations. *Journal of Medical Ethics, 34,* 810–814.

Fitzgerald, P., Brown, T., Marston, N., Daskalakis, J., de Castella, A., & Kulkarni, J. (2003). *Archives of General Psychiatry, 60,* 1002–1008.

Frankl, V. (1959). *Man's search for meaning.* Boston: Beacon Press.

Freud, S. (1920/1960). *Beyond the pleasure principle.* New York: Norton.

Gilligan, J. (1997). *Violence: Reflections on a national epidemic.* Berkeley, CA: University of California Press.

Güroğlu, B., van den Bos, W. Rombouts, A. R. B., & Crone, E. (2010). Unfair? It depends: Neural correlates of fairness in social context. *Social Cognitive and Affective Neuroscience, 5,* 414–423.

Grossman, D. (1995). *On killing.* New York: Little, Brown.

Guileyardo, J., Prahlow, J., & Barnard, J. (1999). Familial filicide and filicide classification. *American Journal of Forensic Medicine & Pathology, 20,* 286–292.

Haidt, J. (2012). *The righteous mind.* New York: Pantheon.

Haidt, J., & Joseph, C. (2008). Evolution and cognition. In P. Carruthers, S. Laurence, & S. Stitch (Eds.). *The innate mind, Volume 3: Foundations and the future* (pp. 367–391). New York: Oxford University Press.

Hames, J., Ribeiro, J., Smith, A., & Joiner, T. (2011). An urge to jump affirms the urge to live: An empirical examination of the high place phenomenon. *Journal of Affective Disorders.* Epub 2011 Nov 25.

Hamilton, W. (1964). The genetical evolution of social behavior, I and II. *Journal of Theoretical Biology, 7,* 1–52.

Hamlin, K., Wynn, K., Bloom, P., & Mahajan, N. (2011). How infants and toddlers react to antisocial others. *Proceedings of the National Academy of Science, 108,* 19931–19936.

Hardy, G. H. (1940). *A mathematician's apology.* Cambridge: Cambridge University Press.

Harris, L., & Fiske, S. (2011). Dehumanized perception: A psychological means to facilitate atrocities, torture, and genocide? *Zeitschrift für Psychologie/Journal of Psychology, 219,* 175–181.

Hatzfield, J. (2005). *A time for machetes.* New York: Farrar, Straus and Giroux.

Hayek, F. A. (1944). *The road to serfdom.* New York: Routledge & Sons.

Heinze, J., & Walter, B. (2010). Moribund ants leave the nest to die. *Current Biology, 20,* 249–252.

Hempel, A., Meloy, J. R., & Richards, T. (1999). Offender and offense characteristics of a nonrandom sample of mass murderers. *Journal of the American Academy of Psychiatry & the Law, 27,* 213–225.

Hendin, H. (1997). *Seduced by death.* New York: Norton.

Herbert, W. (2010). *On second thought.* New York: Crown.

Holm-Denoma, J. M., Witte, T. K., Gordon, K. H., Herzog, D. B., Franko, D. L., Fichter, M., Quaflieg, N., & Joiner, T. E. (2008). Deaths by suicide among individuals with anorexia as arbiters between competing explanations of the anorexia-suicide link. *Journal of Affective Disorders, 107,* 231–236.

Huxley, T. H., & Huxley, L. (1916). *The life and letters of Thomas Henry Huxley,* Vol. 1. New York: D. Appleton.

Isbell, L. (2010). *The fruit, the tree, and the serpent: why we see so well.* Cambridge, MA: Harvard University Press.

James, W. (1903). *The varieties of religious experience.* New York: Longmans, Green & Co.

James, W. (1910). *The moral equivalent of war, and other essays: and selections from some problems in philosophy.* New York: Harper & Row.

Jamison, K. R. (1995). *An unquiet mind.* New York: Random House.

Jaynes, J. (1976). *The origin of consciousness in the breakdown of the bicameral mind.* New York: Houghton Mifflin.

Jenyns, S. (1756). *A free enquiry into the nature and origin of evil.* Pall-Mall: J. Dodsley.

Joiner, T. (2005). *Why people die by suicide.* Cambridge, MA: Harvard University Press.

Joiner, T. (2010). *Myths about suicide.* Cambridge, MA: Harvard University Press.

Joiner, T. (2011). *Lonely at the top.* New York: Macmillan Palgrave.

Joiner, T., Pettit, J. W., Walker, R. L., Voelz, Z. R., Cruz, J., Rudd, M. D., & Lester, D. (2002). Perceived burdensomeness and suicidality: Two studies on the suicide notes of those attempting and those completing suicide. *Journal of Social & Clinical Psychology, 21*, 531–545.

Joiner, T., Petty, S., Perez, M., Sachs-Ericsson, N., & Rudd, M. D. (2008). Depressive symptoms induce paranoid symptoms in narcissistic personalities (but not narcissistic symptoms in paranoid personalities). *Psychiatry Research, 159*, 237–244.

Judt, T. (2005). *Postwar.* New York: Penguin.

Judt, T. (2010). *The memory chalet.* New York: Penguin.

Kahnneman, D. (2011). *Thinking, fast and slow.* New York: Farrar, Straus and Giroux.

Karson, C., Berman, K., Donnelly, E., Mendelson, W., Kleinman, J., & Wyatt, R. J. (1981). Speaking, thinking, and blinking. *Psychiatry Research, 5*, 243–246.

Kessler, R., Berglund, P., Demler, O., Jin, R., Koretz, D., Merikangas, K., Rush, A. J., Walters, E., & Wang, P. (2003). The epidemiology of major depressive disorder: Results from the National Comorbidity Survey Replication (NCS-R). *Journal of the American Medical Association, 289*, 3095–3105.

Klomek, A., Marrocco, F., Kleinman, M., Schonfeld, I., & Gould, M. (2007). Bullying, depression, and suicidality in adolescents. *Journal of the American Academy of Child & Adolescent Psychiatry, 46*, 40–49.

Koestler, A. (1957). *Reflections on hanging.* New York: Macmillan.

Koren, Y., & Negev, E. (2006). *Lover of unreason: The biography of Assia Wevill.* London: Robson Books.

Krakauer, J. (1996). *Into the wild.* New York: Anchor.

Krakauer, J. (2003). *Under the banner of heaven.* New York: Doubleday.

Kruglanski, A., Chen, X., Dechesne, M., Fishman, S., & Orehek, S. (2009). Fully committed: Suicide bombers' motivation and the quest for personal significance. *Political Psychology, 30*, 331–357.

Large, M., Smith, G., & Nielssen, O. (2010). The epidemiology of homicide followed by suicide: A systematic and quantitative review. *Suicide & Life-Threatening Behavior, 39*, 294–306.

Liem, M., & Nieuwbeerta, P. (2010). Homicide followed by suicide: A comparison with homicide and suicide. *Suicide & Life-Threatening Behavior, 40*, 133–145.

Liem, M., & Roberts, D. (2009). Intimate partner violence by presence of absence of a self-destructive act. *Homicide Studies, 13,* 339–354.

Linde, P. (2010). *Danger to self.* Berkeley: University of California Press.

Logan, J., Hill, H., Black, M., Crosby, A., Karch, D., Barnes, J., & Lubell, K. (2008). Characteristics of perpetrators in homicide-followed-by-suicide incidents: National Violent Death Reporting System-17 U.S. States, 2003-2005. *American Journal of Epidemiology, 168,* 1056–1064.

Mackintosh, J. H., Kumar, R., & Kitamura, T. (1983). Blink rate in psychiatric illness. *British Journal of Psychiatry, 143,* 55–57.

Malphurs, J., & Cohen, D. (2005). A statewide case-control study of spousal homicide-suicide in older persons. *Amercan Journal of Geriatric Psychiatry, 13,* 211–217.

Maris, R. (1981). *Pathways to suicide.* Baltimore: Johns Hopkins University Press.

Marzuk, P., Tardiff, K., & Hirsch, C. (1992). The epidemiology of murder-suicide. *Journal of the American Medical Association, 267,* 3179–3183.

Masters, A. (2006). *Stuart: A life backwards.* New York: HarperCollins.

McAllister, M., Roitberg, B., & Weldon, K. (1990). Adaptive suicide in pea aphids: Decisions are cost-sensitive. *Animal Behaviour, 40,* 167–175.

Meloy, J. R. (1999). Predatory violence during mass murder. *Journal of Forensic Sciences, 42,* 326–329.

Meloy, J. R. (2004). Indirect personality assessment of the violent true believer. *Journal of Personality Assessment, 82,* 138–146.

Meloy, J. R. (2006). Empirical basis and forensic application of affective and predatory violence. *Australian & New Zealand Journal of Psychiatry, 40,* 539–547.

Merari, A., Diamant, I., Bibi, A., Broshi, Y., & Zakin, G. (2009). Personality characteristics of "self martyrs"/"suicide bombers" and organizers of suicide attacks. *Terrorism & Political Violence, 22,* 87–101.

Merari, A. (2010). *Driven to death.* New York: Oxford University Press.

Menninger, K. (1938). *Man against himself.* New York: Harcourt, Brace, Jovanovich.

Michel, L., & Herbeck, D. (2001). *American terrorist.* New York: Regan Books.

Miles, R. (2011). *Carthage must be destroyed.* New York: Viking.

Milroy, C. (1995). The epidemiology of homicide-suicide (dyadic death). *Forensic Science International, 71,* 117–122.

Minois, G. (1999). *A history of suicide.* Baltimore: Johns Hopkins.

Mischel, W., Ebbesen, E., & Zeiss, A. (1972). Cognitive and attentional mechanisms in delay of gratification. *Journal of Personality & Social Psychology, 21,* 204–218.

Mitani, J., Watts, D., & Amsler, S. (2010). Lethal intergroup aggression leads to territorial expansion in wild chimpanzees. *Current Biology, 20,* R507–R508.

Moffitt, T., Arseneault, L., Belsky, D., Dickson, N., Hancox, R., Harrington, H., Houts, R., Poulton, R., Roberts, B., Ross, S., Sears, M., Thomson, W. M., & Caspi, A. (2011). A gradient of childhood self-control predicts health, wealth, and public safety. *Proceedings of the National Academy of Science, 108,* 2693–2698.

Monahan, J. (2012). The individual risk assessment of terrorism. *Psychology, Public Policy, & Law, 18,* 167–205.

Nearing, H. (1992). *Loving and leaving the good life.* White River Junction, VT: Chelsea Green Publishing Company.

Nowak, M., Tarnita, C., & Wilson, E.O. (2010). The evolution of eusociality. *Nature, 466,* 1057–1062.

Pape, R. (2003). The strategic logic of suicide terrorism. *American Political Science Review, 97*(3), 1–19.

Pascal, B. (1670/1995). *Pensées.* Oxford: Oxford University Press.

Peterson, C., & Seligman, M. (2004). *Character strengths and virtues.* New York: Oxford.

Pyszczynski, T., Greenberg, J., & Solomon, S. (1999). A dual-process model of defense against conscious and unconscious death-related thoughts: An extension of terror management theory. *Psychological Review, 106,* 835–845.

Raskin, R., & Shaw, R. (1988). Narcissism and the use of personal pronouns. *Journal of Personality, 56,* 393–404.

Robins, E. (1981). *The final months.* Oxford: Oxford University Press.

Rosen, D. (1975). A follow-up study of persons who survived jumping form the Golden Gate and San Francisco-Oakland Bay bridges. *Western Journal of Medicine, 122,* 289–294.

Roth, R. (2009). *American homicide.* Cambridge, MA: Harvard University Press.

Rudd, M. D., Berman, A., Joiner, T., Nock, M., Mandrusiak, M., Van Orden, K., & Witte, T. (2006). Warning signs for suicide: Theory, research, and clinical applications. *Suicide & Life-Threatening Behavior, 36,* 255–271.

Ryan, R., & Deci, E. (2000). Self-determination theory and the facilitation of intrinsic motivation, social development, and well-being. *American Psychologist, 55,* 68–78.

Santayana, G. (1905). *The life of reason.* New York: Dover.

Selden, B., Goodman, J., Cordell, W., Rodman, G., & Schnitzer, P. (1988). Outcome of self-inflicted gunshot wounds of the brain. *Annals of Emergency Medicine, 17,* 247–253.

Selzer, R. (2002). *The exact location of the soul.* New York: Picador.

Sheehan-Miles, C. (2008). How it feels to kill. In M. S. Robbins (Ed.), *Peace not terror,* pp. 79–86. Lanham, MD: Lexington Books.

Shevardnadze, E. (1991). *The future belongs to freedom.* London: The Free Press.

Sheybani, M.-M. (1987). Cultural defense: One person's culture is another's crime. *Loyola of Los Angeles International and Comparative Law Review, 9,* 751–783.

Shneidman, E. S. (1996). *The suicidal mind.* Oxford: Oxford University Press.

Shorter, J., & Rueppell, O. (2012). A review on self-destructive defense behaviors in social insects. *Insectes Sociaux, 59,* 1–10.

Simms, W. G. (1811). *The life of Francis Marion.* New York: Cooledge & Brother.

Simon, G., & Savarino, J. (2007). Suicide attempts among patients starting depression treatment with medications of psychotherapy. *American Journal of Psychiatry, 164,* 1029–1034.

Skeem, J., Polaschek, D., Patrick, C., & Lilienfeld, S. (2011). Psychopathic personality: Bridging the gap between scientific evidence and public policy. *Psychological Science in the Public Interest, 12,* 95–162.

Solomon, R. L. (1980). The opponent-process theory of acquired motivation: The costs of pleasure and the benefits of pain. *American Psychologist, 35,* 691–712.

Solzhenitsyn, A. (1973). *The Gulag Archipelago.* New York: Harper & Row.

Spedding, J., Ellis, R. L., & Heath, D. D. (1869). *The works of Francis Bacon*. New York: Hurd.

Stack, S. (1997). Homicide followed by suicide: an analysis of Chicago data. *Criminology, 35,* 435–453.

Sullivan, H. S. (1953). *Conceptions of modern psychiatry*. New York: Norton.

Thomson, J. (1985). The trolley problem. *Yale Law Journal, 94,* 1395–1415.

Türk, E., & Tsokos, M. (2004). Pathologic features of falls from heights. *American Journal of Forensic Medicine & Pathology, 25,* 194–199.

Vaillant, J. (2010). *The tiger*. New York: Knopf.

Van Orden, K., Witte, T., Cukrowicz, K., Braithwaite, S., Selby, E., & Joiner, T. (2010). The interpersonal theory of suicide. *Psychological Review, 117,* 575–600.

van Wormer, K., & Odiah, C. (1999). The psychology of suicide-murder and the death penalty. *Journal of Criminal Justice, 27,* 361–370.

van Wormer, K., & Roberts, A. (2009). *Death by domestic violence*. Westport, CT: Greenwood.

Vandello, J. A., Bosson, J. K., Cohen, D., Burnaford, R. M., & Weaver, J. R. (2008). Precarious manhood. *Journal of Personality and Social Psychology, 95,* 1325–1339.

West, D. (1966). *Murder followed by suicide*. Cambridge, MA: Harvard University Press.

Wilson, E. (2010). *The mercy of eternity*. Evanston, IL: Northwestern University Press.

Wortman, M. (2006). *The millionaire's unit*. New York: Public Affairs.

Young, L., Camprodon, J., Hauser, M., Pascual-Leone, A., & Saxe, R. (2010). Disruption of the right temporoparietal junction with transcranial magnetic stimulation reduces the role of beliefs in moral judgments. *Proceedings of the National Academy of Science*, published ahead of print March 29, 2010, doi:10.1073/pnas.0914826107.

Zimring, F. (2011). *The city that became safe*. New York: Oxford University Press.

Index

Note: Page numbers followed by the letter "f" indicate material found in figures; page numbers followed by the letter "n" indicate material found in notes.

accidents
  deaths as, 102
  as perversion of fate, 181–186, 188
adrenaline, role of, 76
affective violence, 15
agitation. *See also* suicidal behavior
  in clinical assessment, 198
  physiological arousal and, 34
  suicide contemplation and, 129
  as warning sign/signal, 100, 166, 194–196, 204
Alanus, de Insulis, 14
alcohol, in murder-suicide, 29–31
"alienation" concept, 91–92, 96–99, 103, 158
ambivalence, 76, 79–81, 84, 86, 102
American Homicide (Roth), 46, 144
American Revolution, 146
amygdala/amygdala functioning, 22–23, 25, 204
analog experimental tests, 210–211
ancient fear module, 24–25
animals
  conflict avoidance among, 54–55
  killing of, 138–139, 169–170, 227n22, 227n23
Anything Goes (Dalrymple), 203
Aquinas, Thomas, 112, 124, 128

arousal
  in affective violence, 15
  physiological, 60–61
  suicide and, 34
asphyxiation, 79
assaults, on police officers, 57–58
assessments, in suicide prevention, 193
assisted suicide, 63–64
automatic fear response, 25
autonomy, 116–117, 210

Barber, C., 46
Baudelaire, Charles, 63
Baumeister, Roy, 62, 73
Beadle family incident, 3, 51, 130, 211
Beccaria, Cesare, 62
Beck, A. T., 90
Becker, Ernest, 113, 171
bereaved family members, 19, 78, 85, 96–97, 150
Biblical perspective, 118
Bin Laden, Osama, 132, 142, 164, 171
Bishop, Amy, 36–37
Blackwelder, John, 89–90
Bleuler, E., 207
blink rate, 195–196, 198, 233n6. *See also* suicidal behavior

blood alcohol content (BAC) data, 30–31
bludgeoning, 50
brain. See also opponent process
    amygdala functioning, 22–23, 24, 25
    temporoparietal junction activity,
        160–161, 200
    violent impulse and, 204
The Bridge (film), 75–76, 78–79, 83. See also
        Hines, Kevin
bridges, jumping from, 22–23
"burdensomeness" concept, 91–93, 96,
        99, 207

Cain and Abel, 67
Camus, Albert, 29, 62, 72, 146–147
care, perversion of, 167–168
caretakers, duty toward others, 165
cars, suicide in, 28, 184–187, 217n67
Character Strengths and Virtues: A
        Handbook and Classification
        (Peterson and Seligman), 106, 152
charity, as root of virtue, 124, 128
child abuse, 162, 168
children. See also parent/children
        murder-suicide
    avenging, 162
    injustice, perception of, 151–152
    killing of, 6–7, 132–133
    as victims, 42, 44, 50
chimps, lethal intergroup aggression in,
        67–68
Cho, Seung-Hui, 13, 158, 161–162, 196
Christ, comparisons to, 13
Cleckley, Hervey, 14, 21, 55, 93, 179
"Cleckley psychopaths," 179–180
clinicians, patients' suicides and, 19
Cohen, Donna, 127–128, 159, 200–201
collectivist virtues, 117–118
Columbine (Cullen), 172, 174
Columbine High School incident, 10–11, 68,
        146, 162, 171–174, 197, 209
Common Sense (Paine), 111
continuity of process, 34, 45
continuum of suicidality, 134
control, emphasis on, 179. See also
        perversion of self-control
"control"-related suicides, 159
corruption, perception of, 144
crisis negotiation, 201
Cullen, Dave, 172, 174
"cultural defense," 138
cyanide usage, 49–50

Dahmer, Jeffrey, 63, 65–66, 72
Dalrymple, Theodore, 59, 63, 110, 121, 153,
        163–164, 203

Daly, M., 167–168
Daniels, Anthony. See Dalrymple, Theodore
Darwin, Charles, 4, 25, 26, 108, 113, 213n5
day-of-week patterns, 28
de-escalation/negotiation, 201
deadly force, by law enforcement, 57–58
DeAngelo, M., 96
death. See also desire for death
    capability, 80–82
    fear of, 4, 56, 88
    "regularization of," 65
"Death Becomes Her" (Falconer), 63
Death by Domestic Violence (van Wormer
        and Roberts), 41
death instinct, 21, 113
death penalty, 89, 138
death wish, 21–24
Death with Dignity Act (Oregon), 5–6
"death worth more than life" calculation,
        95–96, 99, 103
decorum, justice and, 141–142
Dele, Bison, 35–37
Dementia Praecox (Bleuler), 207
demographics, of murder-suicide, 41–45
The Denial of Death (Becker), 113, 171
Department of Defense, 98
depersonalized incidents, 158–159
depressive illnesses/disorder
    in desire for death, 90–92
    in murder-suicide, 31
desire for death
    "alienation" concept in, 91–92, 96–99,
        103, 158
    "burdensomeness" concept in, 91–93, 96,
        99, 207
    "death worth more than life" calculation,
        95–96, 99, 103
    depressive disorder and, 90–92
    fearlessness and, 90
    inclusive fitness and, 93–96
    low self-esteem and, 92
    reason to live/die distinction, 90–91
    "self-destruct" mechanisms and, 93
    withdrawal and, 99–100
desire to die, 49, 76, 87, 133
desire to live, 76–77
Devji, Faisal, 132
Dewey, Larry, 56, 58, 70, 87, 139, 152
Dignitas, 64–65
domestic violence, 41, 201
Dostoevsky, Fyodor, 103, 153, 232–233n12
driving into oncoming traffic, 28, 184–187,
        217n67
duty. See also perversion of duty
    caretakers and, 165
    interpersonal nature of, 109–111

nature of, 163–164
sense of obligation and, 143

Ecclesiastes, Book of, 62
Elder, Robert, 107
Eliason, Scott, 29–30
Elliot, Carl, 83
Emerson, Ralph Waldo, 171–172
emotional pain, 90–93, 95
emotionality, temperament and, 68
empathy, derangement of, 112–118
"escalation of appetite," 63. *See also*
    opponent process
ethnic groups, killing among, 72
Evil (Baumeister), 62
evolutionary psychology, 167–168
The Exact Location of the Soul (Selzer),
    125
Exodus, Book of, 56, 108
experiments. *See* analog experimental tests
*The Expression of the Emotions in Man and
    Animals* (Darwin), 25
"eye-for-an-eye" concept, 108, 118
eyes. *See* "thousand-yard stare"

Facebook, 234n16
"fair deal," 152
Falconer, Bruce, 63
false-positive/false-negative scenarios, 198
The Family (cult), 162, 168
family violence, 127
far-away look. *See* "thousand-yard stare"
fate. *See* perversion of fate
Faulkner, William, 63, 176, 202, 209, 211
Fawcett, Percy, 21
fear, ancient module of, 24–25
fear of death, 4, 56, 88
fear processing, 22, 204
fear response, 25
fearlessness
    learned, 86–89
    suicide and, 4, 158
Ferguson, Adam, 111
fiction, murder-suicide in, 153
fighter pilots' views, 70. *See also* military
    combatants/soldiers
The Final Months (Robins), 31, 42, 47–48,
    81, 100, 147, 165–166, 194
financial motives, 85
firearm usage, 47–48
first principles assumptions, 7, 11, 137, 174
"flash-in-the-pan" thoughts, 20–27
flinching, at last moment, 136
Frankl, Viktor, 64–65
freedom, 8, 111, 115, 210, 225n18, 228n12
Freud, Sigmund, 21, 67, 113

*The Fruit, the Tree, and the Serpent: Why
    We See So Well* (Isbell), 21–22
Ft. Hood incident, 13, 197
fumes, toxic, 147–149
future research, 210

Garcia, Stephen, 207–208
gender, in murder-suicide, 42–43, 131, 151
Genesis, Book of, 67, 74
Georgia Commission on Family
    Violence, 127
Gilligan, James, 141
global murder-suicide rates, 45–47
glory. *See also* perversion of glory
    derivation of, 176
    interpersonal nature of, 109–111
    nature of, 171–172
God
    intervention of, 58–59
    voice of, 24, 58–59, 87–88
Golden Gate Bridge, 18, 75–78, 80, 87
Good Samaritan, 75, 110, 143
"grand score," 150
Great Expectations (Dickens), 151
Grizzly Man (film), 101–102
Grossman, Dave, 56, 70, 180
Guileyardo, J., 122
"guillotine fever," 62
gun usage, 47–48

habituation, 61, 63, 65, 186, 224n39
Haidt, Jonathan, 115–116
Hames, J., 23–24
Hamlet (Shakespeare), 203
hand-binding, 84, 150
hanging, death by, 82–83, 84, 150–151
happiness, 90
Hardy, G. H., 4, 111
Harris, Eric, 10–11, 68, 171–174. *See also*
    Columbine High School incident
Harris, Thomas, 62–63
Hasan, Nidal Malik, 197
Hatzfield, Jean, 72
Hayek, F. A., 117–118, 228n12
health plans/public health, 19–20
Herbert, Wray, 24
heroism
    nature of, 171–172
    perversion of, 172–176
"high place phenomenon," 23–24, 26
Hines, Kevin, 76–81, 84
homicidal ideation, 197
"homicide-suicide," 28
honor, defense of, 151–152
Hoover, Herbert, 141
hopelessness, 90–92, 95

Hughes, Ted, 137
Huguenard, Amy, 101–102
human nature
    in clinical assessment, 199
    death wishes and, 23
    evil and, 66
    heroism in, 173
    incapacity to kill and, 60
    interpersonal virtues and, 115
    murder-suicide and, 54, 107
    psychopathy and, 69
Humane Borders, 146
humanitarianism, language of, 132
humility, murder-suicide perpetrators and,
    128
hunting, opponent process in, 71
Hutus, 71–72
Huxley, Thomas Henry, 4

"if-then" reasoning, 12
imagination, murder-suicide perpetrators
    and, 128
"impulsive suicide" myth, 16–20, 183
inclusive fitness, 93–96, 215n41
independent phenomena, 34–35
inflated self-concept, 73–74
insomnia, 100, 133, 166, 194, 196, 198. See
    also suicidal behavior
insurance, 222n10
intent/intention
    to die, 4, 76, 101–102, 134, 136
    in murder-suicide, 9
    transparency of, 20
international murder-suicide rates, 45–47
interpersonal virtues, 8, 12, 109–111,
    115–116, 210
intimate relationships, 41
Into the Wild (Krakauer), 102–103
intoxication, suicide and, 30
Isbell, Lynne, 21–22

James, William, 98, 173
Jamison, Kay Redfield, 17
jealously, role of, 153
Jefferson, Thomas, 145
Job, Biblical tale of, 181
Johnson, Scott, 72–74
Jordan, Michael, 49–50
Joseph, C., 116
jumping
    from bridges, 22–23
    daunting nature of, 182–183
justice. See also perversion of justice
    as ancient/primitive, 146
    nature of, 141–143
    in non-human primates, 108

Kazmierczak, Steve, 174–175
killing
    effects of, 70
    as "fascinating," 58–60, 62
    for first time, 62
    as gendered, 131–132
    as loathsome, 56, 88
    physiological arousal and, 34, 60–61
    potentiality for, 67, 72
killing, within-species
    law enforcement and, 57–58
    law of nature and, 33–34
    military combatants and, 55–57
    natural barrier against, 54–60
    of self vs. others, 89–90, 131
Kimura, Fumiko, 138
King Lear (Shakespeare), 66, 118
King, Martin Luther, Jr., 110
Klebold, Dylan, 10–11, 68, 172–174. See also
    Columbine High School incident
knife usage, 49
Koestler, Arthur, 89, 128
Krakauer, Jon, 58, 102
Kruglanski, Arie, 175

La Rochefoucauld, François, 86
Landscapes of the Jihad (Devji), 132
language of humanitarianism, 132
Large, M., 46
"last grand score," 150
last moment flinching, 136
last words, 106–107
Last Words of the Executed (Elder), 107
law enforcement officers, deadly force use
    by, 57–58
learned fearlessness, 86–89, 158
"lethal intergroup aggression," 67–68
Life at the Bottom (Dalrymple), 121, 153,
    163–164
life insurance, 222n10
Life's Preservative Against Self-Killing
    (Sym), 97
loneliness, 10, 96–97, 151, 158, 204
Lonely at the Top (Joiner), 151
"Looking Back on the Spanish Civil War"
    (Orwell), 55
Loving and Leaving the Good Life
    (Nearing), 92
low self-esteem, 92
Lupoe family incident, 6–7, 10, 125,
    130–132, 174, 211

male-linked murder, 43. See also gender, in
    murder-suicide
male loneliness, 151. See also loneliness
Man Against Himself (Menninger), 67

manslaughter-suicide, 9
Marion, Francis, 142–143
Martin, Clancy, 103
Marzuk, P., 28, 121
The Mask of Sanity (Cleckley), 14, 21, 55, 93, 179
A Mathematician's Apology (Hardy), 4, 111
Maximes (La Rochefoucauld), 86
McCandless, Christopher, 102–103
McNair, Steve, 160
McVeigh, Timothy, 10, 145–146, 197
medication, lethal doses of, 6
Meloy, J. R., 15
Menninger, Karl, 67
mental disorders, in murder-suicide, 31–32
Merari, A., 175
The Merchant of Venice (Shakespeare), 134
mercy. *See also* perversion of mercy
    as evolutionarily ancient, 109
    as murder-suicide motive, 6
    nature of, 125–126
    vs. vengeance, 139–140
"mercy killings," 126–128
The Mercy of Eternity (Wilson), 17
method choice, in murder-suicide
    asphyxiation, 79
    bludgeoning, 50
    cars, 27n67, 28, 184–187
    cyanide, 49–50
    hanging, 82–83, 84, 150–151
    knife, 49
    poisoning, 49, 165
    toxic fumes, 147–149
military combatants/soldiers
    acts of villainy vs. mercy, 125–126
    battlefield justice, 152
    reluctance to kill, 55–57, 70
    rights and duties of, 164
    "saving voices" and, 87–88
    social alienation and, 98
    suicidal crisis of, 88
Military Suicide Research Consortium, 98
The Millionaires' Unit (Wortman), 66, 70
Minelli, Ludwig, 63–64
Minutemen, 146
"misericordia," 112
moral judgments, brain's role in, 160–161
motives, in murder-suicide, 5–10, 85, 172, 182–183, 185
motor vehicle accidents, 184–186. *See also* driving into oncoming traffic
murder-suicide. *See also* perpetrators, of murder-suicide; perversion of duty; perversion of glory; perversion of justice; perversion of mercy
    alcohol as factor in, 29–31

behavioral sequencing in, 27
categorization of, 208–209
component relations, 40f
day-of-week patterns in, 28
definition of, 14–16, 27, 40
demographics of, 41–45
discontinuity in process, 32, 35–38
duty-related, 125, 165
empathy in, 112–118
gender in, 42–43, 131, 151
glory-motivated, 68
involving strangers, 159
killing pets/animals in, 138–139, 169–170
mental disorders and, 31–32
method choice in, 47–51
motives for, 5–10
murder as incidental in, 39
perversion of virtue and, 5, 8–16
as premeditated, 15, 16–20, 27, 149, 156–157
prevention, 193
as selfish, 168
suicide terrorism as, 38–41
suicide warning signs and, 194–196
terminology in, 27–29
time-lag in, 15–16, 32–35, 36
typologies of, 121–123
virtue-based mental process in, 33
worldwide incidence of, 45–47
murder, urge to, 67
Myths About Suicide (Joiner), 4, 30, 93, 104, 117, 147
myths, in suicide
    impulsivity, 16–20, 183
    selfishness, 4–5, 93

narcissism/narcissists, 73, 74, 143
National Suicide Prevention Lifeline, 234n16
nature. *See* human nature
Navy SEALS, 171–172
Nearing, Helen, 92
negative self-views, 92
negotiation/de-escalation, 201
nicotine's effects, 66
Nietzsche, Friedrich, 121
nightmares, 100, 194, 196, 198. *See also* suicidal behavior
911 calls, 77, 136, 144, 148–149, 167
1984 (Orwell), 103, 111, 158, 181
non-interpersonal virtue, 115, 210
Not With a Bang But a Whimper (Dalrymple), 59, 110

Obama, Barack, 13, 142, 215n24
obligation
    sense of duty and, 143
    transfer of, 164–165

On Killing (Grossman), 56, 70, 180
On Second Thought (Herbert), 24
openness, assumption of, 19
opponent process
    "mundane" people and, 70
    reaction to death and, 65
    role of experience in, 60–63
Oregon's Death with Dignity Act, 5–6, 137
Orwell, George, 22, 55, 103, 111, 158, 181,
    229–230n38
Othello (Shakespeare), 153
others. *See also* perversion of fate
    endangerment of, 147–149
    responsibility to, 163
    rights of, 145
    risk to, 183
"others-better-off" calculation, 50–51
Our Culture, What's Left Of It
    (Dalrymple), 63
overdose/overdose effects, 78–79, 131, 134,
    174, 182

Packing for Mars (Roach), 98–99
pain, emotional, 90–93, 95
Paine, Thomas, 111
Pape, Robert, 38
Pardo, Bruce, 11–12, 177–178, 180
Paré, Ambroise, 125–126
"parent-child suicide" (*oyako-shinju*), 138
parent/children murder-suicide. *See also*
    Lupoe family incident
    continuum of suicidality in, 134
    "cultural defense" in, 138
    evolutionary psychology and, 167–168
    last moment flinching, 136
    parental conflict and, 207–208
    perversion of duty in, 167
    police investigation of, 135–136
    stepparents/biological parents in, 167
    typologies of, 122–123
    willing participants in, 132–133
Pascal, Blaise, 90
patient self-reporting, 194
Peixoto, Helder "Sonny," 179–180
penitence, 107
Pensées (Pascal), 90
perpetrators, of murder-suicide. *See also*
    parent/children murder-suicide
    beliefs of, 131
    clinical attention and, 193
    control emphasis of, 159
    duty emphasis of, 164–165
    empathy and, 112
    justice-motivation and, 143–144, 149, 155
    lack of humility/imagination in, 128
    mental health problems of, 159–160

perceived injustices and, 144
philosophical vantage point of, 107
preoccupation with others' death, 188
preoccupation with virtues, 114
psychological autopsy of, 210
rights of others and, 145
sense of innocence/self-acquittal in,
    146–147
typologies of, 121–123
personal responsibility, 143
"perspective-taking," 112
perversion of care, 167–168
perversion of duty. *See also* parent/children
    murder-suicide
    burdensome obligations and, 164–165
    evolutionary psychology and, 167–168
    in murder's mind, 27
    perversion of mercy and, 166
    perverted glory and, 10, 165
    suicidal males and, 43
    as virtue category, 8
perversion of fate
    accidental deaths, 9, 181–186, 188
    callous actions in, 184–185
    intention/motive/mindset in,
        182–183, 185
    in murder-suicide typology, 123–124
    "suicide by cop" as, 187
perversion of glory, 172–176
    Columbine incident as, 10–11
    in murder's mind, 27
    suicidal males and, 43
    in suicide terrorism, 38–40
    Virginia Tech incident as, 13
    as virtue category, 8
perversion of heroism, 172–176
perversion of justice
    brain's role in, 160–161
    depersonalization in, 158–159
    foundational role of, 124–125
    honor, defense of, 143–144
    loneliness in, 157–158
    in murder-suicide, 8–13, 39–41
    in murder's mind, 27
    need for revenge in, 162
    perception of corruption in, 144
    premeditation in, 144–145, 156, 206
    punishment, infliction of, 143
    rebels/rebellion and, 145–146
    suicidal males and, 43–44
    time-lag in, 16
perversion of mercy. *See also* Lupoe
    family incident; parent/children
    murder-suicide
    foundational role of, 124–125
    killing of animals, 138–139

for loved-ones, 169
"mercy killings," 126–128
misperception/misunderstanding of
    situation, 126–128, 137
in murder-suicide, 8–10, 41, 50–51
in murder's mind, 27
physician's and, 6
Pimienta family incident, 128–130, 132
suicidal males and, 43–44
perversion of self-control, 123–124, 177–180
perversion of virtue, 5, 8–16
Peterson, C., 106, 108, 109, 118, 152, 208
pets, as victims, 169–170. *See also* animals
physicians, terminally ill patients and, 6
physiological arousal, 34, 60–61
Pimienta family incident, 128–130, 132
pity, concept of, 125
Plath, Slyvia, 137
Plato, 144
poisoning, 49, 165
police officers, deadly force use by, 57–58
political vs. personal motives, 39
Popper, Karl, 21, 203
Powers, William, 146
predatory violence, 15
premeditation, 144–145, 206
prescriptions, for lethal doses of
    medication, 6
prevention, of suicide, 11, 20, 50, 153,
    193, 198
primates, justice in non-human, 108
Proverbs, Book of, 177, 179
psychoanalysis, suspicion of, 26
psychological autopsy methodology, 210
psychopathic patients, resistance of, 55
psychopathic personality
    "Cleckley psychopaths," 179–180
    emotional style, 68
    genetics and, 69
    pleasure in killing of, 71
    selfishness and, 93
psychotherapy, approaches to, 200
PTSD symptoms, 58
punishment
    deterrent effect of, 62, 143
    in murder-suicide, 160
"pushing the envelope," 63, 65, 174

rebels/rebellion, 145–146
Red Dragon (Harris), 62–63
redemption, 139
Reflections on Hanging (Koestler), 89, 128
Reflections on the Guillotine (Camus), 29,
    62, 72, 146–147
regret, 18, 77–78
"regularization of death," 65

religion
    justice/humanity in, 106, 107
    suicide terrorism and, 38
religious settings, 24
reluctance to kill. *See* killing, within-species
reputation, 151
research, future, 210
responsibility, personal, 143
Revelation, Book of, 87
revenge, 10, 12, 150–151. *See also* vengeance
right temporoparietal junction activity,
    160–161, 200
Roach, Mary, 98–99
The Road to Serfdom (Hayek), 117, 228n12
Robins, Eli
    on justice-motivated incident, 149
    on mental disorders/states, 31, 147
    on murder-suicide rates, 42, 47–48
    perverted mercy example, 165–166, 169
    on suicide communications, 81
    on withdrawal/social withdrawal, 100, 194
Rodriguez, Rick, 162, 168
Roosevelt, Theodore, 173
Roth, Randolph, 46, 144
Rudolph, Eric, 154
Rwandan genocide, 71–72

Salvation on Sand Mountain
    (Covington), 24
"Santa Claus" killer, 11–12, 35–37, 40–41,
    153, 161, 177–178, 180
Santayana, George, 51
"saving voices," 87
schizophrenic patients, 207
school shootings, 174, 214n17. *See also*
    Columbine High School incident;
    Kazmierczak, Steve; Virginia Tech
    incident
self-concept, inflated, 73–74
self-control
    perversion of, 123–124, 177–180
    as virtue, 115–117
"self-destruct" mechanisms, 93
self-determination, respect for, 6
Self-Determination Theory, 116
self-esteem, 92
self-injury, 96, 98, 224n39, 234n13
self-preservation instinct, 4, 24, 78, 84, 150
self-reporting, 194
self-sacrifice, 94–96, 99, 116
selfishness
    of murder-suicides, 168
    in psychopathic personality, 68
    suicide and, 4–5, 93
Seligman, M., 106, 108, 109, 118, 152, 208
Selzer, Richard, 125–126

"senseless," meaning of, 5
serial killers
    behavior of, 54
    opponent process and, 65, 68
    psychopathic mind of, 69
    suicide and, 53
    transformation of, 62–63
service members. See military combatants/
        soldiers
Shakespeare, William, 66, 74, 103,
        134, 153
Sharpe, Richard, 36
Shneidman, E., 90
snake-handling, 24
snakes, conscious awareness and,
        21–22, 25
social alienation, 91, 96, 98–99, 103
social hierarchy, 151
social misfits, 162
social withdrawal/withdrawal, 99–100,
        129, 194–196, 198. See also suicidal
        behavior
soldiers. See military combatants/soldiers
Solzhenitsyn, Aleksandr, 215n24
species, killing one's own
    law enforcement and, 57–58
    law of nature and, 33–34
    military combatants and, 55–57
    natural barrier against, 54–60
    of self vs. others, 89–90, 131
"spur of the moment" myth, 16–20
Stack, Steve, 123
starvation/self-starvation, 95, 102
Steel, Kevin, 75
stigma/stigmatization, 82, 84–86, 88,
        104, 194
strangers, murder-suicide and, 159
Stuart: A Life Backwards
        (Masters), 28
suffering, suicide and, 5–6
suicidal behavior. See also desire
        for death
    agitation, 34, 100, 129, 166, 194–196,
        198, 204
    ambivalence, 76, 79–81, 84–86, 102
    blink rate, 195–196, 198, 233n6
    capability, 80–82
    fearlessness and, 86–89
    financial motives in, 85
    impulsivity and, 215n35
    insincerity vs. constraints in, 83
    insomnia, 100, 133, 166, 194,
        196, 198
    internal debate, 80
    nightmares, 100, 194, 196, 198
    periodic monitoring of, 82

resolve and, 86, 134, 157–158, 167,
        186, 187
    signatures of, 17
    stigma, role of, 82, 84–86, 88,
        104, 194
    "thousand-yard stare," 100, 195, 198
    withdrawal/social withdrawal, 99–100,
        129, 194–196, 198
suicidal ideation
    burdensomeness/alienation concepts and,
        91–92, 100
    chronic, 81–82
    clinical assessments and, 196–197
    continuum of suicidality in, 134
    decedents' history of, 37
    "high place phenomenon" and, 23
    self-preservation instincts and, 78
    suicide attempts and, 174
suicidal mind, 76, 86, 103, 158,
        184, 207
suicidal thoughts, 20
suicidality, continuum of, 134
suicide
    assisted, 63–64
    day-of-week patterns in, 28
    decedents' loved ones and, 18–19
    as "double offense," 88
    endangerment of others, 147–149
    fearlessness and, 4, 158
    as fearsome, 104–105
    as "last grand score," 150
    as premeditated, 16–20
    primacy of, 9, 11, 27–28
    regret and, 18
    as revenge-motivated, 147
suicide bombers, 94, 95, 132, 175
"suicide by cop," 73, 187, 221–222n59
suicide decedents
    autonomy/self-control and, 117
    BAC in, 30–31, 226n11
    beliefs of, 96
    "grand score" concept and, 150
    murder-suicide plans of, 186
    as murderers, 37
suicide notes, 97, 100, 106, 188, 194
suicide pacts, 130–131, 133
suicide prevention, 11, 20, 50, 153,
        193, 198
suicide risk assessment, 193–196
suicide terrorism, 38–41, 95, 96, 132,
        175–176
suicide, understanding
    ambivalence and, 76, 79–81, 84,
        86, 102
    bereaved family members, 19, 78, 85,
        96–97, 150

desire to die, 49, 76, 87, 133
desire to live, 76–77
impulsive myth in, 16–20, 183, 215n35
intent, concept of, 101–102
intent to die, 4, 76, 101–102, 134, 136
killing self vs. others, 89–90
revenge, role of, 150–151
self-preservation instinct, 4, 24, 78,
    84, 150
"suicide is selfish" myth, 4–5, 93
suicide notes, 97, 100, 106, 194
what it is/is not, 101–105
Sullivan, Harry Stack, 3, 26, 66
survive, urge to, 77
Sym, John, 97

temperament, emotionality and, 68
temporoparietal junction activity,
    160–161, 200
Terence (Roman playwright), 3
terminally ill patients, 5–6
terminology, for murder-suicide, 27–29
Terror Management Theory, 113–114
terrorism. *See* suicide terrorism
The Terrorist in Search of Humanity
    (Devji), 132
terrorists. *See* suicide terrorism
The Odyssey (Homer), 142
Thompson, D. L., 114
Thornton, Omar, 144–145
"thousand-yard stare," 100, 195, 198. *See*
    also suicidal behavior
"threatened egotism" model, 73
Thus Spake Zarathustra (Nietzsche), 121
The Tiger (Vaillant), 108
A Time for Machetes (Hatzfield), 72
"time lag" problem, in murder-suicide,
    15–16, 32–35, 36
toxic fumes, 147–149
toxicology reports, on suicide
    decedents, 30
Treadwell, Timothy, 101–102
Tutsis, 71–72

Under the Banner of Heaven (Krakauer), 58
An Unquiet Mind (Jamison), 17
"unseen force," 58–59
urge
    to murder, 67
    to survive, 77

Vaillant, John, 108
Vann, David, 174
vengeance, 107, 130–131, 139–140, 155, 157,
    161, 208
veterans. *See* military combatants/soldiers

victim/perpetrator relationships,
    121–123. *See also* perpetrators, of
    murder-suicide
victimhood rates, 43
violence
    to achieve justice, 141
    affective/predatory distinction, 15
    domestic, 41, 201
    ideation about, 197
    previous experience with, 68
Violence Policy Center, 42, 44
Violence: Reflections on a National Epidemic
    (Gilligan), 141
violent crime, 3–4
Virginia Tech incident, 13, 158, 161–162,
    165, 196, 197, 209, 215n24
virtue/virtues
    collectivist, 117–118
    connections among, 209f
    discussion in clinical settings, 196–201
    interpersonal nature of, 109–111, 115–116
    as murder-suicide motive, 5–6
    perversion of, 5, 8–16
    in religious/philosophical traditions,
        106, 107
visual cliff, 61
voice of God, 24, 58–59, 87–88

Wallace, David Foster, 150–151
War and Redemption (Dewey), 56, 70, 87,
    139, 152
war, within-species killing in, 55–57. *See*
    also military combatants/soldiers
warning signs, 194–196. *See also* suicidal
    behavior
weight loss, 194–195. *See also* suicidal
    behavior
West, D., 41
West, Frederick, 54, 68–69, 71
Wevill, Assia, 137, 165
Whitman, Charles, 203–205
Why People Die By Suicide (Joiner), 4
will to live, 76–77
Williams, Brian. *See* Dele, Bison
Wilson, Eric, 17
Wilson, M., 167–168
Winnicott, D. W., 26
withdrawal/social withdrawal, 99–100,
    129, 194–196, 198. *See also* suicidal
    behavior
within-species killing
    law enforcement and, 57–58
    law of nature and, 33–34
    military combatants and, 55–57
    natural barrier against, 54–60
    veterans' war experiences, 55–57

women, as victims, 44
Wong, Jiverly, 205–207
Woods, Tiger, 195, 233n6
worldwide murder-suicide rates,
    45–47
Wortman, Marc, 66, 70

youth, as victims, 44. *See also* children

Zawahiri, Ayman al-, 132
"zero suicide" policy, 19
Zinkhan, George, III, 153–155, 174, 177,
    199–200